# Lecture Notes in Computer Science 9975

Commenced Publication in 1973
Founding and Former Series Editors:
Gerhard Goos, Juris Hartmanis, and Jan van Leeuwen

More information about this series at http://www.springer.com/series/7409

Sebastian Link · Juan C. Trujillo (Eds.)

# Advances in Conceptual Modeling

ER 2016 Workshops, AHA, MoBiD, MORE-BI,
MReBA, QMMQ, SCME, and WM2SP
Gifu, Japan, November 14–17, 2016
Proceedings

 Springer

*Editors*
Sebastian Link
University of Auckland
Auckland
New Zealand

Juan C. Trujillo
University of Alicante
Alicante
Spain

ISSN 0302-9743          ISSN 1611-3349  (electronic)
Lecture Notes in Computer Science
ISBN 978-3-319-47716-9      ISBN 978-3-319-47717-6  (eBook)
DOI 10.1007/978-3-319-47717-6

Library of Congress Control Number: 2016954469

LNCS Sublibrary: SL3 – Information Systems and Applications, incl. Internet/Web, and HCI

Printed on acid-free paper

This Springer imprint is published by Springer Nature
The registered company is Springer International Publishing AG
The registered company address is: Gewerbestrasse 11, 6330 Cham, Switzerland

# Preface

This volume contains the proceedings of the workshops associated with the 35th International Conference on Conceptual Modelling (ER 2016) and one paper associated with the Demonstration Session of ER 2016.

The International Conference on Conceptual Modelling (ER) is the leading international forum for presenting and discussing research and applications of conceptual modelling. Topics of interest include foundations of conceptual models, theories of concepts, ontology-driven conceptual modelling and analysis, methods and tools for developing, communicating, consolidating, and evolving conceptual models, and techniques for transforming conceptual models into effective implementations.

Continuing a long tradition, ER 2016 hosted seven workshops that were held in conjunction with the main ER conference. The workshops served as an intensive collaborative forum for exchanging innovative ideas about conceptual modelling and for discovering new frontiers for its use. In addition, a demonstration session was organized in which participants show-cased their latest tools for conceptual modelling.

After a Call for Workshops proposal, we finally accept seven high-quality workshops. Therefore, this volume contains articles from the following seven accepted workshops:

- AHA 2016 – Conceptual Modelling for Ambient Assistance and Healthy Ageing
- MoBiD 2016 – Modelling and Management of Big Data
- MORE-BI 2016 – Modelling and Reasoning for Business Intelligence
- MReBA 2016 – Conceptual Modelling in Requirements and Business Analysis
- QMMQ 2016 – Quality of Modelling and Modelling of Quality
- SCME 2015 – Conceptual Modelling Education
- WM2SP 2016 – Models and Modelling on Security and Privacy

The volume also includes one of the four presented demonstration papers.

In its 2016 edition, the ER workshop series focused on the use of conceptual modelling to increase end-user satisfaction by aligning technical systems to the goals of a given domain. The MoBiD, MReBA, and MORE-BI workshops aimed at improving our understanding of how better data management, requirements engineering, and business intelligence lead to better organizational values. Similarly, the AHA workshop aimed at designing and developing systems that ensure a better quality of life. More generally, the QMMQ workshop addressed the issue of ensuring the quality of systems and developing techniques to manage quality aspects. The impact of security and privacy on conceptual modelling was discussed in the WM2SP workshop. The SCME symposium examined methods of teaching and educating conceptual modelling to research and industry communities.

The workshop program of ER 2016 provided a place for participants to discuss, deliberate, and provoke, with the primary goal of setting an agenda for future research in the areas of the workshops.

Across all workshop events, 52 papers were submitted from the following 16 countries: Belgium, Brazil, Colombia, Finland, France, Germany, Israel, Japan, New Zealand, Poland, Russia, Spain, Sweden, The Netherlands, UK, and USA. Following the rule of the ER workshops, the respective workshop Program Committees carried out peer reviews and accepted a total number of 19 papers, resulting in an acceptance rate of 36 %. Furthermore, three of the workshops featured a keynote talk, which significantly enhanced the perspective and quality of the ER 2016 workshops.

We would like to express our sincere gratitude to all authors and reviewers of the regular papers and keynotes, to the co-chairs of the individual workshops and other events, and to the entire ER organization team for an unforgettable event in Gifu. Our biggest thanks go to Motoshi Saeki, who was always there to help us with any problems we put forward. Finally, we would like to thank the Springer team for producing another memorable ER workshop volume.

November 2016                                                    Sebastian Link
                                                                Juan C. Trujillo

# ER 2016 Workshop Organization

## Honorary Chair

Kiyoshi Agusa            Nanzan University, Japan

## Conference Co-chairs

Shuichiro Yamamoto      Nagoya University, Japan
Motoshi Saeki            Tokyo Institute of Technology, Japan

## Program Committee Co-chairs

Isabelle Comyn-wattiau     CEDRIC-CNAM and ESSEC Business School, France
Katsumi Tanaka          Kyoto University, Japan
Il-Yeol Song            Drexel University, USA

## Workshop Co-chairs

Sebastian Link          The University of Auckland, New Zealand
Juan C. Trujillo         University of Alicante, Spain

## Tutorial Co-chairs

Atsushi Ohnishi         Ritsumeikan University, Japan
Panos Vassiliadis       Univesity of Ioannia, Greece

## Panel Co-chairs

Sudha Ram            University of Arizona, USA
Esteban Zimanyi         Universite Libre de Bruxelles, Belgium

## Tool Demonstration and Poster Co-chairs

Aditya Ghose           University of Wollongong, Australia
Takashi Kobayahsi       Tokyo Institute of Technology, Japan

## PhD Symposium Co-chairs

Tsuneo Ajisaka         Wakayama University, Japan
Carson Woo           The University of British Columbia, Canada

## Symposium on Conceptual Modelling Education

Karen Davis                 University of Cincinnatti, USA (Co-chair)
Xavier Franch               Universitat Politecnica de Catalunya, Spain (Co-chair)

## Treasurer

Takako Nakatani             The Open University of Japan, Japan

## Local Organizing Co-chairs

Shuji Morisaki             Nagoya University, Japan
Atsushi Yoshida            Nanzan University, Japan

## Liasons to IPSJ

Isamu Hasegawa             Square Enix, Japan

## Publicity Chair and Web Master

Shinpei Hayashi            Tokyo Institute of Technology, Japan

## Student Volunteer Co-chairs

Noritoshi Atsumi           Kyoto University, Japan
Hiroaki Kuwabara           Nanzan University, Japan

## Liaison to Steering Committee

Sudha Ram                  University of Arizona, USA

## Advisory

Mikio Aoyama               Nanzan University, Japan

## Conceptual Modelling for Ambient Assistance and Healthy Ageing

### Organizing and Program Committee

Heinrich C. Mayr              Alpen-Adria-Universität Klagenfurt, Austria (Co-chair)
Ulrich Frank                  Universität Essen-Duisburg, Germany (Co-chair)
J. Palazzo M. de Oliveira     UFRGS Porto Alegre, Brazil (Co-chair)
Fadi Al Machot                Alpen-Adria-Universität Klagenfurt, Austria
Vadim Ermolayev               Zaporozhye National University, Ukraine
Hans-Georg Fill               Universität Wien, Austria
Athula Ginige                 University of Western Sydney, Australia
Sven Hartmann                 Universität Clausthal, Germany

| | |
|---|---|
| Marion A. Hersh | University of Glasgow, UK |
| Dimitris Karagiannis | Universität Wien, Austria |
| Yuichi Kurita | Hioshima University, Japan |
| Gerhard Lakemeyer | RWTH Aachen, Germany |
| Stephen Liddle | Kevin and Debra Rollins Center for e-Business, USA |
| Elisabeth Métais | Laboratory CEDRIC, Paris, France |
| Judith Michael | Alpen-Adria-Universität Klagenfurt, Austria |
| Johannes Oberzaucher | FH Kärnten, Austria |
| Leif Oppermann | Fraunhofer Gesellschaft, Germany |
| Oscar Pastor | University of Valencia, Spain |
| Wolfgang Reisig | Humboldt-Universität Berlin, Germany |
| Dominique Rieu | UPMF Grenoble, France |
| Elmar Sinz | Universität Bamberg, Germany |
| Vladimir Shekhovtsov | National Technical University of Kharkiv, Ukraine |
| Markus Stumptner | University of South Australia, Australia |
| Bernhard Thalheim | Universität Kiel, Germany |
| Benkt Wangler | Stockholm University, Sweden |
| Tatjana Welzer | University of Maribor, Slovenia |

## Modelling and Management of Big Data

### Organizing and Program Committee

| | |
|---|---|
| David Gill | University of Alicante, Spain (Co-chair) |
| Il-Yeol Song | Drexel University, USA (Co-chair) |
| Yuan An | Drexel University, USA (Co-chair) |
| Jesus Peral | University of Alicante, Spain (Co-chair) |
| Marie-Aude Aufaure | Ecole Centrale Paris, France |
| Rafael Berlanga | Universitat Jaume I, Spain |
| Sandro Bimonte | Irstea, France |
| Michael Blaha | Yahoo Inc., USA |
| Gennaro Cordasco | Università di Salerno, Italy |
| Dickson Chiu | University of Hong Kong, SAR Hong Kong |
| Gill Dobbie | The University of Auckland, New Zealand |
| Pedro Furtado | Universidade de Coimbra, Portugal |
| Matteo Golfarelli | University of Bologna, Italy |
| Magnus Johnsson | University of Lund, Sweden |
| Nectarios Koziris | National Technical University of Athens, Greece |
| Jiexun Li | Drexel University, USA |
| Stephen W. Liddle | Brigham Young University, USA |
| Antoni Olivé | Universitat Politècnica de Catalunya, Spain |
| Jeffrey Parsons | Memorial University of Newfoundland, Canada |
| Oscar Pastor | Universidad Politécnica de Valencia, Spain |
| Mario Piattini | University of Castilla-La Mancha, Spain |
| Nicolas Prat | ESSEC Business School, France |
| Sudha Ram | University of Arizona, USA |

| Carlos Rivero | University of Idaho, USA |
|---|---|
| Colette Rolland | Université Paris 1, France |
| Keng Siau | University of Nebraska-Lincoln, USA |
| Alkis Simitsis | Hewlett-Packard Co., USA |
| Alejandro Vaisman | Université Libre de Bruxelles, Belgium |
| Panos Vassiliadis | University of Ioannina, Greece |

## Modelling and Reasoning for Business Intelligence

### Organizing and Program Committee

| Ivan J. Jureta | FNRS and University of Namur, Belgium (Co-chair) |
|---|---|
| Corentin Burnay | FNRS and University of Namur, Belgium (Co-chair) |
| Stéphane Faulkner | University of Namur, Belgium (Co-chair) |
| Alberto Abelló | Universitat Politècnica de Catalunya, Spain |
| Ladjel Bellatreche | Ecole Nationale Supérieure de Mécanique et d'Aérotechnique, France |
| Sandro Bimonte | Irstea Clermont Ferrand, France |
| Olivier Corby | Inria, France |
| Alfredo Cuzzocrea | ICAR-CNR and University of Calabria, Italy |
| Neil Ernst | University of British Columbia, Canada |
| Cécile Favre | Université Lyon 2, France |
| Jennifer Horkoff | University of Trento, Italy |
| Dimitris Karagiannis | University of Vienna, Austria |
| Alexei Lapouchnian | University of Trento, Italy |
| Isabelle Linden | University of Namur, Belgium |
| Patrick Marcel | Université François Rabelais de Tours, France |
| Jose-Norberto Mazón | University of Alicante, Spain |
| Catherine Roussey | Irstea Clermont Ferrand, France |
| Monique Snoeck | Katholieke Universiteit Leuven, Belgium |
| Thodoros Topaloglou | University of Toronto, Canada |
| Juan C. Trujillo | University of Alicante, Spain |
| Robert Wrembel | Poznań University of Technology, Poland |

## Conceptual Modelling in Requirements and Business Analysis

### Organizing and Program Committee

| Takako Nakatani | The Open University of Japan, Japan (Co-chair) |
|---|---|
| Jennifer Horkoff | City University London, UK (Co-chair) |
| Jelena Zdravkovic | Stockholm University, Sweden (Co-chair) |
| Okhaide Akhigbe | University of Ottawa, Canada |
| Claudia Cappelli | NP2TEC/Universidade Federal do Estado do Rio de Janeiro, Brazil |
| Aditya Ghose | University of Wollongong, Australia |
| Paul Johannesson | KTH Royal Institute of Technology, Sweden |
| Sotirios Liaskos | York University, Canada |

| | |
|---|---|
| Lin Liu | Tsinghua University, China |
| Lidia Lopez | Universitat Politècnica de Catalunya, Spain |
| Pericles Loucopoulos | University of Manchester, UK |
| Joshua Nwokeji | University of Kent, UK |
| Andreas Opdahl | University of Bergen, Norway |
| Anna Perini | Fondazione Bruno Kessler, Italy |
| Jolita Ralyté | University of Geneva, Switzerland |
| Kevin Ryan | University of Limerick, Ireland |
| Junko Shirogane | Tokyo Woman's Christian University, Japan |
| Samira Si-Said Cherfi | Conservatoire National des Arts et Métiers, France |
| Vitor Souza | Universidade Federal do Espírito Santo, Brazil |
| Sam Supakkul | Sabre Travel Network, USA |
| Lucineia Thom | Universidade Federal do Rio Grande do Sul, Brazil |

## Models and Modelling on Security and Privacy

### Organizing and Program Committee

| | |
|---|---|
| Eduardo Fernandez | Florida Atlantic University, USA (Co-chair) |
| Atsuo Hazeyama | Tokyo Gakugei Univerity, Japan (Co-chair) |
| Takao Okubo | Institute of Information Security, Japan (Co-chair) |
| Arosha Bandara | The Open University, UK |
| Shinpei Hayashi | Tokyo Institute of Technology, Japan |
| Haruhiko Kaiya | Kanagawa University, Japan |
| Masaru Matsunami | Sony Digital Network Applications, Japan |
| Nancy Mead | CMU/SEI, USA |
| Haris Mouratidis | University of Brighton, UK |
| Seiji Munetoh | IBM Research Tokyo, Japan |
| Shinpei Ogata | Shinshu University, Japan |
| Liliana Pasquale | Lero, Ireland |
| Motoshi Saeki | Tokyo Institute of Technology, Japan |
| Kenji Taguchi | AIST, Japan |
| Yasuyuki Tahara | The University of Electro-Communication, Japan |
| Thein Tun | The Open University, UK |
| Hironori Washizaki | Waseda University, Japan |
| Nobukazu Yoshioka | National Institute of Informatics, Japan |
| Yijun Yu | The Open University, UK |

## Quality of Models and Models of Quality

### Organizing and Program Committee

| | |
|---|---|
| Samira Si-Said Cherfi | National Conservatory of Arts and Crafts, France (Co-chair) |
| Oscar Pastor | Valencia University of Technology, Spain (Co-chair) |

| | |
|---|---|
| Elena Kornyshova | National Conservatory of Arts and Crafts, France (Co-chair) |
| Jacky Akoka | CNAM, France |
| Said Assar | Telecom Ecole de Management, France |
| Marko Bajec | University of Ljubljana, Slovenia |
| Lotfi Bouzguenda | ISMIS, Tunisia |
| Cristina Cachero | Universidad de Alicante, Spain |
| Isabelle Comyn-Wattiau | CNAM-ESSEC, France |
| Sophie Dupuy-Chessa | UPMF-Grenoble 2, France |
| Cesar Gonzalez-Perez | Spanish National Research Council, Institute of Heritage Sciences, Spain |
| Roberto E. Lopez-Herrejon | Johannes Kepler Universität, Austria |
| Raimundas Matulevicius | University of Tartu, Estonia |
| Jeffrey Parsons | University of Newfoundland, Canada |
| Jolita Ralyte | University of Geneva, Switzerland |
| Sudha Ram | University of Arizona, USA |
| Camille Salinesi | Université de Paris 1, France |
| Guttorm Sindre | Norwegian University of Science and Technology, Norway |
| Pnina Soffer | University of Haifa, Israel |

## Conceptual Modelling Education

### Organizing and Program Committee

| | |
|---|---|
| Karen Davis | University of Cincinnati, USA (Co-chair) |
| Xavier Franch | Universitat Politecnica de Catalunya, Spain (Co-chair) |
| Alberto Abello | Universitat Politecnica de Catalunya, Spain |
| Fabiano Dalpiaz | Utrecht University, The Netherlands |
| Suzanne W. Dietrich | Arizona State University, USA |
| Renata Guizzardi | Universidade Federal do Espirito Santo, Brazil |
| Nenad Jukic | Loyola University Chicago, USA |
| Haruhiko Kaiya | Kanagawa University, Japan |
| Petra Leimich | Edinburgh Napier University, UK |
| Don Schwartz | Marist College, USA |

### Organized by

- Special Interest Group on Software Engineering, Information Processing Society of Japan
- The ER Institute (ER Steering Committee)

### In Cooperation with

- The Database Society of Japan
- Special Interest Group on Database Systems, Information Processing Society of Japan

- Information and Systems Society and Technical Committee on Data Engineering, The Institute of Electronics, Information and Communication Engineers
- IEEE Computer Society Japan Chapter
- ACM SIGMOD Japan
- Software Engineers Association

**Industrial Sponsors**

HITACHI
Inspire the Next

株式会社 デンソークリエイト

# Abstracts of Keynotes

# Managing and Exploring GPS Trajectories

Baihua Zheng

School of Information Systems, Singapore Management University
Stanford Road 80, Singapore 178902
bhzheng@smu.edu.sg

**Abstract.** In the era of big data, quantities of data reach almost incomprehensible proportions. As we move forward, we're going to have more and more huge data collections. The collection of GPS trajectories generated by moving objects in urban spaces is just one example. What are the research opportunities and the business values of the big collection of GPS trajectories? The keynote answers the above question via several projects, including taxi sharing, trajectory compression, map auto-updating, and single GPS point location.

**Keywords:** GPS trajectories · Map updating · Taxi sharing · Trajectory compression

# A Capability-Driven Development Approach for Requirements and Business Process Modeling

Oscar Pastor

Centro de I+D+i en Métodos de Producción de Software –PROS-Universitat
Politècnica de València
Camino de Vera s/n, 46022 València, Spain
opastor@dsic.upv.es

**Abstract.** Requirements modeling and business process modeling are two essential activities in the earliest steps of any sound software production process. A precise conceptual alignment between them is required in order to assess that requirements are "operationalized" through an adequate set of processes. Complementary, the trip from requirements to code should benefit from using a precise model driven development connection, intended to characterize not only the involved conceptual models, but also their corresponding model transformations. Selecting the most appropriate conceptual models for specifying the different system perspective becomes a crucial task. This conceptual modeling-based solution requires to use a holistic conceptual framework to determine those modeling elements to be taken into account. Surprisingly, the link with MDD approaches to provide a rigorous link with the software components of a final software application has not been analyzed in a clear and convincing way. Exploring the notion of capability, this keynote will present a capability driven development approach together with its associated meta-model as the selected conceptual framework. Additionally, it will be shown how this framework facilitates the selection of the most appropriate method components in order to design an effective software process and in order to make feasible a sound MDD connection.

# Grounding for Ontological Architecture Quality: Metaphysical Choices

Chris Partridge[1,2] and Sergio de Cesare[1]

[1] Brunel University London, Uxbridge, UK
{chris.partridge, sergio.decesare}@brunel.ac.uk
[2] BORO Solution Ltd., London, UK
partridgec@borogroup.co.uk

**Keywords:** Information grounding · Gargantuan systems · Ontological architecture · Foundational ontology · Metaphysical choices · Criterion of identity · BORO · Intersubjectively reliable criteria of identity · Space-time maps

# Contents

**Conceptual Modeling in Requirements and Business Analysis**

**Quality of Models and Models of Quality**

**Conceptual Modelling Education**

**Models and Modelling on Security and Privacy**

**Tool Demonstrations**

# Keynotes

# A Capability-Driven Development Approach for Requirements and Business Process Modeling

Oscar Pastor[✉]

Centro de I+D+i en Métodos de Producción de Software–PROS-Universitat Politècnica de València, Camino de Vera s/n, 46022 València, Spain
opastor@dsic.upv.es

**Abstract.** Requirements modeling and business process modeling are two essential activities in the earliest steps of any sound software production process. A precise conceptual alignment between them is required in order to assess that requirements are "operationalized" through an adequate set of processes. Complementary, the trip from requirements to code should benefit from using a precise model driven development connection, intended to characterize not only the involved conceptual models, but also their corresponding model transformations. Selecting the most appropriate conceptual models for specifying the different system perspective becomes a crucial task. This conceptual modeling-based solution requires to use a holistic conceptual framework to determine those modeling elements to be taken into account. Surprisingly, the link with MDD approaches to provide a rigorous link with the software components of a final software application has not been analyzed in a clear and convincing way. Exploring the notion of capability, this keynote will present a capability driven development approach together with its associated meta-model as the selected conceptual framework. Additionally, it will be shown how this framework facilitates the selection of the most appropriate method components in order to design an effective software process and in order to make feasible a sound MDD connection.

## 1 Introduction

Requirements Engineering (RE) is widely accepted to be an essential initial step for any successful software production process. Requirements must be correctly and precisely specified, and they have to be properly aligned with the business processes that conform any enterprise activity. If capturing the desired system functionality and qualities is such an essential process, to model them adequately becomes a fundamental need. Too often, the corresponding information is specified in natural language what appears to be clearly insufficient. Conceptual modeling emerges as the right strategy for sharing a collaborative perception of requirements, to facilitate analysis, and to transform the designed conceptual models into architecture design and code.

Additionally, in practical terms requirements activities often fall under the heading of Business Analysis (BA), the goal being to create a Business Process Model (BPM) that has to determine and specify the processes of an organization. The design of such a BPM allows for an explicit consideration of the selected business strategy, providing

© Springer International Publishing AG 2016
S. Link and J.C. Trujillo (Eds.): ER 2016 Workshops, LNCS 9975, pp. 3–8, 2016.
DOI: 10.1007/978-3-319-47717-6_1

a basic component for any method intended to operationalize it, always according and compliant to the system requirements. The resultant BPM must then be conceptually aligned with those system requirements that justify their existence. This can determine how a business will make use of technology in order to provide a software product that improves its operations and meet the business goals.

Being the MReBA workshop a very convenient forum for discussing the interplay between RE, BPM and conceptual models, this keynote will develop the idea of using the notion of capability in a conceptual modeling context. The main goal is to discuss how capability-driven development (CDD) can be effectively used to link RE and BPM under a unifying methodological perspective.

## 2   Why a CDD-Based Approach?

The first question to be answered is why selecting a CDD-based approach. Why using a framework based on the notion of capability? In a business context, the notion of capability mainly refers to the resources and expertise that an enterprise needs to offer its functions. As pointed out by Zdravkovic et al. [1], it is a notion that has gained more and more attention in the last years because it directs business investment focus, it can be used as a baseline for business planning and it leads directly to service specification and design. It has been intensively argued that capability-oriented enterprise modeling can provide an effective and promising solution to face adequately well-known problems related to how to select the most convenient enterprise architecture, how to link strategy, context and operation, how to deal with changing business contexts and how to integrate applications designed for different execution contexts that are part of a common business process. This has an immediate application over our intention of providing a sound conceptual modeling framework for modeling requirements and business processes, using the most convenient method components and connecting with advanced model-driven development (MDD) practices.

While capabilities have subsequently being used quite extensively in the context of business architecture, enterprise modeling and enterprise architecture [2], the link with MDD approaches to provide a rigorous link with the software components of a final software application has not been analyzed in a clear and convincing way. In this keynote, we will focus on the link of a CDD-based approach with the methodological guidance required to design a sound software production process where the RE and BPM perspectives are adequately included.

This work aims to explore this integration aspect by using an open framework to model capabilities, assuming that different views require different modeling approaches. The holistic framework should make possible to incorporate the most accurate techniques for modeling a particular component. Different conceptual models are needed to specify a conceptual map to be used for building a global business model where the relevant different views (i.e., strategy, process, information, organization…) are to be properly integrated.

# 3   The Methodological Approach

We start from the definition of capability used in the FP7 CaaS project [3], as "the ability and capacity that enables an enterprise to achieve a business goal in a certain operational context". A capability meta-model (CMM) determines the main conceptual primitives that conforms the approach. How to specify the different modeling perspectives that are present in this CMM becomes the essential decision to instantiate it in a particular method. Following the CaaS proposal, three main aspects are used to structure the CMM (see Fig. 1): context, enterprise modelling, reuse and variability, each one requiring a particular conceptual modeling approach, but without loosing the global, unified point of view. These three aspects provides an effective conceptual coverage to face the RE - BPM connection problem that we are exploring. To have an open architecture, it should be possible to select different modeling proposals to cover those modeling perspectives that are delimited with the meta-model. In this keynote, the idea is to provide an effective capability-driven development method where the most accurate pieces for context, enterprise modeling and reuse and variability could be selected according to the modeler's choices. Based on this CMM, the open architecture assumption will have a precise methodological support.

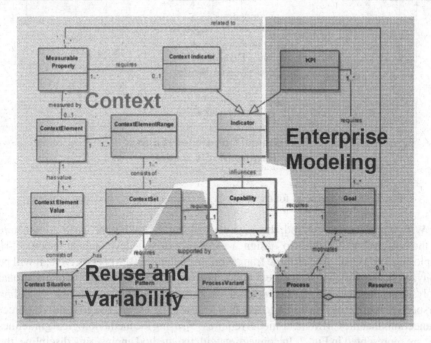

**Fig. 1.**  The three main aspects of the capability meta-model

Concretely, we will focus on the enterprise modeling perspective (see Fig. 2), to select the business process model meta-class. In the scope of the RE/BPM connection that we are interested in, we use this figure as a starting point to determine how to use a capability-based design to select the method components to be used in order to model the relevant concepts. Assuming that the notion of process is the most relevant in the Business Process Model context, we will consider that a process is a series of actions that are performed in order to achieve a particular result, supporting goals and consuming resources. We will use communicational analysis as the methodological approach to describe processes. This decision is based on the fact that the concepts included in the meta-model underlying communicational analysis [4] covers well the ones selected from the presented capability meta-model. This use of communicational analysis in a CDD environment is a significant part of the presented work.

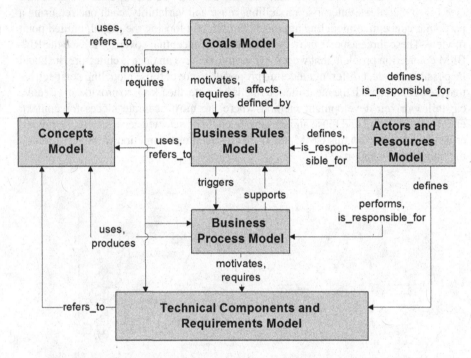

**Fig. 2.** A starting point for capability design in an enterprise modeling scope.

With this objective in mind, this keynote will start by taking the CaaS architecture as the selected architecture to design a capability-driven development method [4], Exploring the "open" aspect of the framework from the RE/BPM perspective, it will be analyzed how to develop the process meta-class component by using communicational analysis as the selected methodological background. Once this relevant modeling perspective is covered, we will also emphasize how to determine the goal and resources connections that the CMM meta-model requires [5], using the methodological guidelines that are represented in Fig. 2. In connection with the method engineering discipline, the proposed framework provides an effective solution to design a sound MDD-based software process able to:

- Provide a holistic perspective for the different method components that are required to go from requirements to code.

- Materialize a concrete starting point for capability-based design in the scope of RM/BPM by using as conceptual modeling strategy a communicational analysis-based approach.
- Connect the selected conceptual models for performing the RM/BPM steps with the model transformation properties of tools that can generate the final application code, making true the MDD goal of going from requirements to code following a process that is as much automated as possible [6, 7].

## 4   Conclusions

As the MReBA series of workshops precisely states, "in practice, requirements activities often fall under the heading of Business Analysis (BA), determining how a business can make use of technology in order to improve its operations, meet targets, and thrive in a competitive economy". To make this goal true, it is essential to have a concrete conceptual framework that characterizes the basic conceptual models that are required to specify a system from its different perspectives.

This keynote shows how the notion of capability can be used as a sound basis to provide such a framework intended to cover the expressiveness that requirements modeling and business process modeling requires. Having in mind that both perspectives must be conceptually aligned in a precise way, a capability meta-model is used to determine the basic notions to be covered by the selected conceptual modeling approach. Using a method engineering-based approach, this meta-model guides the different modeling components that have to be properly integrated to conform an efficient software product process capable to go from systems requirements and the business process model that operationalize them, to the final software product that constitutes their representation in practice.

As an example, a method based on communication analysis can be used as the central RE/BPM modeling strategy, taking advantage of its code generation capacity to design a powerful MDD-based method, in order to show how the proposed approach, based on capability driven development, can provide the desired conceptual modeling-based framework for connecting requirements and business process modeling.

## References

1. Zdravkovic, J., Stirna, J., Kuhr, J.-C., Koç, H.: Requirements engineering for capability driven development. In: Frank, U., Loucopoulos, P., Pastor, Ó., Petrounias, I. (eds.) PoEM 2014. LNBIP, vol. 197, pp. 193–207. Springer, Heidelberg (2014). doi:10.1007/978-3-662-45501-2_14
2. Zdravkovic, J., Stirna, J., Henkel, M., Grabis, J.: Modeling business capabilities and context dependent delivery by cloud services. In: Salinesi, C., Norrie, M.C., Pastor, Ó. (eds.) CAiSE 2013. LNCS, vol. 7908, pp. 369–383. Springer, Heidelberg (2013). doi:10.1007/978-3-642-38709-8_24

3. Bērziša, S., Bravos, G., Gonzalez, T., Czubayko, U., España, S., Grabis, J., Henkel, M., Jokste, L., Kampars, J., Koç, H., Kuhr, J., Llorca, C., Loucopoulos, P., Juenes Pascual, R., Pastor, O., Sandkuhl, K., Simic, H., Stirna, J., Valverde, F., Zdravkovic, J.: Capability driven development: an approach to designing digital enterprises. J. Bus. Inf. Syst. Eng. **57**(1), 15–25 (2015). Special Issue "Advanced Enterprise Modeling", Springer
4. España, S., González, A., Pastor, Ó.: Communication analysis: a requirements engineering method for information systems. In: Eck, P., Gordijn, J., Wieringa, R. (eds.) CAiSE 2009. LNCS, vol. 5565, pp. 530–545. Springer, Heidelberg (2009). doi:10.1007/978-3-642-02144-2_41
5. Ruiz, M., Costal, D., España, S., Franch, X., Pastor, Ó.: Integrating the goal and business process perspectives in information system analysis. In: Jarke, M., Mylopoulos, J., Quix, C., Rolland, C., Manolopoulos, Y., Mouratidis, H., Horkoff, J. (eds.) CAiSE 2014. LNCS, vol. 8484, pp. 332–346. Springer, Heidelberg (2014). doi:10.1007/978-3-319-07881-6_23
6. Embley, D.W., Liddle, S.W., Pastor, O.: Conceptual-model programming: a manifesto. In: Embley, D.W., Thalheim, B. (eds.) Handbook of Conceptual Modeling, pp. 3–16. Springer, Heidelberg (2011)
7. Pastor, O., Molina, J.C.: Model-Driven Architecture in Practice - A Software Production Environment Based on Conceptual Modeling. Springer, Heidelberg (2007). ISBN 978-3-540-71867-3, pp. I–XVI, 1–302

# Grounding for Ontological Architecture Quality: Metaphysical Choices

Chris Partridge[1,2] and Sergio de Cesare[1(✉)]

[1] Brunel University London, Uxbridge, UK
{chris.partridge,sergio.decesare}@brunel.ac.uk
[2] BORO Solution Ltd., London, UK
partridgec@borogroup.co.uk

**Keywords:** Information grounding · Gargantuan systems · Ontological architecture · Foundational ontology · Metaphysical choices · Criterion of identity · BORO · Intersubjectively reliable criteria of identity · Space-time maps

## 1 Introduction

Information systems (IS) are getting larger and more complex, becoming 'gargantuan'. IS practices have not evolved in step to handle the development and maintenance of these gargantuan systems, leading to a variety of quality issues. The community recognises that they need to develop an appropriate organising architecture and are making significant efforts [1]. Examples include the System Engineering Modeling Language (SysML), the Reference Model for Open Distributed Processing (RM-ODP) and 4 + 1 Architectural Blueprints [2]. Most of these follow IEEE 1471-2000's [3] recommendation to use view models.

We believe that these efforts are missing a key component – an information grounding view. In this paper, we firstly describe this view. Then we suggest a way to provide an architecture for it – foundational ontologies – and a way of assessing them – metaphysical choices. We illustrate how the metaphysical choices are made and how this can affect information modelling.

## 2 Information Grounding

The basic elements of the information grounding view are not new. It can be linked to the discussion of a 'Universe of Discourse' (UoD) found as far back as Boole's 1854 Laws of Thought [4]. The underlying idea is much older; that given some discourse there is a collection of things the discourse is about, i.e. its UoD. In the IS community the terminology was adopted for a different purpose (see e.g. ISO/TR 9007:1987 [5]). In this, a pre-existing system (discourse) is seen as containing a 'Universe of Discourse Description' (UoDD) which describes the UoD. What this suggests is that the information component of a new, yet-to-be-built, system can be developed by starting with its UoD and describing this, building the UoDD from the UoD. This suggests an attractive symmetry with models of a system; where a system model is a description of the system.

© Springer International Publishing AG 2016
S. Link and J.C. Trujillo (Eds.): ER 2016 Workshops, LNCS 9975, pp. 9–15, 2016.
DOI: 10.1007/978-3-319-47717-6_2

And so the system model contains a description of a description of the UoD – creating a chain of descriptions.

For our purposes, we will talk about an 'information grounding' rather than a describing relation, where the elements of information in a system are grounded by the things the information is about (or expressed in the language of truthmakers [6, 7], one can say by the things that make them true). From this new perspective, the UoD is more naturally called the 'information ground' of the system. This raises questions about exactly what the UoDD is. Is it the model of the information ground – the information ground model? Or is it the information in the system – the system information – which is grounded by the information ground? From a grounding perspective these are different; in the following sections we clarify this distinction.

There is a literature on the confusions that can arise around information grounding relations. Korzybski [8] talks of confusing the map with the territory. 20th century analytic philosophy cautions against use-mention confusion [9]. Lewis Carroll illustrates this in *Through the Looking-Glass* [10] with Alice's confusion at the Knight's discussion of Haddocks' Eyes (which uses a chain of information grounding levels). In these cases, the typical confusion is mistaking one level for its neighbor.

In IS development, it is common to make a similar kind of mistake and talk of a model at one time as if it modelled the system and another time as if it modelled the information ground. The RM-ODP architecture appears to do this; the 4 + 1 architecture, like many software focused approaches, appears to avoid consideration of the information ground almost entirely.

However, the problem goes deeper. Once the system is developed, the relationship between the information ground, the system (information) and the system (information) model is a clear case of an information grounding hierarchy. However, during development things are less clear. In the early stages, one works with design artefacts. One builds the information ground model and uses this to build the system model. But what legitimises this? The relation between the two cannot be simple grounding; the system itself grounds the system model and the information ground model is a design artefact – clearly not the system. The grounding relation is indirect, it is that the system information and the information ground model shared the same information ground, so are in some way isomorphic. The information grounding view will need to account for this kind of indirect isomorphic grounding.

There are other refinements that will be needed. For example, it is usual to represent the information ground outside the system. However, there are many cases where they overlap. (Davidson [11] makes a similar point about the use-mention distinction.) Obvious cases are operating systems, where the objects of interest (for examples, files) are clearly inside the system. Less obvious, but common, cases would be internet orders, which are processed almost completely online. In these cases, the order is inside the system. In these cases, the system information does not clearly map into a level in the information grounding hierarchy. This leads to a requirement for a more intricate mapping of the information grounding hierarchy onto the design models.

## 3    First-Third Person Divergence

The original UoD/UoDD literature and subsequent work assumes a simple grounding structure, where the UoDD inside the system is a simple model/description of the UoD (in our terms, that the system information is just an information ground model). However, the system is often an agent and as such the information content is not a simple description – so more than simple grounding is at play. We discuss two ways it is less simple: indexical and epistemic. There are others that need to be catered for, such as the deontic and doxastic aspects.

In philosophy, particularly philosophy of mind there is much debate about the relation between first and third person perspectives [12], and the reducibility of the first to the third person. One aspect of these are the indexicals typically linked to the first person (the most prominent being 'I', 'here' and 'now'), whose meaning depends upon the context of the utterance. These indexicals are also studied in philosophy of language, where Perry [13] made a convincing argument that they are irreducible.

There seems to be a similar phenomenon in information systems. Statements giving a person's age are linked to the 'now' time of utterance – 'Boris Johnson is 52 (now)' is true at the time of writing, but will be false when read in a few years. A typical information design manoeuvre is to talk about a static date of birth rather than dynamic age. This merely pushes back the need for the 'now' indexical; in order to recover the age, one needs to calculate the time between the date of birth and now. So it is no surprise that programming languages cater for this; C#'s DateTime.Now property being an example. In an analogous way, one may convert a mobile phone's dynamic 'here' location into static coordinates, but one still needs the equivalent of 'here' to find one's current location.

A business application often has a requirement for designed blindness – a restriction on its information about its domain. A topical example is name and age blindness in a curriculum vitae register – to avoid discrimination. We call what the system knows a 'first person epistemology' here – it is what the application as agent is designed to know. In [14] this is called just 'epistemology' and the designed blindness 'epistemic divergence'.

Hopefully the preceding discussion has both clarified what information grounding is and the kind of attention to detail needed to expose the underlying structure. We have developed a view that this exemplifies a wider problem of a lack of attention to fundamental meta-ontological issues that become particularly acute in gargantuan systems. It is a common theme among metaphysicians that metaphysics is unavoidable; that most positions involve an array of metaphysical assumptions [15, 16]. And that if one does not make the effort to understand the choices one has made, then it is likely that they will be uninformed, often ill-formed. This view suggests a way forward.

## 4    Information Grounding Architectural Framework

The way forward is to use a framework in which these metaphysical issues, including information grounding, are explicitly addressed. One such framework is a foundational ontology; where this "defines a range of top-level domain-independent ontological categories, which form a general foundation for more elaborated domain-specific ontologies" [17].

However, the mere adoption of a foundational ontology in itself is insufficient to ensure the right level of quality. One also needs a framework from within which one can assess the metaphysical quality; whether and how the issues have been dealt with.

Within philosophy, there is not a consensus on the 'right' ontology. But there is a reasonable consensus on ways a particular ontology can be characterised. One is its position on ontological topics such as identity or space and time. These are useful headings under which to understand an individual foundational ontology. There is also a reasonable consensus on the range of metaphysical choices one can make. These can be helpful when deciding between foundational ontologies, as they can help to characterise commonalties and differences.

We have been developing a range of choices for a while. The choices (listed in Table 1) were first published in [18], and subsequently in [19–21]. They have been discussed in [22]. Together these texts contain a quite detailed explanation of these choices, which we will not repeat here. There are undoubtedly refinements and additions that could (and should) be made to this list, but we have found it a useful starting point.

**Table 1.** Metaphysical Choices (BORO choices highlighted)

| Choice 1 | Choice 2 | Related Topics |
| --- | --- | --- |
| Endurantism | Perdurantism | Existence. Change. |
| Eternalism | Presentism | Existence. Change. |
| Single Space-Time Continuum | Separate Space and Time Continua | Change. |
| Modally Extended | Modally Flat | Modality/Possibility. Counterparts. |
| First Order Universals Only | Higher Order Universals | Existence. |
| Universals – Metaphysical Realism | Universals – Nominalism | Identity. Can two different universals have the same extension? |
| Particulars – Extensional Identity | Particulars - Coincident | Identity. Incudes mereology. |
| Materialism | Non-Materialism (Abstract) | Existence. |
| Branching Time | Linear Time | Existence. Possibility. |

We now provide an example of how to characterise a foundational ontology using metaphysical choices, using one we are familiar with – the BORO ontology (for an example of how one could use the choices to compare two ontologies see [23]). It is useful to understand the external drivers for the choices. One way to frame these is in terms of concerns, topics and choices – we provide two examples below.

Reproducibility is key to science, one expects different scientists to be able to get the same results when reproducing experiments. Unfortunately, in the practice of domain modelling, there is little reproducibility of models, as expert domain modellers often have fundamental disagreements. This is a result, in large part, of a lack of criteria of identity, mechanisms for understanding identity and difference.

A more stringent (and potentially more useful) desideratum is intersubjectively reliable criteria of identity; a mechanism that different people can use to reliably arrive at and agree upon the same result. This is not a new idea. Quine worried about this reliability question and this motivated his metaphysical choices. Decock [24] explores this in some detail. BORO makes similar choices to Quine for similar reasons (BORO's choices are highlighted in Table 1). For example, Quine (like BORO) selects materialism to avoid abstract objects which are notoriously difficult to agree on. Like Quine, BORO settles on a four-dimensional spatio-temporal extensional criterion of identity. Unlike Quine (but like Lewis) BORO chooses modally flat possible worlds. Like Quine, BORO's types are extensional. So this single concern has motivated most of the choices.

One way to appreciate how the choices shape the foundational ontology is looking at the tools and techniques they enable. The space-time maps used in BORO analysis (an example in Table 1) provide a good example. Given that four-dimensional spatio-temporal extent is a criterion of identity for particulars, then this kind of map of spatio-temporal extents is a way of characterising their identity (Fig. 1).

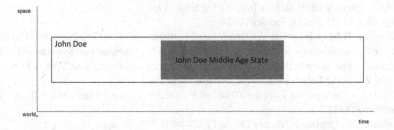

**Fig. 1.** An example of a BORO space-time map

This provides a clear way of visualising the ontological commitment, though one only available within a foundational ontology that has made these specific choices. Each object will occupy an area on the map (while objects can overlap no two objects can occupy the same exact area) – so one can unequivocally count the objects. One can also visualise mereological relations – overlaps and containments are clearly visible. This is analogous to the way Venn and Euler diagrams diagrammatically reason [25] over extensional sets, the way the spatial arrangement captures the identity criteria. Given BORO's space-time maps work with similar extensional identity criteria, then they could also be seen as a form of diagrammatical reasoning (see also Casati and Varzi's [26] Chapter 11 for the semantics of maps – though these are only spatial, they share some extensional characteristics).

## 5 Summary

We have highlighted the need for an information grounding view in IS architectures when working with gargantuan systems. We showed how this view reveals intricacies central to the structure of the IS development process that are missed by contemporary efforts. We have proposed foundational ontologies as architectures for the information grounding approach and shown how metaphysical choices can be used to assess them.

**Acknowledgements.** The authors would like to thank the UK Engineering and Physical Sciences Research Council (grant EP/K009923/1) for funding this research.

# References

1. Shames, P., Skipper, J.: Toward a framework for modeling space systems architectures. In: Proceedings of the Jet Propulsion Laboratory, National Aeronautics and Space Administration, Pasadena, CA (2006)
2. Kruchten, P.B.: The 4 + 1 view model of architecture. IEEE Softw. **12**, 42–50 (1995). IEEE
3. Hilliard, R.: Ieee-Std-1471-2000 Recommended Practice for Architectural Description of Software-Intensive Systems (2000)
4. Boole, G.: An Investigation of the Laws of Thought: On which are Founded the Mathematical Theories of Logic and Probabilities. Walton and Maberly, London (1854)
5. ISO: ISO/TR 9007:1987 - Information Processing Systems – Concepts and Terminology for the Conceptual Schema and the Information Base (1987)
6. Bergmann, G.: Logic and Reality (1964)
7. Armstrong, D.M.: Universals: An Opinionated Introduction. Westview Press, Boulder (1989)
8. Korzybski, A.: Science and Sanity: An Introduction to Non-Aristotelian Systems and General Semantics. The Science Press Printing Company, Lancaster, Penn./New York (1933)
9. Quine, W.V.O.: Mathematical Logic. Norton, New York (1940)
10. Carroll, L.: Through the Looking-Glass, and what Alice found There. Macmillan, United Kingdom (1871)
11. Davidson, D.: Quotation. Theory Decis. 11, 27–40 (1979). Springer
12. Baker, L.R.: Naturalism and the First-Person Perspective. Oxford University Press, New York (2013)
13. Perry, J.: The problem of the essential indexical. Noûs 13, 3–21 (1979). Wiley
14. Lycett, M., Partridge, C.: The challenge of epistemic divergence in is development. Commun. ACM **52**, 127–131 (2009). ACM
15. Lowe, E.J.: The Possibility of Metaphysics: Substance, Identity, and Time. Clarendon Press, Oxford University Press, Oxford, New York (1998)
16. Peirce, C.S.: Collected Papers of Charles Sanders Peirce. Harvard University Press, Cambridge (1932)
17. Guizzardi, G., Wagner, G.: A unified foundational ontology and some applications of it in business modeling. In: Proceedings of the CAiSE Workshops, pp. 129–143 (2004)
18. Partridge, C.: LADSEB-CNR - Technical Report 06/02 - Note: A Couple of Meta-Ontological Choices for Ontological Architectures. The BORO Program, LADSEB CNR, Italy, Padova (2002)
19. Semy, S.K., Pulvermacher, M.K., Obrst, L.J.: Toward the use of an Upper Ontology for US Government and US Military Domains: An Evaluation. The MITRE Corporation, Bedford (2004)
20. Masolo, C., Borgo, S., Gangemi, A., Guarino, N., Oltramari, A.: Wonderweb Deliverable D18. Ontology Library (Final). Laboratory for Applied Ontology, ISTC-CNR, Trento (2003)

21. Borgo, S., Gangemi, A., Guarino, N., Masolo, C., Oltramari, A.: WonderWeb Deliverable D15 Ontology RoadMap. The WonderWeb Library of Foundational Ontologies and the DOLCE Ontology, ISTC-CNR, Padova (2002)
22. Partridge, C., Mitchell, A., De Cesare, S.: Guidelines for developing ontological architectures in modelling and simulation. In: Tolk, A. (ed.) Ontology, Epistemology, and Teleology for Modeling and Simulation. ISRL, pp. 27–57. Springer, Heidelberg (2012)
23. de Cesare, Sergio, Henderson-Sellers, Brian, Partridge, Chris, Lycett, Mark: Improving model quality through foundational ontologies: two contrasting approaches to the representation of roles. In: Jeusfeld, Manfred A., et al. (eds.) ER 2015 Workshops. LNCS, vol. 9382, pp. 304–314. Springer, Heidelberg (2015). doi:10.1007/978-3-319-25747-1_30
24. Decock, L.: Trading Ontology for Ideology: The Interplay of Logic, Set Theory and Semantics in Quine's Philosophy. Synthese Library, vol. 313. Springer Science & Business Media (2002)
25. Shin, S.: The Logical Status of Diagrams. Cambridge University Press, New York (1994)
26. Casati, R., Varzi, A.C.: Parts and Places: the Structure of Spatial Representation. MIT Press, Cambridge (1999)

# Conceptual Modelling for Ambient Assistance and Healthy Ageing

## Preface: Conceptual Modeling for Ambient Assistance and Healthy Ageing

Heinrich C. Mayr[1], Ulrich Frank[2], and J. Palazzo M. de Oliveira[3]

[1] Alpen-Adria-Universität Klagenfurt, Klagenfurt, Austria
heinrich.mayr@aau.at
[2] Universität Essen-Duisburg, Duisburg, Germany
ulrich.frank@uni-duisburg-essen.de
[3] UFRGS Porto Alegre, Porto Alegre, Brazil
palazzo@inf.ufrgs.br

"Health, demographic change and wellbeing" is not only a designated "Grand Challenge" of the European Union but an upcoming challenge of the entire world. Endeavors are made in various directions to meet that challenge, amongst which the fields of "Active and Assisted Living (AAL)" and "Healthy Ageing (HA)" are rather prominent.

The design of innovative and beneficial IT solutions in these domains recommends "thinking out of the box", i.e. looking beyond current ways of living in the older age. For innovation to work, it is also important to get various stakeholders of future assistance systems involved in time, i.e. to offer them comprehensible representations of possible solutions that enable them to express their concerns and demands. Therefore, the realization of advanced systems to support "Active and Assisted Living (AAL)" and "Healthy Ageing (HA)" recommends powerful abstractions, or, in other words, the design and use of conceptual models.

Although most projects dealing with AAL and HA use models in some way, only few systematic approaches to modeling methods for these fields have been reported so far. Therefore, the workshop "Conceptual Modeling for Ambient Assistance and Healthy Ageing" was designed and firstly held at ER2015 to reveal the existing and potential contributions, which can be made by the modeling community to AAL and HA. A particular emphasis was on Conceptual Modeling within the context of designing and developing systems for assisting humans in their everyday live and in healthy ageing. A discussion at the end of the 2015 AHA instance came to the clear conviction of all participants that this had been a successful begin and should be continued in the next years as the model focused view of AHA will become increasing importance.

Questions to be discussed at AHA2016 were, among others, which modeling method might be useful for which purpose, how the requirements of the end users could be met by using (conceptual) modeling techniques, and how to relate modeling tools to common standards in the fields of Ambient Assistance, Ambient Assisted Living and Healthy Ageing. `

All submitted papers have been peer reviewed by members of the program committee. This chapter contains those papers, which have been accepted by the program committee, and carefully revised following the reviewers' comments.

The paper "*A Model-Driven Engineering Approach for the Well-Being of Ageing People*" by Amanuel Koshima, Vincent Englebert, Moussa Amani, Abdelmounaim Debieche and Amanuel Wakjira presents a model-driven framework for handling high-level specifications of AAL concerns like being notified of events (e.g., a ringing phone) or receiving adequate assistance (e.g., after a fall). The framework focuses on the following aspects to be modeled explicitly: (1) agent's goals that formally capture users' concerns, (2) abstract solutions, and (3) concrete solutions in terms of APIs or various combination of APIs.

Bernhard Thalheim and Hannu Jaakkola address in their paper "*The Cultural Background and Support for Smart Web Information Systems*" the challenge of designing and implementing web information systems that are 'smart' in the sense that they adapt to the user's 'culture' independently on her/his age, abilities, habits and environments. The authors propose a generic approach based on stereotypes reflecting cultures.

We thank all authors for submitting to AHA2016 as well as the members of our renowned program committee for their careful and intensive collaboration.

## Program Committee

| | |
|---|---|
| Heinrich C. Mayr | Alpen-Adria-Universität Klagenfurt (chair person) |
| Ulrich Frank | Universität Duisburg-Essen (chair person) |
| J. Palazzo M. de Oliveira | UFRGS Porto Alegre (chair person) |
| Fadi Al Machot | Alpen-Adria-Universität Klagenfurt, Austria |
| Vadim Ermolayev | Zaporozhye National University, Ukraine |
| Hans-Georg Fill | Universität Wien, Austria |
| Athula Ginige | University of Western Sydney, Australia |
| Sven Hartmann | Universität Clausthal, Germany |
| Marion A. Hersh | University of Glasgow, UK |
| Dimitris Karagiannis | Universität Wien, Austria |
| Yuichi Kurita | Hiroshima University, JP |
| Gerhard Lakemeyer | RWTH Aachen, Germany |
| Stephen Liddle | Kevin and Debra Rollins Center for e-Business, USA |
| Elisabeth Métais | Laboratory CEDRIC, Paris, France |
| Judith Michael | Alpen-Adria-Universität Klagenfurt, Austria |
| Johannes Oberzaucher | FH Kärnten, Austria |
| Leif Oppermann | Fraunhofer Gesellschaft, Germany |

| Oscar Pastor | University of Valencia, Spain |
| Wolfgang Reisig | Humboldt-Universität zu Berlin, Germany |
| Dominique Rieu | UPMF Grenoble, France |
| Elmar Sinz | Universität Bamberg, Germany |
| Vladimir Shekhovtsov | National Technical Univ. "KhPI", Kharkiv, Ukraine |
| Markus Stumptner | University of South Australia, Australia |
| Bermhard Thalheim | Universität Kiel, Germany |
| Benkt Wangler | Stockholm University, Sweden |
| Tatjana Welzer | University of Maribor, Slovenia |

# A Model-Driven Engineering Approach for the Well-Being of Ageing People

Amanuel Alemayehu Koshima[1], Vincent Englebert[1(✉)], Moussa Amani[1],
Abdelmounaim Debieche[1], and Amanuel Wakjira[2]

[1] PReCISE Research Center, University of Namur, Namur, Belgium
{Amanuel.Koshima,Vincent.Englebert,Moussa.Amrani,
Abdelmounaim.Debieche}@unamur.be
[2] Vrije Universiteit Brussel, ETRO, Brussel, Belgium
acwakjir@etro.vub.ac.be

**Abstract.** Ambient Assisted Living has been widely perceived as a
viable solution to mitigate the astronomical increase in the cost of health
care. In the context of our Geras Project, we propose a Model-Driven
Engineering framework for handling high-level specifications that capture the concerns of elderly people still living at home. These concerns
are related to concrete living issues, like being notified of a ringing phone
for a deaf people, or receiving adequate assistance after a fall. The framework explicitly models three aspects: agent's goals, formally capturing
users' concerns; abstract solutions, defining a canvas for answering the
goal; and concrete solutions in terms of APIs or various combination of
APIs, for their operationalisation. We illustrate the usage of our framework on two simple scenarios.

**Keywords:** Ambient assisting ageing people · Smart home · Model-
driven engineering · Goal elicitation · Software factory

## 1 Introduction

According to the World Health Organization report on ageing and health [12], the
life expectancy of people has improved and most people can expect to live into
their 60s and beyond. The increase in life expectancy augmented with low fer-
tility rates result in an uneven demographic composition in developed countries
[9,15]. For instance, the ages of 30 % of the European population are expected
to be 65 years or above in 2050 [8]. Ageing people are more susceptible to frailty,
chronic diseases, and increased multimorbidity, higher hospitalization rates and
prevalence of health risk [9]. The demographic change and inadequate number of
health care professionals will make the future costs of an ageing society unsustainable in terms of health care and social services [15]. Ambient Assisted Living
(AAL) has been widely perceived as a viable solution to mitigate the astronomical increase in the cost of health care. Besides, it provides a new model of positive
ageing that empowers older adults to maintain independence, functionality, well-
being and higher quality of life in their residence [9].

S. Link and J.C. Trujillo (Eds.): ER 2016 Workshops, LNCS 9975, pp. 21–29, 2016.
DOI: 10.1007/978-3-319-47717-6_3

AAL is a residential setting equipped with embedded technologies (sensors, actuators, cameras, and similar electronic devices) so as to support elderly people in their daily life by monitoring themselves and their environments [15]. This potential of smart home attracts industries and academia to provide different smart home based solutions for elderly citizens. However, the interoperability of different smart home solutions is far-fetched due to the fact that they address a limited set of requirements and problems, and they are usually developed in isolation and target different architectures and operating systems [13]. Model Driven Engineering (MDE) approach is proven to address interoperability problems among heterogeneous software systems [6].

In the context of our project Geras, we present in this paper a theoretical framework for handling high-level specifications aimed at capturing the concerns of elderly people living at home, and assisting them by deploying concrete solutions tailored to their home equipment, taking into account possibly conflicting concerns of residents.

The rest of the paper is organized as follows: Sect. 2 presents the Geras Framework. In Sect. 3, we demonstrate the running example to motivate our work. Section 4 discuses related work, and Sect. 5 presents conclusion and future work.

## 2   Geras Framework

The Geras framework aims to be a software factory to assemble and generate concrete smart home solutions from high-level abstract specifications. Geras adopts a Model Driven Engineering (MDE) approach.

MDE is a software engineering methodology that is adopted to deal with an ever increasing complexity of software solutions. MDE raises the level of abstractions of software development from technological details (i.e., source codes and underlying platforms) to the problem domain. In MDE, models are the principal artifacts that give full descriptions of software systems and are used for analysis, simulation, and source code generation of a software system [11]. Domain concepts are defined using well-suited Domain Specific Modeling Languages (DSML) at acceptable levels of abstraction [11].

MDE applies separation of concern principles that reduces complexity, improves reusability, and ensures simpler evolution of modeling languages [11]. It separates the domain knowledge from the underlying implementation details, as a result, the business domain and the underlying smart home technologies could evolve separately. These benefits of the MDE approach motivates the adoption of MDE in the Geras framework.

The Geras framework uses DSML tool-chains to generate IoT-based smart home solutions. Figure 1 demonstrates the general architecture of the Geras framework. Although our concepts could be spread on several modeling levels (i.e. Agent and AgentType in Fig. 2), we decided to present them at the same level (M2) for sake of simplicity. A generic goal represents a high level user concern (e.g. listening phone calls or having a quiet environment). Each goal may be associated with related abstract solutions. An abstract solution (AS) is

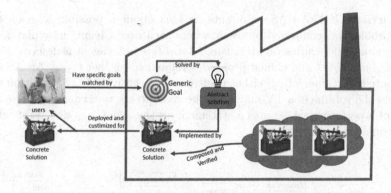

**Fig. 1.** General architecture of the Geras framework

akin to the concept of a patent, and does not provide much details about its implementation. The user profiles (e.g. environment, constraints, etc.) are used to tune the software generation process at design time. Besides, contextual information can also be used at runtime to equip the framework with context-aware capabilities.

In Geras, the mapping between a goal and an AS is performed in two steps. The AS is firstly described using a feature model that captures the variability of different product configurations (the technical solutions) [1]. Afterwards, the goal is mapped to the feature model. One goal can be achieved by one or more features of the solution. Apel *et al.* define a feature as "a characteristic or end-user-visible behavior of a software system" [1]. Of course, users do not usually live in isolation, therefore, the Geras framework should support social goal modeling as well.

One of the main challenge in social goal modeling is to detect conflicting goals automatically. In order to detect conflicts, we merge the feature selection of each user into one consolidated model. Afterwards, we use the feature configurator to validate whether this is consistent or not, for instance, two goals mapped to features that belong to a same parent and have an *alternative (XOR)* relationship denote a conflict. This case can be illustrated with an example: a husband who is deaf wants to listen a phone call, and this goal is mapped to a `high-volume` feature in the feature model. On the other hand, his wife who has a depressive character and wants to have a `quiet environment`. The `quiet environment` goal is mapped to a `low-volume` feature. In the merged model, both the `high-volume` and the `low-volume` features are selected, although they have an XOR relationship in the feature model. Hence, the configurator automatically detects this conflict.

The software factory is guided by a DSML that allows us to model both the "problem" and the "technical" spaces. Figure 2 depicts the problem space meta-model. Meta-models are defined with an Extented Entity Relationship notation [7]. This meta-model specifies the knowledge about which kinds of solutions, (*AbstractSolution* AS), are available to address certain kinds of goals

(*GenericGoal* GG). An AS represents an idea about a possible solution that solves problems encountered by users, where each user (*Agent*) may play a role (*Performance*) depending on his nature (*AgentType*). An agent is described with a set of *AgentTypes* and valued *properties* related to his/her types. An AS may contribute to a *GenericGoal* either positively or negatively (e.g. a solution that increases the volume of a TV may alter the goal `quiet environment`). The condition of a performance denotes a statement on the agent, e.g. `not deaf` where `deaf` would be a property.

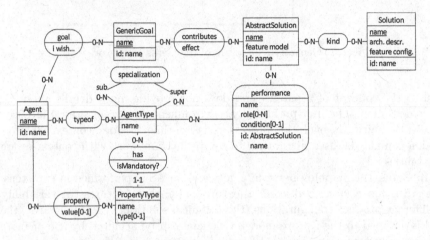

**Fig. 2.** Metamodel of the problem space

The technical space meta-model (see Fig. 3) describes the available solutions (considered here as a shelf of reusable technological assets — COTS). A *Solution* is considered as a prototypical assembly of services (*Service*), software components (*Soft Component*), or hardware (*Equipment*). The *role* of each one is defined as well as its possible occurrences (*min-max*) by the *usage* relationship. The *equipment* can be arbitrarily complex and have IO devices. IO Devices, software components and services can have provided/required API. API can be defined by an implementation or be defined in an ontological way, independently from any provider's constraint. If an API subsumes another one, then a *wrapper* can be defined with a set of *matching rules*. A solution can denote a very simple assembly (a plug and its wireless switch) as well as more complex solutions based on sensors, actuators, hubs, computers, software and cloud applications. A *solution* can be defined as a composite of other solutions, where the assembling mechanism is defined with a set of *composition rules*. A solution can be deployed and customized for a set of agents identified by their role. This information can be used to ensure that the safety preconditions are met.

These both meta-models are two facets of a global meta-model where the *solution* concept is the hinge. This meta-model does not intend to be exhaustive but rather to be a transversal backbone among several concerns and offers

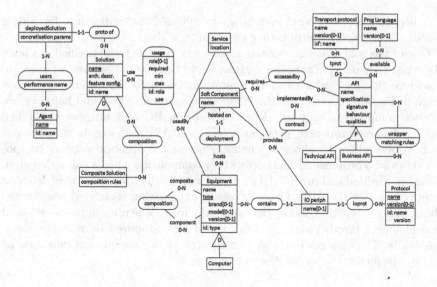

**Fig. 3.** Metamodel of the technical space

alignment to other modeling languages such as goal modeling languages (GRL http://www.cs.toronto.edu/km/GRL, I* http://www.cs.toronto.edu/km/istar, KAOS http://www.objectiver.com/index.php?id=25), architecture description languages, other DSL for IoT for instance (ThingML[1]), or other languages (SySML[2]). The DSML has been defined with three specific goals in mind: designing user-centred AAL solutions by tuning or assembling existing solutions (i) at the lowest cost (ii) and with a good ROI (iii) in order to have a viable business model.

## 3    Running Example

We demonstrate the Geras framework with the following use case: *Albert, 70, and his wife Beth, 68, are a fictitious couple that lives in the country side of Belgium. Both are capable of using a smart home solution. Albert is deaf and can only hear sounds in a limited spectrum. Hence, he needs a smart home solution that assists him to be notified when his phone rings. Beth has muscular problems and needs to be assisted whenever she falls.* This use case is captured in Fig. 4: it proposes a concrete instance of the previous meta-models (Figs. 2 and 3). *Albert* is an instance of the *Agent* with *Deaf Person* as *AgentType*: a deaf person is characterized by the fact that they only hear a portion of the sound spectrum. Agents' properties detail their characteristics according to the property types declared for their agent type. For example, Albert's property able is set to true, indicating his ability to assist other persons (moving and calling) in their

---

[1] http://thingml.org/.

[2] http://sysml.org/.

daily life; and property `spectrum` is set to 600-3000Hz, indicating, for a deaf person, which sound spectrum they can hear.

One of the goal of a deaf person, as an agent type, is to be notified of phone calls when they occur: `increase volume` could be a potential abstract solution to achieve this goal, which can be operationalized into the concrete solutions shown in Fig. 4 (red icons). In the `POPUP4Win` solution, `Popup` and `Monitor` are software components that are deployed resp. on PC and Raspberry Pi. The Popup software component provides a technical API that lets its environment notify Albert when the phone is ringing, whereas the Monitor software component relies on a business API to notify other components when a call is detected. When the required and provided API do not match, the framework may deliver a wrapper to adapt the APIs. Other elements' explanation is omitted here for the sake of brevity, but they follow the same principles. When a solution is selected for deployment (`Deployed solution`), it can be customized to meet the users' constraints. The `concretisation parameters` of this deployment can then be used by the factory to automatise the process.

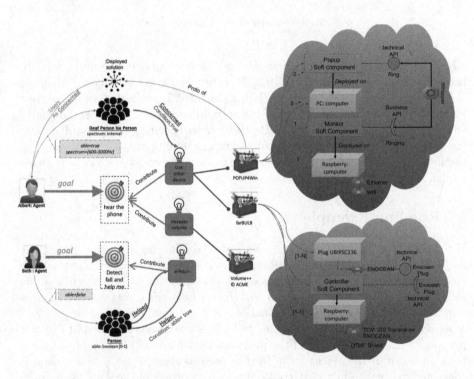

**Fig. 4.** Use case (Color figure online)

## 4   Related Work

The main challenge of IoT-based smart home solutions is an efficient management of interconnected resource-constrained (i.e., low power, small size) devices.
The IoT reference architecture [2] eases the development of interoperable IoT
applications by providing a common structure and guidelines for dealing with
core aspects of developing, using and analyzing IoT systems. In [14], Pramudianto *et al.* develop the IoTLink toolkit by adopting an MDE approach and
the IoT reference architecture. The MDE approach is used to ensure portability,
interoperability and reusability of applications through separation of concerns
[3]. The IoTLink is not a context-aware system. The context awareness capability is crucial for a smart home solution in order to leverage information about
the end users and improves the quality of their interaction [16]. In [5], Fleurey
*et al.* use a model-driven approach to develop adaptive firmwares. However, their
work does not fully support the contextual information presented in [4].

The aforementioned work focus on using the MDE approach to ensure interoperability, but they provide little support for modeling the underlying motivation of the user in terms of stakeholder concerns and the high-level goals that
address these concerns. Massacci *et al.* present a goal-oriented access control
model for ambient assisted living [10], but their work has a limited scope and
it does not use goal modeling techniques to generate and refine smart home
solutions. In [15], Rafferty *et al.* adopt the goal oriented modeling approach to
develop a smart home. However, the authors do not apply the MDE approach in
their work that could ensure interoperability among heterogeneous smart home
applications.

## 5   Conclusion and Future Work

AAL appears to become a widely adopted solution to mitigate the increasing
costs of health care for elderly people. In this context, we propose a new framework that aims at (i) capturing high-level concerns through abstract goals people living in their smart home encounter in their daily life; (ii) associating these
concerns to abstract solutions that describe a way to overcome these concerns;
and (iii) operationalizing these solutions according to the equipment the smart
home possess. We proposed a conceptual meta-model capturing all aspects of our
framework, and demonstrated its use through two illustrating examples coming
from real-life situations.

We are currently focusing on two aspects. The first one targets interoperability between the many devices a smart home can contain. In order for our
concrete solutions to work, independently of the APIs, protocols, manufactur-
ers or concrete capabilities the devices in the smart home present, we plan
to design a DSML targeting the centralized inter-communication of devices,
based on business rules that implement the requirements expressed by abstract
solutions.

At a earlier stage in our framework, the second aspect targets the capture of
high-level concerns through the elicitation of the residents' concerns expressed

as goals. This crucial step requires an explicit modeling of the user profiles, the many contexts of an abstract solution, spanning from the devices' network to a lightweight description of the home's environment. In turn, this explicit representation should allow to analyze adequately the compliance of the proposed abstract solutions, and the potential conflicts that will inevitably occur throughout the use of our framework.

# References

1. Apel, S., Batory, D., Kästner, C., Saake, G.: Feature-Oriented Software Product Lines: Concepts and Implementation. Springer, Heidelberg (2013)
2. Bauer, M., Bui, N., De Loof, J., Magerkurth, C., Nettsträter, A., Stefa, J., Walewski, J.W.: IoT reference model. In: Bassi, A., Bauer, M., Fiedler, M., Kramp, T., van Kranenburg, R., Lange, S., Meissner, S. (eds.) Enabling Things to Talk, pp. 113–162. Springer, Heidelberg (2013)
3. Belaunde, M., Casanave, C., DSouza, D., Duddy, K., El Kaim, W., Kennedy, A., Frank, W., Frankel, D., Hauch, R., Hendryx, S. et al.: Mda guide version 1.0 (2003)
4. Dey, A.K., Abowd, G.D., Salber, D.: A conceptual framework and a toolkit for supporting the rapid prototyping of context-aware applications. Hum. Comput. Interact. $16(2)$, 97–166 (2001)
5. Fleurey, F., Morin, B., Solberg, A.: A model-driven approach to develop adaptive firmwares. In: Proceedings of the 6th SEAMS (2011)
6. Fleurey, F., Morin, B., Solberg, A., Barais, O.: MDE to manage communications with and between resource-constrained systems. In: Whittle, J., Clark, T., Kühne, T. (eds.) MODELS 2011. LNCS, vol. 6981, pp. 349–363. Springer, Heidelberg (2011). doi:10.1007/978-3-642-24485-8_25
7. Hainaut, J.-L., Hick, J.-M., Englebert, V., Henrard, J., Roland, D.: Understanding the implementation of IS-A relations. In: Thalheim, B. (ed.) ER 1996. LNCS, vol. 1157, pp. 42–57. Springer, Heidelberg (1996). doi:10.1007/BFb0019914
8. Herradi, N., Hamdi, F., Métais, E., Ghorbel, F., Soukane, A.: PersonLink: an ontology representing family relationships for the CAPTAIN MEMO memory prosthesis. In: Jeusfeld, M.A., Karlapalem, K. (eds.) ER 2015. LNCS, vol. 9382, pp. 3–13. Springer, Heidelberg (2015). doi:10.1007/978-3-319-25747-1_1
9. Lê, Q., Nguyen, H.B., Barnett, T.: Smart homes for older people: positive aging in a digital world. Future Internet $4(2)$, 607–617 (2012)
10. Massacci, F., Hung Nguyen, V.: Goal-oriented access control model for ambient assisted living. In: Bezzi, M., Duquenoy, P., Fischer-Hübner, S., Hansen, M., Zhang, G. (eds.) Privacy and Identity 2009. IAICT, vol. 320, pp. 160–173. Springer, Heidelberg (2010). doi:10.1007/978-3-642-14282-6_13
11. Meyers, B., Vangheluwe, H.: A framework for evolution of modelling languages. Sci. Comput. Program. $76(12)$, 1223–1246 (2011)
12. World Health Organization, et al.: World report on ageing and health. World Health Organization (2015)
13. Perumal, T., Ramli, A.R., Leong, C.Y., Mansor, S., Samsudin, K.: Interoperability for smart home environment using web services. Int. J. Smart Home $2(4)$, 1–16 (2008)
14. Pramudianto, F., Kamienski, C.A., Souto, E., Borelli, F., Gomes, L.L., Sadok, D., Jarke, M.: IoTLink: an internet of things prototyping toolkit. In: UTC-ATC-ScalCom. IEEE (2014)

15. Rafferty, J., Chen, L., Nugent, C.: Ontological goal modelling for proactive assistive living in smart environments. In: Urzaiz, G., Ochoa, S.F., Bravo, J., Chen, L.L., Oliveira, J. (eds.) UCAmI 2013. LNCS, vol. 8276, pp. 262–269. Springer, Heidelberg (2013). doi:10.1007/978-3-319-03176-7_34

16. Robles, R.J., Kim, T.: Review: context aware tools for smart home development. Int. J. Smart Home 4(1), 1–11 (2010)

# The Cultural Background and Support for Smart Web Information Systems

Bernhard Thalheim[1]([✉]) and Hannu Jaakkola[2]

[1] Christian-Albrechts-University Kiel,
Computer Science Institute, 24098 Kiel, Germany
thalheim@is.informatik.uni-kiel.de
[2] Tampere University of Technology, P.O. Box 300, 28101 Pori, Finland
hannu.jaakkola@tut.fi
http://www.is.informatik.uni-kiel.de/~thalheim,
http://www.pori.tut.fi/~hj

**Abstract.** Applications and technical solutions change very quickly. Societies change also change to certain extent. Users do not change in the same manner. They want to use systems in a way they are used to. So a systems should be smart in the sense that users may stay within their habits, their way of working, their ways of accessing systems, and their circumstances. We introduce a culture-based approach to smart systems. Such smart systems may adapt to the current user independently on her/his age, abilities, habits, environments, and collaborators of them.

**Keywords:** Smart web information systems · Information system development · Culture based approach

## 1 The HOME Approach to Systems

### 1.1 The Janus Head for Web Information System Development

Classical software engineering starts with a holistic approach to systems and users of such systems. A web information system represents three facets in a holistic manner: humans, tasks and information/communication systems. The system supports the user according to the tasks the users has to resolve. Therefore, software development approaches derive requirements to systems from the task portfolio of users. Next, the system specification is developed. The specification can be based on some system architecture, e.g. on a separation into the application interface, a technical system, and the technical infrastructure in the QuASAR framework. The system should reflect all needs of the user. Computer engineering thus assumed that users must become knowledgeable with the system and must learn how a system behaves.

In reality there are however different requirements from different users, different approaches to task fulfillment, different technical environments, and different collaboration approaches for user communities [35]. With the advent of

© Springer International Publishing AG 2016
S. Link and J.C. Trujillo (Eds.): ER 2016 Workshops, LNCS 9975, pp. 30–45, 2016.
DOI: 10.1007/978-3-319-47717-6_4

web applications and web information systems it became apparent that the classical approach does not work. We have to separate two different viewpoints and support these viewpoints in a different form during system development.

**The social viewpoint** reflects the environment of the user with
  - the life cases (i.e. real life application cases) that are important for the user,
  - the tasks that must be solved by the user in order to overcome problems of their daily life,
  - the context of the user, e.g., cultural, language, and
  - the collaboration with other users within a community of practice or society depending on the organisational structure, the user information space, and the user features.

**The technical viewpoint** is based on systems with a reflection of the application logic and the needs of the user. Such systems may consist of
  - a database system with the database and the database management system,
  - an ensemble of logical procedures that might be of use for the system deployment, and
  - supporting facilities such as analysis machines or data warehouses.

**The mediating connector** connects the two viewpoints based on views and with functions that allow a user to act with the system.

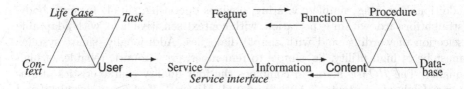

**Fig. 1.** Service architectures for web information systems

Figure 1 displays the *'Janus' head* of *socio-technical systems* based on service interfaces. The user world is driven by life cases, tasks and context. The information system world is composed of a database system, on views defined on top of the database, on procedures which are supported by the database management system, and on functions which support the user work. A web information system is a specific information system that additionally supports users by web technology. Its flow of work can be represented by stories which are combined into a story space on the based of a storyboard language [4]. The service interface is the mediating connector that allows the user to satisfy his/her information and activity demand. This demand depends on the support needed, e.g. for workplace and workspace requested, for data consumed or produced by the user, and for the environment and context of the user. The user is characterised by a profile, e.g. the work profile, the education profile, and the personality profile.

## 1.2  Towards Smart Systems Supporting Users with Their Life Cases

*Smart systems* support different people in their way of system usage within their contexts. They can make intelligent response to different kinds of needs, including daily livelihood, environmental protection, public safety and city services, industrial and commercial activities.

Modern information systems must support a large variety of users that have different educational, work and personality profiles. These users perform tasks in dependence on their life cases, their habits and abilities, and their flow of work. Classical systems cannot meet such requirements due to the large variety of flows of work, of viewpoints on data, and of collaborations among users. It would require thousands of different variants of a system. It is thus infeasible to develop them.

Users typically have their own background and history, their own experiences and system usage approaches, their specific environment, their specific daily life requirement at work and at home, and their specific system understanding. I.e. users have their own *culture* of system usage. The half-life time of systems is far shorter than the abilities of users to adapt their behaviour to systems. So, systems must become freely customisable to any user, any age, any behaviour, and any specific life circumstance.

We thus derive a super-requirement: adaptable [5] and easy to use systems without any additional learning effort. Website development approaches used to call such systems *'grandmother-proof'* [29] or with ease of use: usable without additional training, simple operating, obvious operating, simple for everybody, straightforward, within expectation, with context-sensitive help, with adaptable selection of wording, and with simple dialogues. Additionally, smart systems must be of high utility, i.e. simple to remember, error robust, reliable, of high quality. The *HOME* acronym combines the four quality characteristics of systems: *H*igh quality content, *O*ften updated, *M*inimal effort (, e.g. download and processing time and space), and *E*ase of use.

Such systems must be supporting any user within his/her life cases and tasks. At the same time, the system should meet the expectations of the user, should stay within their normal habits, should also be robust against any specific treatment of tasks, and might be adaptable to the current accomplishment of the task.

Applications are becoming **smart** if they are *S*imple in any step of usage that any user might request, are *M*otivational for any user independently on the way of working of the given user, are *A*ttainable for the goals the user has in mind, tend to be *R*ewarding since they seem to be worthwhile, right time, match efforts and needs, and are *T*ime-efficient within the limits and expectations of users.

*Ambient assistance* and *healthy aging* systems are a specific kind of smart systems. People want to stay within their habits, within the way of working, within their traditions, and within their traditional life cases, i.e. within their daily culture. Moreover, they do not want to pay a lot of attention to the way how systems work beside those they are used to. So, active and assisted living requires highly adaptive systems.

### 1.3  Adaptation of Dynamic or Generic Systems

Classical static systems cannot be smart whenever users are different. Dynamic systems [26] react to changes in its environment in a quick and flexible way. They support process agility on the basis of product and service variability and ensure business IT alignment. They are called process-aware information systems (PAIS) since they might change the flow of action in dependence on some parameters. The variability is based on parameters that are used for selection of the most appropriate flow of action and provision of data. It turns however out that the parameter instantiation results in a combinatorial explosion of variants that might be selected. Moreover, such systems cannot yet support users in their manifold.

Generic systems and generic functionality [2] might be a better solution. An application can often be described in a general form. Handicraft education is based on this approach. Craftsmen learn the general approaches and adaptation of them to specific situations. We are not yet able to develop generic systems. We might however specify specific systems for specific applications. These systems may be then adapted to become specialised to the user. Such systems have already be developed for advanced applications such as disaster management [38, 39].

We might try to build generic or dynamic systems on the logical or physical level. It turns out however that this becomes infeasible due to the variety in applications, the velocity of changes, the variations we would need, and the different viewpoints. So, a better way is to model this adaptability at the conceptual level. We thus need a general conceptual model of such systems which can be adapted to users. If we know main general behavioural pattern of users and some context then we can adapt systems on a basis of a *conceptual generic model* with some *adaptation model*. The adaptation model is a *governing strategic and tactical model.*

### 1.4  The Paper

This paper investigates one way of constructing smart web information systems. These systems adapt to the culture of the user. We delineate the technological support for such systems. The social space of users remains to be untouched. The technical space provides adaptability. The mediator can become thus generic.

## 2  Cultures of System Users Matter

### 2.1  National and Regional Cultures of Users

G. Hofstede [7,8] defines culture as "*a collective phenomenon, which is shared with people who live or lived within the same social environment, which is where it was learned; culture consists of the unwritten rules of the social game; it is the collective programming of the mind that separates the member of one group or category of people from others.*" Culture has different facets: *National culture* (language, educational tradition, religion, beliefs, attitudes, and social context), *regional cultures* (as a specialisation of national cultures), *organisational (work) culture* within an organisation, *professional culture* based on education and adopted practices, and *project culture* or *team culture*. Hofstede and his followers [27,28,36] characterise users based on parameters such as power distance (PDI), individualism/collectivism (IDV), masculinity/femininity (MAS), uncertainty avoidance (UIA), Long-term/short term orientation (LTO), and indulgence/restraint (IVR).

R. Lewis [16,17] recognises three *basic stereotypes of cultures*. *Linear-active culture* is task-oriented and value is given to technical competence and facts. They are cool, factual and decisive planners. *Multi-active culture* is extrovert and human force is seen as an inspirational factor. They are warm, emotional, loquacious and impulsive. *Reactive culture* is people-oriented and dominated by knowledge, patience and silent control. They are courteous, amiable, accommodating, compromisers and good listeners.

It seems to be infeasible to support all possible cultures for any user independently on the application. Instead of providing a sophisticated, fully flexible and completely adaptable system we base our approach on generic systems [2,38] and develop a generalisation of cultural varieties and manifold.

## 2.2 Cultural Varieties and Their Way of System Usage

In this paper we concentrate on the cultural background of users and show how users can be supported based on their culture. The user support for assistance systems should incorporate these findings. Users prefer systems that behave in a similar way as humans supporting them. With the advent of Web 2.0 (or more challenging Web x.y) they request additional features according to their circumstances such as smart infrastructures, smart collaboration with other users, smart governance, smart mobility, smart economy, smart lifestyle, smart technology adaptation, smart service integration, and smart feedback response. Therefore, our approach should be considered as a step towards smart web information systems.

Lewis has collected the common traits of the three basic categories [16] (pp. 33–34). These categories result in different behavioural pattern. Table 1 summarises the findings in [12].

It is not surprising that each of the stereotypes must be supported in a different way. For instance, linear-active people prefer a well-structured website that follows a linear activity pattern, that provides activity-oriented data on place and continuously, that has high-quality content on hand, and that has the right feedback also in cases of failures and errors. In a similar form we may derive user data structures and functionality of web information systems in dependence on the Hofstede stereotypes.

**Table 1.** Characteristics of cultural stereotypes according to Lewis' model, applied in WIS context

| Linear-active | Multi-active | Reactive |
|---|---|---|
| introvert | extrovert | introvert |
| patient | impatient | patient |
| plans ahead | plans grand outline | looks at general principles |
| does one thing at a time | does several things at once | reacts |
| punctual | not punctual | punctual |
| compartmentalises activities | one activity influences another | sees the whole picture |
| sticks to plans | changes plans | makes slight changes |
| sticks to facts | juggles facts | statements are promises |
| gets information from official sources | prefers oral information | information from official and oral sources |
| follows correct procedures | pulls strings | networks |
| completes action changes | completes human transactions | react to partners |
| likes fixed agendas | interrelates everything | thoughtful |
| uses memos | rarely writes memos | plans slowly |
| dislikes losing face | has ready excuses | must not lose face |

## 2.3 Cultural Stereotypes for Dynamic or Generic Systems

*Cultural stereotypes* help to understand common patterns typical to national cultures. National culture is the basement of the personality and explains a lot of the behavioural pattern of an individual. Each kind of culture brings in its specific stereotype[1]. Since culture is a complex phenomenon and culture may be overlayed by other cultures whenever a user changes its environment it seems that the development of a general pattern is infeasible. In the past, workflow and other systems have been enhanced by dynamic approaches.

The cultural variety of successful national websites has been analysed for checkout procedures in [12]. We discovered that the variety is large and cannot be supported by a singleton story although these procedures seem to follow a common general confirm-pay story. It is not surprising that webshop users prefer their culture-specific systems and thus webshops are adapted to the local

---

[1] Stereotypes should satisfy at least five properties: (1) they must be accurate; (2) the quality of the stereotype allows it to be used consciously; (3) they should be descriptive, not evaluative; (4) they should be flexible so that they can be modified from time to time; (5) they can be used as a first "best guess".

cultures. We will now combine our approaches [9,11–13] to a general framework for smart web information systems.

## 2.4  User Stereotypes

Stereotypes of users can be combined into personae [22,30]. A *personae* is characterised by an expressive name characterising the stereotype, by culture, by nationality, by organisations or teams, by a bundle of projects the person might be engaged in, by a profession, by intents, by typical technical equipment, by behaviour pattern, by skills and profile, by disabilities, and by specific properties such as hobbies and habits. A personae is set into a task, personal, environmental, social, temporal, regional etc. context. A personae is stereotype that describes a typical individual, the context, the portfolio, and the profile. This description can be extended by an identity with name, pictures, etc., by personal characteristics such as age, gender, location, and socio-economic status, by a characterisation of reaction to possible users error, by specific observed behaviour including skill sets, behavioural pattern, expertise and background, and by specific relationships, requirements, and expectations. A typical stereotype is the German Jack-of-all-trades that represents a specific kind of a business man in Germany.

User models can be developed based on three specific profiles: *education*, *work* and *personality* profiles [11]. A *portfolio* of a user combines responsibilities and a collection of tasks assigned to or intended by a user and for which s/he has the authority and control, and a description of involvement within the task solution [31].

A *user stereotype* thus is given by three dimensions: (1) personae, (2) user model, and (3) user portfolio.

## 3  Support for Cultures

### 3.1  The Six Dimensions of Web Information Systems

It seems that the specification of web information systems is an overly difficult task. We may however separate the following six different concerns [12]:

**Intention:** The intention aspect is a very general one, centered around a mission statement for the system. The primary question is: what is the purpose of the system? Which users will use the system? Which skills and capabilities can be expected? What kind of support is needed? Users typically have their own specific behavior.

**Usage and the resulting story space:** Once some clarity with respect to the intentions of the web-based system has been obtained, the question arises of how the system will be used and by whom? As web-based systems are open systems, it is important to anticipate the behaviour of the users. We model usage through storyboards that allow the specification of the stories that users might use with the web information system. The story space is the combination of all the stories supported.

**Content:** The content aspect concerns the question: Which information should be provided to which user at which stage of the work? It is coupled with the problem of designing an adequate database. However, the organization of the data presented to the user via a website is significantly different from the organization of data in a database.

**Functionality:** The functionality aspect is coupled with the question of whether the site should be passive or active. A passive site only allows a user to navigate through the pages without any action or to search for corresponding content. It can be combined with guidance and help support. In an active site, input is also required from the user. Specific functions allow the processing of user input and the provision of features such as searching, printing, marking, and extraction.

**Context:** The context aspect deals with the context of the web information system with respect to society, time, expected users, the history of utilisation, and the paths of these users through the system. One major element of the context is culture in all its peculiarities, e.g. national and regional, organisational, website provider, and work environment cultures.

**Presentation:** The presentation aspect concerns the final realisation in web pages. The presentation can be separated into layout and playout. It follows principles of screenography [21] and is based on principles of visuality such as visual communication, visual cognition and visual design [34]. Design also depends on the support of technical end-devices such as computer screens, television, cell phones, etc., and the set layout preferences.

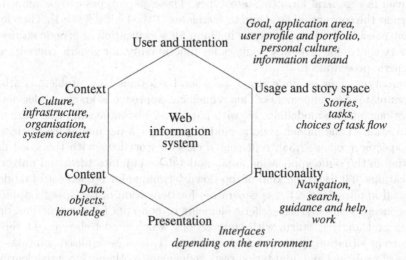

**Fig. 2.** The six concerns for web information system and the conceptual facilities

The concerns can directly be represented by separate conceptual structures. For instance, the intention dimension can be specified on the basis of life cases

[32] and solutions to them. It is typically combined with a user model that has a profile describing the user properties and with a portfolio of tasks that the user has to complete. Users can be stereotyped. The stereotype must then reflect the specific personal culture of a group of users. Figure 2 displays the concerns with their specific elements.

The adaptation possibilities discussed in [28] are: (1) information density, (2) navigation, (3) accessibility of functions, (4) guidance, (5) structure, (6) colourfulness, (7) saturation, and (8) support. Information density is a special property of content; functionality must reflect (2), (3) (4), and (8); presentation also considers (5), (6), and (7).

Our separation into six concerns goes beyond these adaptation facilities. Depending on the given culture and on the given application, we can develop specific stereotypes that appropriately support the user and can be refined depending on the chosen system environment. The following section develops these stereotypes.

## 3.2   Stereotypes as Generic Models

We concentrate on smart web information systems in this paper. In order to be smart, a system must be adaptable to its users and the context of its users. Therefore, we may assume that the context and users and their intention govern the other four dimensions. In the case of context, we restrict our consideration to the cultural context. The infrastructure, organisation and the systems are left to an extended version of this paper. We also assume that users and culture are given in a general form by stereotypes. These stereotypes can be refined to *pattern* at the conceptual level and to *templates* at the logical level [1]. Therefore, we may consider stereotypes as the linchpin for specification of generic stories in the story space, for generic workflows for functionality, for generic content, and for generic presentation.

Stereotypes can be understood as general solutions to a problem. Pattern and templates are refinements. This refinement approach is known under different notions: inverse modelling [18] with parameter instantiation, calibration and optimisation of the model; generic models represent a parameter-based class of more specific models [2,38]; represent a class of workflows with the same flow of action in the same application area. model-driven architectures and universal applications [33] use some kind of top-down technique for refinement of models; universal applications [24] use generators for derivation of the specific application; concept spaces [1] use generic elements or concepts for construction; data mining and analysis starts with suppositions which model class might reflect the current situation; pattern-based reasoning [1] uses generalised solutions for a class of problems and adaptation resp. refinement methods; inductive learning [40] starts with a supposition that a certain kind of explanation can be used; patient modelling [15] starts with a very general model of combinations of sicknesses and adapts the patient-specific, individualised model in accordance to the observations and data.

In this paper we restrain from details of refinement (specialisation, adaptation, calibration, contextualisation, instantiation, reorganisation, augmentation/distorcion, amplification, and idealisation) for the triad stereotype-pattern-template. We illustrate the path and the basics of stereotypes for the four concerns of web information systems starting with contexts and users and the corresponding refinement in dependence on the culture stereotype.

### 3.3 Deploying the Culture Stereotypes for Story Space Development

Storyboarding has been developed for website development. Stories of groups of users with similar behavioural stereotypes (called actors) are combined in a story space. A story has its structure and an adherence and cohesion among scenes in a story, i.e. scene collections that are more dependent on each other than all others. For instance, we observe in electronic commerce: (1) advertise and quote; (2) request and response; (3) select and collect; (4) bargain and contract; (5) requisition and order; (6) deliver and invoice; (7) pay or return. A *mini-story* [6,37] typically captures a small, self-contained, tightly connected set of scenes similar to a movie clip.

As in daily life, these mini-stories follow general stereotypes that follow the same kind of behaviour. It turns out [12,23] that mini-stories can be parameterised on the basis of the W*H framework [3]. Typical parameters are: wherefore, whereof, wherewith, worthiness, why, whereto, for when, for what reason, by whom, to whom, whatever, wherein, where, for what, wherefrom, whence, what, how, whereat, whereabouts, whither, when, why, what properties, what scenario, which restrictions.

There are several refinement facilities of such mini-story collections:

**Mini-story adaptation:** The specific culture may be a refinement of the stereotype. In this case adaptation of mini-stories follows the culture refinement.

**Adaptation of mini-story combination:** Cultures - esp. multi-active ones - may follow general multi-tasking, multi-facetted and concurrent flow of activities. In this case, the combination of a given story from mini-stories is correspondingly refined.

**Meshing and twisting together:** Cultures - esp. reactive and also multi-active ones - may have their own specific stereotypes for activities. These stereotypes are meshed with the mini-stories and then twisted again together. The result is shuffle product of generic stories and culture-specific stories.

### 3.4 Deploying the Culture Stereotypes for Content Development

Web information systems are based on databases and a collection of views that are derived from these databases. We assume generalised views in the sense of [11] where a view is structured by its own database schema and is combined with a bundle of queries for derivation of data. This local-as-view approach is centred around the database system. It is not acceptable for any culture of the user.

K. Reinecke and A. Bernstein [28] have shown that low PDI cultures do not accept complex views. Low UIA cultures tend to accept confusing situations and thus also content. Users within a certain culture may tolerate some ordering of items, may request specific effects that support the work, and the layout and playout of screens including the content. We can derive cultural guidelines based on the principle of *proper organisation* depending on the user model, on the principle of *economy*, e.g. non-redundancy of actions, on the principle of *collaboration* depending on the skills and abilities of the user, and on system design *standards* [11,23]. These guidelines can now be used for refinement of the information system specification.

A given web information system specification may now be transformed according to the user culture. The specification itself may also be categorised: (a) strictly incremental constructions of database schema (e.g. eER schemata); (b) local schemata with global integration; (c) strictly document-oriented or hierarchal schemata; (d) classical global-as-view schema with local viewpoints; etc. This categorisation may now be used to adapt the specification to the user culture. For instance, linear-active cultures tend to prefer the specification category (b), especially within a high LTI or low IND value [12].

Therefore, we need at least the following refinement approaches for local-as-view web information system content:

**Restructuring global schemata:** The global schema can be transformed by infomorphisms, i.e. schema mappings that associate databases with equal content but different schemata, e.g. classical eER schemata in the Salami slice setting with those in the Venetian blind setting [14].

**View derivation for content consumption:** View schemata can also be a source for another view schema. We may now build an incrementally defined view tower [12] that reflects the specific cultures of users within their specific tasks.

**View representation schema reorganisation:** View towers can also be used to refine the schemata of users for direct representation of the their very specific needs and demands. These view collections provide views for each of the tasks a user performs.

**Auxiliary database integration:** Task portfolio may be more complex and require also the integration of other database systems. This integration is additionally driven by collaboration pattern [10]. It provides also information on the quality of content due to foreign content.

Instead of concentrating on local-as-view approaches we may develop generic specifications on the basis of parameterised schemata and view collections [12].

### 3.5 Deploying the Culture Stereotypes for Functionality Development

Functionality development became important for web information systems since main function families (search, import/export, navigation) must be properly supported for any kind of user and especially for those that cannot program their specific requests. According to [7,8,16,17,27,28,36] and our research [9–13], there is no unifiable functionality. Functionality differs in the same manner as natural languages have their specific expressivity, their specific utterance style, and their specific form of narration. Research on preferring Yahoo over Google in some cultural setting results in the requirement of flexible and adaptable functionality for users within their specific personal culture.

Genericity is then an appropriate approach for development of generic functions [2] and of generic workflows based on these functions [38,39]. Search adaptation has been investigated in [13]. Let us illustrate refinement and adaptation for navigation functionality. Navigation features are based on scenario trees or graphs which are supported by navigation aids: thematic maps with weights, site maps, etc. Users may use different paths, pre-fetching, side traps, actor-controlled navigation, sub-sites, and shortcuts. There is redundant information presentation and the non-redundant one. Typical navigation styles are positioning, escorting, pull down, navigation bars, breadcrumbs (instead of actor bookmark), breadth versus depth, fisheye, and panorama (three-dimensional structures). Navigation is often based on different link types such as embedded links, structural links (siblings, shortcuts, associative (might be of interest), selective/-hierarchical linking, within-page links, outbound links, and incoming links. One should avoid tunnelling and splash screens.

Navigation is however also driven by the culture (national culture, organisational (work) culture, professional culture, project culture, team culture, and personal habits) due to culture integration via personal adaption to the given environment. Linear-active cultures have their segmented navigation agenda, try to use this segmentation into issues, and need support for summarisation. Multi-active cultures start with some support-seeking steps, use a breadth-oriented concurrent navigation, think of wide-ranging all-embracing seeking, and quit with side reflections. Reactive cultures prefer to see the full picture, then converge the opportunities, and finally merge all into one point. So, culture stereotypes heavily influence the style of navigation.

Support for navigation may however been build based on the content structure and the story space. Which trace through the content and the story space is preferred depends thus on the culture stereotype. Navigation thus combines different features beyond the manifold of linking in dependence on the stereotype, e.g. the following ones:

**Uni-directional navigation** uses linear or almost linear flow of activities. Each step determines the set of next potential steps.

**Qualified navigation** is based on qualifiers for simpler selection of the set of next steps.

**Navigation by generalization or specialisation** is based on a tree-like organisation. We may distinguish upward, downwards, or collection-oriented navigation where the last one is based on combination of results into singleton summary.

**Navigation toggling between explicit and content-based styles** is based on a user-driven combination of the workspace and the provided navigation. **Filtered navigation** uses content for selection of the next item in the agenda. **Value-based navigation** supports traverse based on specific values within the content.

### 3.6  Deploying the Culture Stereotypes for Presentation Development

K. Reinecke developed a workbench MOCCA for generation of various layout and playout interfaces based on different cultures [27]. This approach extends and can easily be combined with the screenography approach [19,21]. The Hofstede separation allows to derive, for instance, that users with low UAI prefer to have complex interfaces with non-linear navigation and with colour, typography and sound support [11,12,27,28]. Multi-active cultures should be supported by colourful pages.

Culture stereotypes may now be used for derivation of general screenography guidelines. Such guidelines include proposals such as the following ones:

- The web page is considered to be a the central exchange medium between system and user.
- Pattern and grids for page layout for general placement, parqueting, colouring, texturing, ... provide a holistic layout for a website.
- The website is based on principles such as
  - *visual communication* (*vision, cognition*, and *processing and memorizing characteristics*) with specific visual features such as contrast, visual analogies, presentation dramaturgy, reading direction, visual closeness, symmetric presentation and space and movement;
  - *visual cognition* (*ordering, effect* delivery, and *visualisation*) with specific decisions on *layout organisation, layout economy, skills of users*, and *standards*;
  - *visual design* based on *optical vicinity , similarity , closeness, symmetry, conciseness, reading direction*:
  - *style of consumption* (shallow, deep, reasoning during)
  - *psychogenesis and psychognosis* ("Fremdbilder") especially for acceptance and reception of layout and playout of web pages.
- The styles for for page composition include descriptions for collages, overlays, floating elements, and tolerated elements.
- The website uses identity elements such as logos, icons, and backgrounds.

A general adaptation and refinement approach for culture-driven presentation is still a matter of research [20,25].

## 4  Conclusion

Smart web information systems combine features of web information systems with the social worlds and thus viewpoints of users. Users will encounter systems that meet their habits, their way of working and behaving, their way to live within an environment, their collaborations, and their current lifestances.

Since a development of web information systems for any user in any culture is infeasible, a generic approach is necessary that allows to adapt systems to specific user groups within their culture. We generalise the approaches developed in [9–13] to a stereotype approach. User cultures can be stereotyped. Four of the six concerns of web information systems (story space, content, functionality, presentation) can be refined in dependence on culture stereotypes.

# References

1. AlBdaiwi, B., Noack, R., Thalheim, B.: Pattern-based conceptual data modelling. In: Information Modelling and Knowledge Bases. Frontiers in Artificial Intelligence and Applications XXVI, vol. 272 pp. 1–20. IOS Press (2014)
2. Bienemann, A., Schewe, K.-D., Thalheim, B.: Towards a theory of genericity based on government and binding. In: Embley, D.W., Olivé, A., Ram, S. (eds.) ER 2006. LNCS, vol. 4215, pp. 311–324. Springer, Heidelberg (2006). doi:10.1007/11901181_24
3. Dahanayake, A., Thalheim, B.: W*H: The conceptual model for services. In: Correct Software in Web Applications and Web Services. Texts & Monographs in Symbolic Computation, pp. 145–176. Springer, Wien (2015)
4. Thalheim, B., Düsterhöft, A.: SiteLang: conceptual modeling of internet sites. In: S.Kunii, H., Jajodia, S., Sølvberg, A. (eds.) ER 2001. LNCS, vol. 2224, pp. 179–192. Springer, Heidelberg (2001). doi:10.1007/3-540-45581-7_15
5. Fischer, G.: User modeling in human-computer interaction. User Model. User-Adapt. Interact. 11(1–2), 65–86 (2001)
6. Förster, F., Thalheim, B.: An effectual approach for a data and information management for humanists. Qual. Quant. Methods Libr. (QQML) (2), 121–128 (2012)
7. Hofstede, G., Hofstede, G.J.: Cultures and Organizations: Software of the Mind: Intercultural Cooperation and its Importance for Survival. McGraw-Hill, New York (2004)
8. Hofstede, G., Hofstede, G.J., Minkow, M.: Cultures and Organizations: Software of the Mind: Intercultural Cooperation and its Importance for Survival. McGraw-Hill, New York (2010)
9. Jaakkola, H., Henno, J., Thalheim, B., Mäkelä, J.: Collaboration, distribution and culture challenges for communication. In: MiPRO, pp. 657–664. IEEE (2015)
10. Jaakkola, H., Nakanishi, T., Sasaki, S., Schewe, K.-D., Thalheim, B.: Conceptual modelling of collaboration for information systems. In: Information Modelling and Knowledge Bases XXV, pp. 272–305. IOS Press (2014)
11. Jaakkola, H., Thalheim, B.: Multicultural adaptive systems. In: Information Modelling and Knowledge Bases XXVI. Frontiers in Artificial Intelligence and Applications, vol. 272, pp. 172–191. IOS Press (2014)
12. Jaakkola, H., Thalheim, B.: Culture-adaptable web information systems. In: Information Modelling and Knowledge Bases XXVII. Frontiersin Artificial Intelligence and Applications, vol. 280, pp. 77–94. IOS Press (2016)
13. Jaakkola, H., Thalheim, B.: Recognising the culture context in information search. In: EJC 2016, pp. 167–185, Tampere (2016)
14. Klettke, M., Thalheim, B.: Evolution and migration of information systems. In: The Handbook of Conceptual Modeling: Its Usage and its Challenges, chap. 12, pp. 381–420. Springer, Berlin (2011)

15. Kretschmer, J., Schranz, C., Riedlinger, A., Schädler, D., Möller, K.: Wissenschaft und Kunst der Modellierung: Modelle, Modellieren, Modellierung, chapter Hierarchische Modellsysteme zur Optimierung der Beatmungstherapie, pp. 369–389. De Gryuter, Boston (2015)
16. Lewis, R.D.: When Cultures Collide. Managing Successfully Across Cultures, 3rd edn. Nicholas Brealey, London (2011)
17. Lewis, R.D.: Richard Lewis resource pages - Cross-culture (2013). http://www.crossculture.com/services/cross-culture/ & http://www.cultureactive.com. Accessed 20 Nov 2013
18. Menke, W.: Geophysical Data Analysis: Discrete Inverse Theory. International Geophysics, vol. 45. Academic Press Inc. (1989)
19. Moritz, T.: Visuelle Gestaltungsraster interaktiver Informationssysteme alsintegrativer Bestandteil des immersiven Bildraumes. Ph.D. thesis, HFF Berlin-Babelsberg (2006)
20. Moritz, T.: Inszenierung von Interaktivität: Screenography alsintegrativer Bestandteil systematischer Entwicklung und Gestaltung interaktivnutzbarer Informations- und Kommunikationssysteme. Lang, Berlin, 2016/17
21. Moritz, T., Noack, R., Schewe, K.-D., Thalheim, B.:Intention-driven screenography. In: ISTA 2007. LNI, vol. 107, pp. 128–139 (2007)
22. Mulder, S., Yaar, Z.: The User is Always Right: A Practical Guide to Creating and Using Personas for the Web. New Riders, Berkeley (2006)
23. Nicholson, P., Thalheim, B.: Culturally adaptive learning objects: challenges for educators and developers. In: UNESCO-SEAMEO Conference Adapting to Changing Times and Needs, Bangkok (2004)
24. Noack, K.: Technologische und methodische Grundlagen von SCOPELAND. White paper (2009). www.scopeland.de
25. Noack, R.: Content- und benutzungsgesteuertes generisches Layout: Screenography. Ph.D. thesis, Christian-Albrechts University of Kiel, Technical Faculty, Kiel (2016)
26. Reichert, M., Weber, B.: Enabling Flexibility in Process-Aware Information Systems. Challenges, Methods, Technologies. Springer, Berlin (2012)
27. Reinecke, K.: Automatic adaptation of user interfaces to cultural preferences. Inf. Technol. **54**(2), 96–101 (2012)
28. Reinecke, K., Bernstein, A.: Knowing what a user likes: a design science approach to interfaces that automatically adapt to the culture. MIS Q. **37**(2), 427–453 (2013)
29. Schewe, K.-D., Thalheim, B.: Modeling interaction and media objects. In: Bouzeghoub, M., Kedad, Z., Métais, E. (eds.) NLDB 2000. LNCS, vol. 1959, pp. 313–324. Springer, Heidelberg (2001). doi:10.1007/3-540-45399-7_26
30. Schewe, K.-D., Thalheim, B.: User models: a contribution to pragmatics of web information systems design. In: Aberer, K., Peng, Z., Rundensteiner, E.A., Zhang, Y., Li, X. (eds.) WISE 2006. LNCS, vol. 4255, pp. 512–523. Springer, Heidelberg (2006). doi:10.1007/11912873_53
31. Schewe, K.-D., Thalheim, B.: Development of collaboration frameworks for web information systems. In: 20th International Joint Conference on Artifical Intelligence, Section EMC07 (Evolutionary models of collaboration), pp. 27–32, Hyderabad (2007)
32. Schewe, K.-D., Thalheim, B.: Life cases: a kernel element for web information systems engineering. In: Filipe, J., Cordeiro, J. (eds.) WEBIST 2007. LNBIP, vol. 8, pp. 139–156. Springer, Heidelberg (2008). doi:10.1007/978-3-540-68262-2_11
33. Stahl, T., Völter, M.: Model-driven software architectures. dPunkt, Heidelberg (2005). (in German)

34. Thalheim, B.: Syntax, semantics and pragmatics of conceptual modelling. In: Bouma, G., Ittoo, A., Métais, E., Wortmann, H. (eds.) NLDB 2012. LNCS, vol. 7337, pp. 1–10. Springer, Heidelberg (2012). doi:10.1007/978-3-642-31178-9_1

35. Thalheim, B., Jaakkola, H., Nakanashi, T., Sasaki, S., Schewe, K.-D.: Conceptual modelling of collaboration for information systems. In: Information Modelling and Knowledge. Frontiers in Artificial Intelligence and Applications Bases XXV, vol. 260, pp. 272–305. IOS Press (2014)

36. Trompenaars, F., Hampden-Turner, C.: Riding the waves of culture. McGraw-Hill, New York (1998)

37. Tropmann, M., Thalheim, B.: Mini story composition for generic workflows in support of disaster management. In: DEXA 2013, pp. 36–40. IEEE Computer Society (2013)

38. Tropmann-Frick, M.: Genericity in Process-Aware Information Systems. Ph.D. thesis, Christian-Albrechts University of Kiel, Technical Faculty, Kiel (2016)

39. Tropmann-Frick, M., Thalheim, B., Leber, D., Czech, G., Liehr, C.: Generic workflows - a utility to govern disastrous situations. In: Information Modelling and Knowledge Bases. Frontiers in Artificial Intelligence and Applications XXVI, vol. 272, pp. 417–428. IOS Press (2014)

40. Zeugmann, T.: Inductive inference of optimal programs a survey and open problems. In: Dix, J., Jantke, K.P., Schmitt, P.H. (eds.) NIL 1990. LNCS, vol. 543, pp. 208–222. Springer, Heidelberg (1991). doi:10.1007/BFb0023325

# Modelling and Management of Big Data

## Preface of the Fifth International Workshop on Modeling and Management of Big Data

In the last decade, technology has advanced tremendously. Currently, a wide variety of devices, including sensor-enabled smart devices, and all types of wearables, connect to the Internet and power newly connected applications and solutions. On the one hand, the cost of technology has sharply decreased, making it possible for everybody to engage in sensing data. The vast amount of real time information can be accessed across the Internet. Furthermore, some of the environments are just online, like social media, where all the information is in the Cloud. As a result, new words as well as new expressions have appeared such as Big Data, Cloud Computing or Internet of Things, among others.

Due to all of these enormous amounts of data generated (Big Data), there is an increasing interest in incorporating them into traditional applications. This new era requires conceptualization and methods to effectively manage big data and accomplish intended business goals. Thus, the objective of MoBiD'16 is to be an international forum for exchanging ideas on the latest and best proposals for modeling and managing big data in this new data-driven paradigm.

The workshop has been announced in the main announcement venues and attracted papers from eight different countries distributed all over the world: USA, Colombia, Germany, New Zealand, India, China, France, and Spain. We have finally received 7 papers and the Program Committee has selected 3 papers, making an acceptance rate of 43 %. We also have an invited keynote on "Managing and exploring GPS trajectories" by Baihua Zheng.

The first paper by Yuan et al. presents a basket recommendation system. They study shopping behaviors of Walmart online grocery customers. In contrast to traditional online shopping, grocery shopping demonstrates more repeated and frequent purchases with large orders. The recommender is based on multi-level cobought (co-purchase) models. The second paper by Ochoa et al. shows a feature modeling metamodel and two automatic processes: (1) for representing domain and implementation alternative models, and (2) for searching optimal solutions considering a set of optimization objectives, that solve specific problems of feature modeling. The last paper by Hartmann et al. proposes an extension of the basic clustering algorithm Label

Propagation Algorithm (LPA) to allow overlaps between communities, since this is more appropriate for (social) networks where vertices may belong to more than one cluster.

David Gil
Il-Yeol Song
Yuan An
Jesús Peral
Program Co-chairs, MoBiD'16

**Acknowledgments.** We would like to express our gratitude to the Program Committee members for their hard work in reviewing papers, the authors for submitting their papers, and the ER 2016 organizing committee for supporting our workshop. MoBiD'16 was organized within the framework of the project SEQUOIA-UA (TIN2015-63502-C3-3-R) from the Spanish Ministry of Economy and Competitiveness, within the project GRE14-10 (University of Alicante, Spain), and under project GV/2016/087 (Comunidad Valenciana, Spain).

# Walmart Online Grocery Personalization: Behavioral Insights and Basket Recommendations

Mindi Yuan[✉], Yannis Pavlidis, Mukesh Jain, and Kristy Caster

@WalmartLabs, 850 Cherry Avenue, San Bruno, CA 94066, USA
{myuan,yannis,mjain,kcaster}@walmartlabs.com

**Abstract.** Food is so personal. Each individual has her own shopping characteristics. In this paper, we introduce personalization for Walmart online grocery. Our contribution is twofold. First, we study shopping behaviors of Walmart online grocery customers. In contrast to traditional online shopping, grocery shopping demonstrates more repeated and frequent purchases with large orders. Secondly, we present a multi-level basket recommendation system. In this system, unlike typical recommender systems which usually concentrate on single item or bundle recommendations, we analyze a customer's shopping basket holistically to understand her shopping tasks. We then use multi-level cobought models to recommend items for each of the purposes. At the stage of selecting particular items, we incorporate both the customers' general and subtle preferences into decisions. We finally recommend the customer a series of items at checkout. Offline experiments show our system can reach 11 % item hit rate, 40 % subcategory hit rate and 70 % category hit rate. Online tests show it can reach more than 25 % order hit rate.

## 1 Introduction

eCommerce has been hot for decades. Amazon.com provides diversified products with convenient shipping. The retail giant, Walmart, started its online shopping services years ago. Online grocery shopping, however, is an emerging field. It is gaining a lot of interests, mostly from industry at the current stage. Several major companies already entered the battlefield. Popular providers include Walmart grocery home shopping [1], Amazon Fresh [2], and Instacart [3] to name but a few. In academia, online grocery shopping remains an under-studied problem. Fewer recommender systems are designed specifically for grocery shopping, compared to the large number of systems for traditional eCommerce.

Recommender systems, nevertheless, are key components to grocery websites. They fundamentally change the way people explore products, by automatically exposing them to new items. This would attract more traffic, explicitly or implicitly increasing sales and revenues. On the other hand, recommender systems help people find items faster. Customers usually buy more than 20 items (Fig. 1) in one trip. It is favorable if grocery websites can have certain "auto-completion"

© Springer International Publishing AG 2016
S. Link and J.C. Trujillo (Eds.): ER 2016 Workshops, LNCS 9975, pp. 49–64, 2016.
DOI: 10.1007/978-3-319-47717-6_5

function, powered by recommender systems, in contrast to adding every single item by time-consuming searching or browsing.

Tradition recommender systems focus more on single item recommendations. It is true that most of their orders are for a single purpose and an individual user (I buy a camera for myself). And focusing on one anchor item has its own advantage in the sense that it makes recommendation algorithms more scalable. Though there are seemingly algorithms on bundle or package recommendations [4–6], we neither predefine nor form bundles on the fly with alternative prices. More importantly, grocery shopping is essentially different from traditional eCommerce in the following ways, making it hard to directly apply a traditional recommender system in the grocery domain.

– Grocery shopping is multitasking (I purchase food while buying laundry detergents), as well as "multi-people" (I buy grocery for the entire family). Grocery thus has bigger orders. As a result, single-item or bundle recommender systems are not directly applicable to grocery.
– Grocery sells consumables, while most of the traditional eCommerce websites focus on durable goods or standardized products. That is why online grocery contains more repeated and frequent purchases. It makes more sense, for grocery, to track each item's inter-purchase interval and make timely recommendations for replenishment. Most of the traditional recommender systems do not have such a feature. On the other hand, repeated purchases imply similar orders. Grocery recommender systems thus need incorporate more dynamics, otherwise customers may always see similar recommendations.
– Grocery is devoted to customers and their preferences. Grocery recommender systems not only find customers the products (bananas, avocados or deli meat), but also pick the right items (green vs yellow bananas, hard vs ripe avocados, or thick vs thin sliced deli meat).

In a nutshell, we are facing a basket of items. We had better investigate shopping activities holistically, understand customers' needs and offer related recommendations with a variety of coverage.

In order to tackle this challenge, we present a multi-level basket recommendation system. Our contribution is twofold. First, we study shopping behaviors of Walmart online grocery customers. In contrast to traditional online shopping, grocery shopping demonstrates more repeated and frequent purchases with large orders. Secondly, we present a multiple-level basket recommendation system. By examining a customer's shopping basket, we understand her shopping tasks and identify items for each purpose. Utilizing a subcategory level cobought (co-purchase) model, we first dig out the subcategories frequently purchased together with the subcategories in the current basket. Subcategory level data is more dense than item level data, resulting in more trustful insights. We then use a more detailed item level cobought model and map the recommended subcategories to the most relevant items. During this step, we incorporate customers' preferences. General preferences include brand affinity, price range, dietary needs, family size, package size, gluten free, organic food and so on. We also consider subtle preferences, as mentioned before, green vs yellow bananas, hard vs ripe avocados, thick vs thin sliced deli meat, as well as estimated time for the customer to buy the item again. Those features are learned incrementally from both the customer's shopping history and the real-time basket (especially for new users). For example, if we detect that the cart has a lot of organic items, the system would try to promote the organic choice of the recommended products. Finally, we present to the customer a series of recommendations, covering her various needs. Offline experiments show our system can reach 11 % item hit rate, 40 % subcategory hit rate and 70 % category hit rate. Online tests show it can reach more than 25 % order hit rate, meaning more than one quarter of the customers add at least one item from our recommendations in practice.

The rest of the paper is organized as follows. Section 2 discusses related work. Section 3 investigates shopping behaviors of Walmart online grocery customers. The algorithms and models are described in Sect. 4. We evaluate the system in Sect. 5 and conclude in Sect. 6.

## 2 Related Work

Recommender systems are a important field in both academia and industry. Various algorithms exist in the domain of traditional eCommerce, but there are fewer works on grocery recommendations. Nevertheless, it is becoming an interesting topic, as more and more people buy grocery online.

In [7], Li et al. described a recommender system for grocery shopping based on basket-sensitive random walk. In their paper, they calculated similarities between each pair of items. In [8], Wu et al. developed a new recommendation scheme especially for online grocery shopping by incorporating two additional considerations, product replenishment and product promotion. In both papers, however, they did not look at the entire basket holistically and identify the customer's shopping tasks. They treated the problem like a traditional recommendation problem but in a grocery context. There is an interesting paper on shopping behaviors for online grocery. In [9], Hand et al. found the adoption of online grocery shopping is an erratic process, driven by circumstances rather than by a cognitive decision. Customers may therefore discontinue online grocery shopping, when the triggering circumstances disappear. For example, a person without a car may have to shop online. However, as long as she buys a car, she could prefer those brick-and-mortar grocery stores again. This may explain why there are a significant number of one-off customers in online grocery.

Underneath our basket recommendation algorithm, cobought models are built to learn association rules or mine frequent item set. Many algorithms have been presented in this field over time. The most well-known algorithms include Apriori [10], Eclat [11], FP-growth [12] and so on. There is also a more advanced algorithm for parallel item set mining [13]. Since we only need item sets of size two, we basically use a simple yet efficient self join to mine frequent patterns in our system.

Most commonly, recommender systems are classified into three categories: collaborative filtering, content-based filtering and hybrid recommendation approaches. Collaborative filtering [14] [15] investigates users' behaviors in the past, typically by examining their purchase history or numerical ratings for certain products, along with similar decisions made by peer customers. The model built after the above step is then used to predict those customers' potential interests in other items. Content-based filtering [16] employs a vector of discrete features of a product in order to offer recommendations of new items with similar characteristics. It tends to recommend similar products to those a customer has liked or purchased in the past. Each recommender system has its (dis)advantages. In the collaborative filtering papers mentioned above, most of them need a large set of data in order to mine concrete information and make accurate recommendations. This is also known as the cold start problem. Later, we will see that our subcategory cobought model is proposed to overcome the data sparsity problem at the item level. Dense data trains higher-quality models. Content-based recommender systems usually require much less information to start. This, however, limits its application scope, meaning it can only recommend similar products to the anchor item. Therefore, hybrid recommendation algorithms [17,18] were proposed.

As outlined before, online grocery shopping demonstrates significantly different characteristics from traditional eCommerce, so those algorithms are not suitable to be directly applied in grocery domain. More specific algorithms need to be designed to address the challenges in grocery.

## 3    Online Grocery Shopping Behaviors

eCommerce started with providing durable goods or standardized items, including books, CDs and TVs to name but a few. Those products are easier for logistics. In recent years, eCommerce has expended its domain to grocery, where most products are soft goods or consumables with significantly shorter lifespan. As a result, people buy these items frequently and repeatedly. In order to fulfill their everyday needs, customers tend to place larger grocery orders with more items.

Few reports were published on online grocery shopping behaviors. In the following studies, we utilize half-year (Feb to Jul, 2015) Walmart online grocery data to analyze customer behaviors. This data set contains about 6 million transactions in terms of $(customer, item)$ pairs, meaning the $customer$ bought the $item$. In the transactions, there are 185 thousand orders, 40 thousand distinct customers and 50 thousand distinct items.

It has been reported that Amazon.com has an average order size of 1.5, while Walmart.com 2.3 [4]. In Walmart online grocery, however, the average order size reaches 25.7 items per order, which is 17.1 times bigger than Amazon.com and 11.2 times larger than Walmart.com. Even if we count $unique$ items, the average order size is still 21.4. Below is a chart, Fig. 1, on the distribution of order sizes, all items vs. unique items. Most of the customers had 20–30 items or 10–20 unique items in one order. The primary reason for grocery shopping, particularly in North America, is stocking up with food for the week or a longer period of

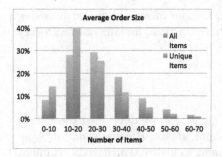

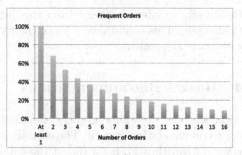

**Fig. 1.** Most customers had 20–30 items or 10–20 unique items per order.

**Fig. 2.** 67.6% out of the at-least-one-order customers placed multiple orders, and 14.4% of them are bi-weekly or more frequent shoppers.

time, which results in large orders. Another reason for big orders is that there is usually a minimum purchase threshold, like $50, for delivery. Since grocery items are cheaper on average than general merchandise, customers need a lot more items to achieve that minimum.

The large size of grocery orders suggests we consider each order or the customer's basket comprehensively. Each item in an order may only function well with other items in that order. They, together, complete one shopping task. In other words, a subset of the entire order satisfies one of the customer's shopping needs. We therefore had better analyze the entire shopping cart holistically to offer high-quality basket recommendations, which, for example, could be an item the customer might forget in this trip, a better substitute product but with a lower price and so on.

We have seen frequent purchases, or small inter-purchase intervals, in the data set. Namely, customers place orders periodically. They can potentially be classified into weekly, biweekly, monthly shoppers. In Fig. 2, we show the cumulative distribution on number of orders among customers who have shopped at least once. The x-axis is the *minimum* number of orders customers have placed. The y-axis shows the percentage. 67.6% of them had multiple orders. 14.4% of them were at least bi-weekly shoppers, who have placed at least 12 orders in 6 months. Though the curve decays rapidly, the tail distribution flats. A next purchase is more likely to happen with accumulation of past orders. Namely, the number of orders from a customer increases, the loyalty of that customer strengthens.

As mentioned above, traditional eCommerce sells more leisure products with non-repeated purchases [7]. Grocery, however, fulfills our daily needs and contains a significant number of repeated purchases. We found 28% of the transactions were repeated in the data. This suggests we build some form of "easy reorder" or subscription services. We could provide customers with a pre-populated *personalized* shopping list of items they have bought. In this list, the items they are most likely to buy in this trip are at the top. Customers could then easily reorder the items from this list, instead of searching and browsing them again. This would save a lot of their shopping time, making online grocery even more convenient.

# 4    Basket Recommendations

After learning the online grocery shopping behaviors, we developed the following recommendation system. The core algorithm, *Basket Recommendation Algorithm* (Algorithm 1), is on top of the cobought models (Algorithm 2). Namely, we mine the Walmart online grocery transaction data to count, for each pair of items (*itemA, itemB*), the cases they were bought together in the same orders, i.e. *cocount*. We then compute a cobought score based on that cocount, as well as each item's popularity. After the cobought models are built, the basket recommendation algorithm consumes their data, incorporates customers' preferences and computes a series of recommended items. Our products have the following taxonomy:

$$(item, subcategory, category, department, superdepartment).$$

## 4.1    Basket Recommendation Algorithm

On a high level, the algorithm works as follows:

- Given a shopping basket, investigate each item's taxonomy (the item's subcategory and super department in particular), and its item cobought data. From the super department distribution of the basket, we later *proportionally* select recommendation items in each of those super departments. From the subcategory distribution, we will select the most frequently cobought (co-purchased) subcategories with those subcategories in the current basket. From the item cobought data, we build a dictionary of the most frequently cobought items with those basket items.
- For each super department presented in the basket, sort the basket subcategories in that super department by its frequency. For each of the sorted basket subcategories, fetch its subcategory cobought data. For each of the cobought subcategories, check if there are items, in that cobought subcategory, in the item cobought dictionary built in the previous step. Otherwise, backfill using the popular items in that cobought subcategory. In both cases, apply the personal preference filters while selecting a particular item in the subcategory. Loop until we find enough recommendation items for that super department.
- Merge the recommendation items from each super department and return.

The pseudo code of the basket recommendation algorithm is shown in Algorithm 1.

This is a 3-step algorithm. We will detail how to build the item-cobought model, subcategory-cobought model and subcategory popular item list later. Let us first go through the algorithm by example. In step one, we analyze the basket and group items from a same super department (*sdept*) together. Items from each super department typically serve for one shopping task. By grouping them together, we can detect the customer's shopping tasks. For each item in the basket, we also get all its cobought items. The cobought item score is a relevance score of this item to the anchor item, quantifying how likely those two items are bought together. Later, we would introduce four methods to calculate the cobought scores. After step 1, we have the *basket*'s *sdept* distribution in *basketSuperDeptDict*, as well as subcategory distribution within each super department in *basketSuperDeptDict*[*sdept*]. For example, suppose total 10 items exist in the basket. After investigating their super departments, we find five are from super department "produce", three from "pets" and two from "household & laundry". Among the three pet items, we further find two are from subcategory "wet cat food" and one from "dry cat food". We also build a cobought item dictionary *subcatListDict*. In that dictionary, key is a subcategory and value is a list of cobought items, pointed from at least one item in the basket, in that subcategory. A same cobought item can be pointed from multiple anchor items in the basket. In that case, we sum up the cobought scores from all the anchor items as in line 11 of the algorithm. Finally, sort each list of cobought items by their accumulated scores in descending order.

In step 2, we start from the subcategory level and compute recommendations for each super department *proportionally*. Still use the above example. If we want to generate 6 final recommendations, we look for $6 * (3/10) = 2$ items from pets. Wet cat food is the first anchor based on its subcategory frequency, which is 2, compared to 1 for dry cat food. Suppose in its subcategory cobought list, dry cat food is at the top. However, the customer already has dry cat food in the basket. Skip and continue. Further suppose the second cobought subcategory is cat treats. The customer does not have any cat treats item in the basket. As a result, choose that subcategory and look into the sorted list of *subcatListDict*["cat treats"]. The first item is "xxx seafood medley flavor cat treats", whose flavor happens to meet the preferences of the customer's cat. Add it to *recommended*. If *subcatListDict*["cat treats"] is null, we backfill one item from the subcategory's popular item list. The second recommended item for this super department is generated in the same way. Repeat the above process for the other super departments, until we finally generate $6 * (5/10) = 3$ items for produce, 2 items for pets and $6 * (2/10) = 1$ item for household &laundry. Store the 6 items in *recommended*.

Lastly in step 3, for each super department, sort the recommended items by their scores accumulated in step 1. Merge and return. In the above example, the final results will be: [1stItemFromProduce, 1stItemFromPets, 1stItemFromHouseholdAndLaundry, 2ndItemFromProduce, 2ndItemFromPets, 3rdItemFromProduce].

**Algorithm 1.** Basket Recommendation

---

1: #**Input: a list of items** *basket*
2: #**Output: a list of items** *recommended*
3: #**Step 1: analyze basket**
4: Get each basket item's cobought item list;
5: Go through each item with its cobought items and build the following dictionaries;
6: **for** each item $i$ in *basket* **do**
7:     $basketSuperDeptDict[i.sdept][\text{"count"}] += 1;$
8:     $basketSuperDeptDict[i.sdept][i.subcat] += 1;$
9:     **for** each item $c$ in $i.coboughtItemList$ **do**
10:         Add $c$ to list $subcatListDict[c.subcat];$
11:         Accumulate $c.score$ if $c$ is already in $subcatListDict[c.subcat];$
12:     **end for**
13: **end for**
14: Sort subcats in each $basketSuperDeptDict[sdept]$ by subcats' frequencies descendingly;
15: Sort items in each $subcatListDict[subcat]$ by $score$ descendingly;
16: #**Step 2: subcat cobought recommendations**
17: According to *basket*'s *sdept* distribution gathered in step 1, <u>proportionally</u> get a certain number of recommendation items from each *sdept* in the following way;
18: **for** each basket *sdept* **do**
19:     **while** target number of recommendation items in *sdept* not met and cobought subcats not exhausted **do**
20:         **for** each sorted basket *subcat* in *sdept* **do**
21:             Get its subcat cobought list $subcatCoboughtList;$
22:             **for** each $s$ in $subcatCoboughtList$ **do**
23:                 Filter items in $subcatListDict[s]$ by customer's preferences and then test each item;
24:                 **if** the item and $s$ are not already in *basket* or *recommended* **then**
25:                     Add it to *recommended* and break;
26:                 **end if**
27:                 **if** $subcatListDict[s]$ is null or no feasible candidates found **then**
28:                     Backfill one item from $s$'s popular item list filtered by customer's preferences and break;
29:                 **end if**
30:             **end for**
31:         **end for**
32:     **end while**
33: **end for**
34: #**Step 3: Sort** *recommended*
35: **for** each *sdept* in *recommended* **do**
36:     Sort its items by score descendingly;
37: **end for**
38: Merge the recommended items from each *sdept* so that the $n$th recommended items from each *sdept* are grouped together before all the $(n+1)$th items for each $n$;
39: Return *recommended*;

## 4.2   Cobought Models

Our production data set is large. We therefore use MapReduce [19] to compute the item cobought and subcategory cobought models as in Algorithm 2. The input to our cobought models is transaction data in the following format: $(orderID, itemID)$. Basically, once a customer places an order on $N$ items, $N$ entries will be stored into our databases: $(order1, item1)$, $(order1, item2)$, ..., $(order1, itemN)$. Therefore, for any pair of items, if their order ID's are the same, they were bought together in the same order.

---

**Algorithm 2.** Cobought model

---

1: **#Input: a table** $D$ **of** $(order, item)$;
2: **#Output: a table** $D11$ **of** $(item, coboughtItemList)$;
3: $D1$ = SELF JOIN $D$ ON $order$;
4: $D2$ = $D1 \rightarrow (order, item1, item2)$;
5: $D3$ = GROUP $D2$ BY $(item1, item2)$;
6: $D4$ = $D3 \rightarrow (item1, item2, cocount)$;
7: $D5$ = FILTER $D4$ BY $(item1 == item2)$;
8: $D6$ = $D5 \rightarrow (item, count)$;
9: $D7$ = JOIN $D4$ and $D6$ ON $item1$ and $item2$ respectively;
10: $D8$ = $D7 \rightarrow (item1, item2, count1, count2, cocount)$;
11: $D9$ = $D8 \rightarrow (item1, item2, coboughtScore)$ BY scoreFunc();
12: $D10$ = GROUP $D9$ BY $item1$;
13: $D11$ = $D10 \rightarrow (item1, coboughtItemList)$;
14: STORE $D11$;

---

At line 11 of the algorithm, we use different scoring methods $scoreFunc()$ to compute a cobought score between $item1$, the anchor item, and $item2$, the cobought item. The following four methods are used in this paper.

– **Cocount**

$$coboughtScore = cocount$$

In this case, we simply use the number of co-occurrences of $item1$ and $item2$ as the cobought score. For example, if $item1$ and $item2$ appeared in 900 same orders, the score between them is 900. This is a symmetric score, meaning $item1$'s cobought score to $item2$ is equal to $item2$'s cobought score to $item1$.

– **IDF**

$$coboughtScore = \frac{cocount}{popularity2}$$

The first method may have the following issue: popular items are always at the top. For instance, bananas are in most orders and a large set of items would therefore point to bananas, because all these items could always have a high cocount with bananas. That is why we discount the score by $popularity2$, the number of occurrences of $item2$. This is an asymmetric score.

– **Square**

$$coboughtScore = \frac{cocount^2}{popularity2}$$

In order to avoid discounting the cocount too much as in method 2, we boost the cocount by a square operation on the nominator. This is an asymmetric score.

– **Jaccard**

$$coboughtScore = \frac{cocount}{popularity1 + popularity2 - cocount}$$

To make a symmetric score again, we divide the cocount by popularities of both the anchor item and the cobought item. This is actually the Jaccard index [20], a statistic commonly used for measuring similarity between finite sample sets.

All the methods *Cocount, IDF, Square* and *Jaccard* try to adjust rankings for cobought items in *itemCobouhtList* of a particular anchor item so that the most relevant items are at the top. Once we mix the cobought items as in step 1 of Algorithm 1, the rankings change again because each cobought item could accumulate scores and they would be compared across anchor items.

At a high level, Algorithm 2 first ingests the transaction data and makes a self join. After that, it gets the cocount of each pair of items (line 6). If the pair of items have the same item ID, the cocount is actually the popularity of that item (line 7 and 8). At line 10, we have all the necessary features ready: the popularity of the anchor item, the popularity of the cobought item and their cocount. Finally, we can use any of the above methods to implement *scoreFunc()* and calculate the cobought score. Each of the operation can be MapReduced, making our model more scalable. The subcategory level cobought model can be computed in a similar way, substituting the itemID with its subcategory.

In order to make relevant recommendations, we limit the subcategory cobought model within each super department. As mentioned before, grocery shopping is multitasking. Unrelated items may be bought in the same order. By limiting the subcategory model within each super department, we can effectively filter the noise. This logic is similar to what we use to identify a customer's shopping tasks in step 1 of Algorithm 1, where we group basket items by each super department and look at each group respectively.

The subcategory popular item list for backfilling (line 28 of Algorithm 1) is computed by counting the number of orders on each item in a particular subcategory. The time window for the orders is set to one month. In this situation, we get a bonus feature "seasonality". That is, items are sorted by their "seasonal" popularities. This is more favorable in practice. For example, Halloween candies are only popular around October. If the popularities are computed based on annual sales data, Halloween candies may never be able to make the top positions in its subcategory. However, if the time window shrinks to one month, Halloween candies would be bubbled up around October.

Our basket algorithms have the following properties. On one hand, it is able to identify shopping tasks and understand our customers: who have pets, who prefer organic products or who is preparing dinner for a large family. On the other hand, powered by the cobought models, it is capable to remind customers of items they might forget or recommend to them related products. It helps customers explore new products, starting from those which are most relevant to what they are already buying.

# 5    Performance

## 5.1    Cobought Models

Cobought models are the heart of our recommendation. To train the models, we use one year's worth of data, which contains about 20 million transactions, 650 thousand orders, 115 thousand distinct customers, 70 thousand distinct items and 4 thousand distinct subcategories. We limit our subcategory model within each super department to enhance relevancy. We filter mutually exclusive subcategories to alleviate embarrassment. We do not impose super department constraints on the item cobought model for item varieties.

**Table 1.** Top cobought relations between subcategories

| Rank | Cocount | IDF |
|------|---------|-----|
| 1 | (Frozen Poultry Meals, Frozen Beef Meals) | (Mixed-3rd Foods, Meat-3rd Foods) |
| 2 | (Cold Cereal, Dry Pasta) | (Frozen Poultry Meals, Poultry) |
| 3 | (Dry Pasta, Pasta & Pizza Sauces) | (Meat & Seafood Soup, Stews) |
| 4 | (Classic Yogurt, Greek Yogurt) | (Snacks-Toddler Food, Cereal-Toddler Food) |
| 5 | (Frozen Poultry Meals, Frozen Veggie Meals) | (Mixed-3rd Foods, Cereal-3rd Foods) |
|  | Square | Jaccard |
| 1 | (Frozen Poultry Meals, Frozen Beef Meals) | (Fruit-1st Foods, Vegetable-1st Foods) |
| 2 | (Frozen Beef Meals, Frozen Poultry Meals) | (Mixed-2nd Foods, Fruit-2nd Foods) |
| 3 | (Dry Pasta, Pasta & Pizza Sauces) | (Mixed-2nd Foods, Vegetable-2nd Foods) |
| 4 | (Fruit-2nd Foods, Vegetable-2nd Foods) | (Frozen Beef Meals, Frozen Poultry Meals) |
| 5 | (Frozen Poultry Meals, Frozen Veggie Meals) | (Fruit-3rd Foods, Mixed-3rd Foods) |

In Table 1, we show the top 5 strongest cobought relations between subcategories identified by the four scoring methods. From the table, we can see (frozen poultry meals, frozen beef meals), (dry pasta, pasta & pizza sauces), and a lot of baby foods are strongly related. Overall, those relations identified by the algorithms are good to use in practice already. A good property of the cobought models we observed is that it can "automatically" find out the preferences of customers. For example, we do not explicitly implement a method to ensure we recommend baby foods within a certain age, but the model is already able to get that bonus feature simply due to the fact that those products are frequently bought together in reality. Similarly, we found this also works for organic food, gluten free food and so on.

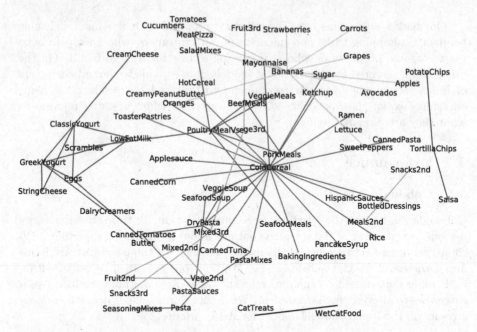

**Fig. 3.** Top 100 strongest relations identified by subcategory cobought model: (cat treats, wet cat food), (pasta, pasta sauces, canned tomatoes), and (tortilla chips, salsa).

In Fig. 3, we further plotted the top 100 strongest cobought relations among subcategories. Different super departments are plotted in different colors. At the bottom left of the red cluster, we can see pasta, pasta sauces and canned tomatoes are frequently bought together. At the bottom, cat treats and wet cat food are another strong cobought pair.

## 5.2   Basket Recommendation Algorithm: Offline Tests

In this section, we examine the basket algorithm and cobought models systematically. We evaluate our algorithms by testing and comparing the four different score functions: *Cocount*, *IDF*, *Square* and *Jaccard*. We fetched real customer orders from the transaction data. We then called our API with the set of items in each order and collected the recommended items. We finally looked into the transaction data to find out how many (*customer, item*) pairs appeared in orders within 3 months, meaning the customer did buy the item we recommended in his or her following orders. The same experiments were conducted on the *customer − subcategory* level and *customer − category* level as well.

In each of the experiments, we tested 13,311 orders sampled from the transaction data. There are 370 thousand transactions with 9,911 distinct customers and 32,135 distinct items. The average order size is 27.7 items. As mentioned before, to train the models to be used by the basket algorithm, we utilized one

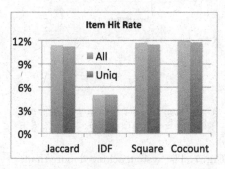

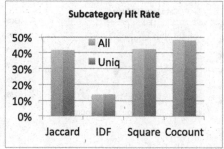

**Fig. 4.** Jaccard, Square and Cocount achieved item hit rates more than 11 %, while IDF only about 5 %.

**Fig. 5.** Jaccard and Square had sub-category hit rates of about 40 %, while Cocount's rates were close to 50 %. However, IDF barely achieved 14 %.

year's worth of data before the testing data. The statistics of the training data set was detailed at the beginning of the previous sub-section. We used the following two performance metrics: *all* hit rate and *unique* hit rate. For every tested order, we got back a series of $(customer, recommendedItem)$ pairs. After gathering all the results from the 13,311 orders, the pairs might not be unique. If a customer placed two similar orders, the recommendations from those two orders could overlap with each other a lot. As a result, we calculated (1) all hit rate, which was the percentage of pairs $(customer, recommendedItem)$ appeared in trans-actions; and (2) unique hit rate, where we first got all the *distinct* $(customer, recommendedItem)$ pairs along with the *unique* $(customer, item)$ transactions, and computed the percentage thereafter.

Figure 4 shows the item level hit rates. All the *Jaccard*, *Square* and *Cocount* can achieve 11 % hit rates. Namely, more than 1 item out of 10 recommended would be purchased by the customer. Among them, a simple cocount model performed the best, with almost 12 % all hit rate. IDF performed relatively worse, with a hit rate around 5 %. In this case, the score was discounted too much by the cobought item's popularity, which potentially caused too many unpopular items to bubble up in the recommendation list.

In terms of subcategory level performance, the rates for *Jaccard*, *Square* and *Cocount* exceeded 40 % as shown in Fig. 5. In other words, the algorithms are able to accurately predict the subcategories the customers want to shop. Items in a subcategory are very similar. In most cases, they only differ in sizes, brands, or flavors. This implies that if we could do the last step of Algorithm 1 better when mapping subcategories back to items for recommendation, we would dra-matically improve our item hit rates. That is, if we can more accurately predict the customers' preferences, we would achieve very high hit rates. However, IDF still performed not that ideally, with hit rates under 15 %.

If we go one level up further to the category, all the four algorithms achieved high hit rates, around 70 % (Fig. 6). There are not so many categories people

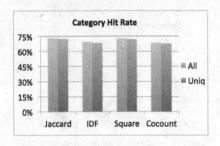

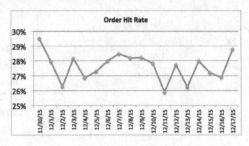

**Fig. 6.** All four algorithms accomplished high category hit rates: around 70 %.

**Fig. 7.** The system achieved more than 25 % order hit rate.

frequently shop. As a result, it is not that hard to predict the categories people buy.

In summary, it is clear that $IDF$ lost to the other three methods, but there was no significant performance difference among the other three. In practice, we chose $Jaccard$ in the current running system after extensive manual evaluations, where human evaluators gave scores to each recommended item and identified embarrassing items.

### 5.3 Basket Recommendation Algorithm: Online Tests

The recommender system is now serving the Walmart online grocery website [1]. When a customer finishes shopping and clicks checkout, she would see a "stock up" page with at most 8 *additional* items recommended, generated by our system.

In this experiment, we used the logs of the recommender system and the transaction data of Walmart online grocery from 2015-11-30 to 2015-12-17 to measure the performance of our system in reality. In the data set, there are 1,604,243 transactions, with 56,022 orders, 37,583 distinct customers, and 42,296 unique items. The Online tests show it reached more than 25 % order hit rate (Fig. 7), meaning more than one quarter of the customers added at least one item from our recommendations.

## 6   Conclusion

In this paper, we analyzed online grocery shopping behaviors. We found the following features are significant: repeated purchases, large orders and frequent purchases. We developed a basket recommendation algorithm based on multi-level cobought models. Through offline evaluations, our system reached 11 % item hit rate, 40 % subcategory hit rate and 70 % category hit rate. From online tests, it achieved more than 25 % order hit rate.

Future work includes but is not limited to (1) improving cobought accuracy, (2) accelerating API responses, (3) tuning systems using user feedback and so on.

# References

1. Walmart. "Grocery home shopping". http://grocery.walmart.com/, Accessed 03-Apr-2016
2. Amazon. "Amazon fresh". http://fresh.amazon.com/, Accessed 03-Apr-2016
3. Instacart. "Instacart". http://www.instacart.com/, Accessed 03-Apr-2016
4. Zhu, T., Harrington, P., Li, J., Tang, L.: Bundle recommendation in eCommerce. In: Proceedings of the 37th International ACM SIGIR Conference on Research & Development in Information Retrieval. Australia, pp. 657–666, July 2014
5. Stremersch, S., Tellis, G.: Strategic bundling of products and prices: A new synthesis for marketing. J. Mark. 66(1), 55–72 (2002)
6. Garfinkel, R., Gopal, R., Tripathi, A., Yin, F.: Design of a shopbot and recommender system for bundle purchases. Decis. Support Syst. 42(3), 1974–1986 (2006)
7. Li, M., Dias, B.M., Jarman, I., El-Deredy, W., Lisboa, P.J.: Grocery shopping recommendations based on basket-sensitive random walk. In: Proceedings of the 15th ACM SIGKDD International Conference on Knowledge Discovery and Data Mining. Paris, France, pp. 1215–1224, June 2009
8. Wu, Y.-J., Teng, W.-G.: An enhanced recommendation scheme for online grocery shopping. In: IEEE 15th International Symposium on Consumer Electronics. Singapore, pp. 410–415, June 2011
9. Hand, C., Riley, F., Harris, P., Singh, J., Rettie, R.: Online grocery shopping: the influence of situational factors. Eur. J. Mark. 43(9), 1205–1219 (2009)
10. Agrawal, R., Srikant, R.: Fast algorithms for mining association rules in large databases. In: Proceedings of the 20th International Conference on Very Large Data Bases. Santiago, Chile, pp. 487–499 (1994)
11. Zaki, M.: Scalable algorithms for association mining. IEEE Trans. Knowl. Data Eng. 12(3), 372–390 (2000)
12. Han, J., Pei, J., Yin, Y.: Mining frequent patterns without candidate generation. In: Proceedings of the 2000 ACM SIGMOD International Conference on Management of Data. Dallas, Texas, USA, pp. 1–12, May 2000
13. Buehrer, G., de Oliveira, R.L., Fuhry, D., Parthasarathy, S.: Towards a parameter-free and parallel itemset mining algorithm in linearithmic time. In: IEEE 31st International Conference on Data Engineering (ICDE). Seoul, South Korea, pp. 1071–1082, April 2015
14. Ekstrand, M., Riedl, J., Konstan, J.: Collaborative filtering recommender systems. Found. Trends Hum. Comput. Inter. 4(2), 81–173 (2011)
15. Shi, Y., Larson, M., Hanjalic, A.: Collaborative filtering beyond the user-item matrix: A survey of the state of the art and future challenges. ACM Comput. Surv. 47(1), 1–45 (2014)
16. Noia, T.D., Mirizzi, R., Ostuni, V.C., Romito, D., Zanker, M.: Linked open data to support content-based recommender systems. In: Proceedings of the 8th International Conference on Semantic Systems, pp. 1–8 (2012)
17. Bostandjiev, S., O'Donovan, J., Hollerer, T.: TasteWeights: a visual interactive hybrid recommender system. In: Proceedings of the Sixth ACM Conference on Recommender Systems. Dublin, Ireland, pp. 35–42, September 2012

18. Kouki, P., Fakhraei, S., Foulds, J., Eirinaki, M., Getoor, L.: Hyper: A flexible and extensible probabilistic framework for hybrid recommender systems. In: Proceedings of the 9th ACM Conference on Recommender Systems. Vienna, Austria, pp. 99–106, September 2015
19. Dean, J., Ghemawat, S.: MapReduce: Simplified data processing on large clusters. Commun. ACM **51**(1), 107–113 (2008)
20. Wikipedia. "Jaccard index". https://en.wikipedia.org/wiki/Jaccard_index, Accessed 03-Apr-2016

# Searching for Optimal Configurations Within Large-Scale Models: A Cloud Computing Domain

Lina Ochoa, Oscar González-Rojas[✉], Mauricio Verano, and Harold Castro

Systems and Computing Engineering Department, School of Engineering,
Universidad de Los Andes, Bogotá D.C., Colombia
{lm.ochoa750,o-gonza1,m.verano239,hcastro}@uniandes.edu.co

**Abstract.** Feature modeling is a widely accepted variability modeling technique for supporting decision-making scenarios, by representing decisions as features. However, there are scenarios where domain concepts have multiple implementation alternatives that have to be analyzed from large-scale data sources. Therefore, a manual selection of an optimal solution from within the alternatives space or even the complete representation of the domain is an unsuitable task. To solve this issue, we created a feature modeling metamodel and two specific processes to represent domain and implementation alternative models, and to search for optimal solutions whilst considering a set of optimization objectives. We applied this approach to a cloud computing case study and obtained an optimal provider configuration for deploying a JEE application.

**Keywords:** Conceptual modeling · Big data · Cloud · Decision-making

## 1 Introduction

Variability modeling is used to represent common and variable characteristics of a given domain [6]. Feature modeling is a variability modeling technique that represents the characteristics of domain concepts (*e.g.* decisions in decision-making domains) as features and the constraints between them through a tree structure. An example of this technique is presented in Sect. 2. Nevertheless, accessing and analyzing a large amount of data from domain scenarios with multiple independent implementation alternatives (*e.g.* cloud computing), is a complex modeling task that requires a multi-dimensional variability modeling [10].

There are approaches that use the separation of concerns for decreasing modeling complexity in general-purpose domains [1,5–7,10] and in concrete scenarios of cloud computing [4,9,13]. However, there is a need to propose a consistent and unified representation, and to make a clear differentiation between the modeling of both domain and implementation alternative concepts. Furthermore, the mapping between models is still not formalized, and the implemented strategies for searching for optimal configurations lack the flexibility to define business preferences (*i.e.* limits, optimization objectives). The non-automated search of a

© Springer International Publishing AG 2016
S. Link and J.C. Trujillo (Eds.): ER 2016 Workshops, LNCS 9975, pp. 65–75, 2016.
DOI: 10.1007/978-3-319-47717-6_6

solution that fulfills a set of requirements and optimization objectives from the stakeholders, is an unsustainable task.

This paper presents a unified modeling method to represent both, the domain and implementation alternative concepts, and their dependencies and decisions metadata (*e.g.* costs). This method is composed of a feature modeling meta-model and two specific processes for supporting decision-making in domains with large-scale data sources to be analyzed. The metamodel represents a set of feature modeling concepts and solution constraints required during the search for optimal solutions (*i.e.* optimization objectives definition [8]). The first process provides a guide on how to model the mentioned scenarios by instantiating the proposed metamodel. The second process enables the search for a set of optimal solutions over the implementation alternatives space, while considering a set of functional and non-functional requirements, including optimization objectives.

We used the Infrastructure as a Service (IaaS) service model of cloud computing as a case study. This case study is suitable for applying our approach due to the high variability and large-scale data sources managed by cloud providers [4,9,13], as well as to the need for defining a set of cloud services, irrespective of the provider's implementation alternatives. We created feature models that represent the IaaS domain and a subset of implementation alternatives (*i.e.* IaaS providers). We managed complexity and readability in the conceptual modeling through a modular representation of domain concerns. Then, we applied a semi-automatic search for optimal configurations that fulfilled a set of requirements for deploying an existing Java Enterprise Edition (JEE) application to the cloud. We obtained one optimal provider configuration as a result.

The remainder of this paper is structured as follows. Section 2 introduces the core terminology and a case study that explains the challenges of this research. Section 3 and Sect. 4 present the proposed metamodel and the processes that were used, respectively. In Sect. 5, we present the results of applying our approach to the cloud computing case study. Finally, related work is presented in Sect. 6, and conclusions and future work are consolidated in Sect. 7.

## 2   Context and Case Study

*Feature modeling* is the process of modeling both, the common and the variable characteristics of a concept as features, whilst considering their dependencies [6]. A *feature* is a visible characteristic of a system that is relevant to a stakeholder [2]. A *feature attribute* refers to the metadata, usually a typed value (*e.g.* integer), that is added to a set of features. A *feature model* defines a complete concept in a tree structure, where the root feature represents the modeled *concept*, the remaining features represent its properties, and the dependencies defined over the tree edges represent *tree constraints*.

A *configuration* is a set of features, selected from the feature model, which represents a particular product. There are four well-known types of tree constraints: *mandatory* relation, which determines the obligatory selection of a feature in any configuration; *optional* relation, which determines that the selection of a particular feature is not obligatory; *alternative* relation, which defines that at most one feature should be selected from the involved features; and *or* relation, which defines that at least one feature should be selected from the involved features. Finally, we can represent dependencies between non-connected features through *cross-tree constraints*, which are specified as propositional formulas.

## 2.1   Case Study: Deploying a JEE Application in the Cloud

We present the deployment of a JEE stateless application in the cloud as a case study. This application was developed by a Colombian software company with several years of experience in designing and developing JEE applications. The main goal of the application is to support business processes related to the management of financial credits. This application was initially deployed on-premise, however, the increasing demand of services resulted in the software company deciding to guarantee elasticity while deploying it in the cloud.

Nonetheless, the JEE application has a set of features that hinder its deployment in the cloud. First, the application had a high dependency on the JBoss application server, which is in turn supported on a few set of Platform as a Service (PaaS) providers under an expensive fee. This situation forbids the usage of this type of providers. Second, the company needs to guarantee elasticity for database concurrency; however, few providers support an auto-scaling configuration of the Oracle database used by the JEE application (not a scaling configuration of the virtual machines). Therefore, we focused the analysis on the comparison and selection of three IaaS providers, mainly Amazon Web Services (AWS), Google Cloud (GC), and Microsoft Azure (*cp.* PaaS solutions are not required). These providers were chosen based on their leadership in the market.

Considering the application requirements, we defined a set of services to be offered by an IaaS provider: virtual machines with *Linux* operating system (OS) and *SSD* block storage, an *Oracle* database, and a *queue* service for supporting time consuming background jobs. The required auto-scaling process should be executed according to a *custom value* of memory usage to control Java's memory consumption in the group of virtual machines. An *alarm* monitoring service is also required to monitor the health state of the application. Moreover, in relation to the monthly pay of the cloud resources, the company seeks the cheapest solution that guarantees a minimum compute and memory capacity of 8 CPU and 16 GB of RAM for the application and the database machines, respectively.

This information was obtained by interviewing two software architects and two managers of the company under study. We identified the following challenges.

**C1:** Modeling decision scenarios in one variability model increases the complexity of the representation, and decreases its readability and understanding [6,10]. A unified variability modeling mechanism is needed to separate concerns, and to have a modular representation of the domain and implementation alternative concepts. This mechanism must control the complexity when modeling and analyzing large-scale data sources for a particular domain.

**C2:** The automatic search for optimal solutions over the alternatives space is required in order to minimize invested time and effort. In this case, domain requirements and a set of solution constraints should induce the search for alternative implementation solutions.

## 3   A Metamodel for Dimensional Variability Modeling

For the multi-dimensional variability modeling, we analyzed the usage of orthogonal models, decision models, and feature models to represent both, the common and variable aspects of a domain. We selected feature modeling due to its visual representation, and its weak dependency on realization artifacts [3,11]. We decided to define our own metamodel due to the need to express metadata, as well as emerging feature modeling concepts (*e.g.* feature attributes, feature solution graphs) that few existing tools support. Figure 1 illustrates the metamodel proposed to express the variability of decision scenarios in which the domain concepts have multiple implementation alternatives. The key contributions of this metamodel are the separation between the domain model and the implementation alternatives, and the definition of cross-model and solution constraints.

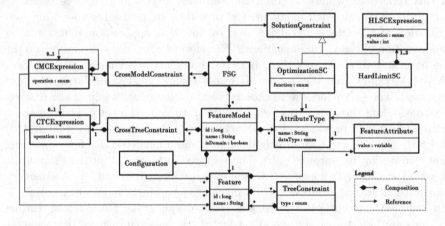

**Fig. 1.** A metamodel for decision-making on crosscutting variability models.

A Feature Solution Graph (*FSG*) is a structure that defines a set of constraints between features in different feature models [1]. We formalized the definition of a FSG as follows (*cp.* Definition 1). Each *FeatureModel* has a boolean variable (*cp.* isDomain) that determines if the model represents a domain (*i.e.* true) or an implementation alternative (*i.e.* false). Only one feature model can be defined as the domain of the FSG. Moreover, each feature model can have one or more *Configurations*, each one of them associated to a set of selected features. In our approach, we defined only one configuration related to the domain model.

**Definition 1.** *A FSG = (FM, CMC, SC) where FM is the set of feature models (FM ≠ ∅), CMC is the set of cross-model constraints, and SC is the set of solution constraints (sc), where each sc is defined as:*

- *An inequality relation $f(x_i)$ operator $f(x_j)$, where operator stands for $\leq, <, \geq$, or $>$, f is a function in terms of an attribute type $x_i$ or $x_j$, and $i, j, n \in \mathbb{Z}$, $1 \geq i, j \geq n$, $i \neq j$.*
- *A one or multi-variable optimization model like minimization$(f(x_1, .., x_n))$ or maximization$(f(x_1, .., x_n))$, where f is a function in terms of a set of attribute types $x_1, .., x_n$, and $i, n \in \mathbb{Z}$, $1 \geq i \geq n$.*

On the other hand, each feature model contains exactly one root feature and as many features as needed. Features are related through tree constraints with *mandatory, optional, or,* and *alternative type* (*cp. TreeConstraint*). Each feature can contain more than one tree constraint, and it is mandatory that each tree constraint contains at least one child feature. In addition, a feature can contain a set of *FeatureAttributes*, which represent metadata related to a previously defined *AttributeType* [8]. For example, we can define an attribute type with the *name* "Costs", and with an "integer" *data type*. Then, a feature could contain a feature attribute related to this type with a value of "100" USD.

We follow the structure defined in the XSD of the feature-oriented framework FeatureIDE [12] to express cross-tree constraints. Accordingly, each feature model must contain one or more *CrossTreeConstraints*. Each cross-tree constraint contains one direct *cross-tree constraint expression* (*cp.* CTCExpression) in order to represent propositional formulas as *p operator q*, where *p* and *q* are logic propositions. Additionally, the *operator* specifies if the child expressions are contained in a logical *and, or, not,* or *implies operation*. Cross-tree constraint expressions that are located in the deepest recursive level must have one or more related features, which define a correct propositional formula.

Similarly, we use the *CrossModelConstraint* entity [1,7] to define constraints between features of different models. This concept has the same possible operations and structure of the cross-tree constraint entity; the main difference is that cross-model constraints are contained in the FSG entity. These type of associations can only be made if there are at least two features contained in two different feature models. In the addressed decision scenarios, a cross-model constraint is defined as an implication that has a set of features in the domain model as a predecessor, and a set of features in the alternatives space as a consequence.

Finally, we propose the usage of *SolutionConstraints* (*cp.* SC in Definition 1) —which were previously presented by Ochoa et al. [8]— as decision rules. We can represent two types of hard constraints by using this concept: (*i*) *HardLimitSC* for defining limits (*cp.* HLSCExpression) over the feature attributes related to a particular attribute type (*e.g.* used to define budget boundaries: the total budget is between 1.000 and 5.000 USD); and (*ii*) *OptimizationSC* for minimizing or maximizing a set of feature attributes of the same type (*e.g.* used to look for the cheapest solution). The detailed description of these constraints is out of the scope of this paper and can be reviewed in the corresponding reference.

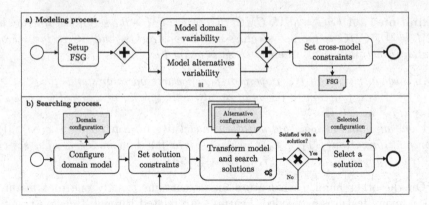

**Fig. 2.** Decision scenario modeling and configuration processes.

## 4   Processes for Searching for Optimal Configurations

Figure 2 illustrates two processes that instantiate the proposed metamodel. The
first process allows modeling the target decision-making scenario. The second
process eases the search for optimal solutions within the alternative models
space, according to a set of functional and non-functional requirements.

A developer executes the modeling process for setting-up the FSG
(*cp.* Fig. 2a). This task includes the instantiation of the metamodel, which is
represented as an Ecore file using the Eclipse Modeling Framework, and the
definition of the required attribute types that are specified with CoCo Domain-
specific Language (DSL) [8]. There are two tasks where the domain and the set
of alternative feature models are instantiated both as XMI and FeatureIDE files.
A semi-automated approach is needed for the alternative models to extract information from large-scale data sources (*e.g.* scraper). Then, the modeler defines a
set of cross-model constraints between the domain and the alternative models.

Each decision-maker executes the search process for defining a configuration
over the domain model. Afterwards, decision-makers define a set of solution
constraints (non-functional requirements) using CoCo DSL. Then, the complete
FSG is transformed into a problem for a given solver, and executed to perform an
automatic exhaustive search for a set of optimal configurations in the alternatives
space. In [8], we presented a transformation to a CSP, however, other techniques
such as evolutionary algorithms or linear programming can be used. The team
decides if the obtained results meet the project's needs, or if they have to define
a new set of solution constraints in order to improve the results. In our case, the
FSG transformation was implemented using Epsilon Languages.

## 5   Application to the Cloud Computing Case Study

**Applying the Modeling Process.** We defined three different attribute types
for the FSG instantiation: *costs*, *memory*, and *compute*. Then, we created four

feature models: one domain feature model representing a set of cloud services, and three alternative feature models representing the corresponding services offered by AWS, GC, and Azure. Three scrapers were built to gather the IaaS provider services information. Each model was included in the instantiated FSG and we manually defined a set of cross-model constraints to relate the domain and the alternative models. In addition, we specified a set of feature attributes related to the previously defined attribute types, considering that all values were calculated for a monthly expenditure.

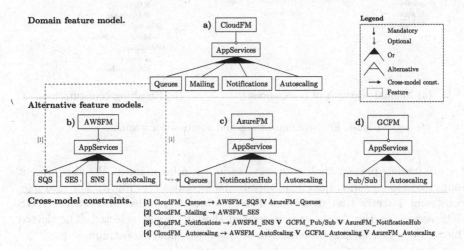

**Fig. 3.** FSG subset for the cloud computing case study.

The cloud model represents a subset of services: the compute service that has a variability related to *Windows* and *Linux* OS; the storage service that includes *block storage*, *object storage*, *SQL* and *No-SQL* databases and *cache* offers; a set of application services like *queues*, *mailing*, *notifications*, and *autoscaling*; network services such as Content Delivery Network (*CDN*), Domain Name System (*DNS*), and *load balancing*; and, finally, monitoring services that offer *alarms*, *dashboards*, and other different types of *metrics*. This subset of services was modeled for each cloud provider[1].

Figure 3 presents a small subset of elements of the instantiated FSG. There, we have represented four *application services* of the cloud model, as well as their corresponding services in the alternative models. For instance, the cloud model (*cp.* Fig. 3.a) has *application services* as an optional feature. This feature has an *or* relation with the *queues*, *mailing*, *notifications*, and *autoscaling* features. In the case of alternative models, the AWS feature model (*cp.* Fig. 3b) presents four services that are also related through an *or* relation: the Simple Queue Service (*SQS*), the Simple Email Service (*SES*), the Simple Notification Service (*SNS*), and the *auto scaling* capacity. The Azure (*cp.* Fig. 3c) and GC (*cp.* Fig. 3d)

---

[1] These models can be found at https://github.com/CoCoResearch/FSGCLoud.

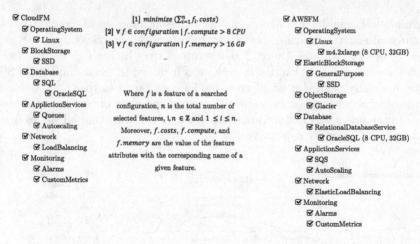

(a) Manual selection of preferences.          (b) Resulting configuration.

**Fig. 4.** FSG configurations and solution constraints.

feature models present their own services in a similar manner. We also present four cross-model constraints as propositional formulas (*cp.* Fig. 3). For example, constraint 1 states that if the cloud *queues* service is selected, then the AWS *SQS* service or the Azure *queues* service should also be selected. The dotted lines show a graphical representation of this cross-model constraint.

**Applying the Searching Process and Obtaining an Optimal Solution.** Once we had modeled the FSG, we created a cloud domain configuration aligned to the JEE application requirements. We also represented the three solution constraints that had been contemplated: (*i*) the minimization of the *costs* type attribute; the definition of hard limits over the (*ii*) *compute* (*i.e.* more than 8 CPU per machine) and the (*iii*) *memory* (*i.e.* more than 16 GB per machine) types in order to guarantee the computational capacity of the application and the database machines. Figure 4a illustrates both, the domain configuration and the set of solution constraints.

Finally, we transformed the FSG to a CSP implementation in order to automate the searching process. The resulting configuration suggested the selection of AWS as cloud provider. The suggested features are also shown in Fig. 4b. Assuming the constant usage of two virtual machines (application and database), the estimated total monthly cost of this solution is $2.496 USD, with a total compute capacity of 8 CPU and 32 GB of memory per machine. The selected services respond to functional and non-functional requirements.

## 6    Related Work

**Approaches to Modular Modeling.** Kang et al. [6] proposed the separation of the problem and the solution space in the variability model. Each space has its own viewpoints. Rosenmüller et al. [10] use propositional formulas to model the domain independently from the implementation variability dimensions. Metzger et al. [7] proposed a separation between the concerns of the product line and the modeling of software artifacts. Technical realizability is represented with feature models and product line representation with orthogonal models. They are related through cross-model links. Similarly, Holl et al. [5] represent multiple systems that collaborate as a System of Systems (SoS) in independent variability models. A set of emerging dependencies are defined during product configuration. Chavarriaga et al. [1] represent different domains in independent feature models, in which their dependencies are defined as *forces* and *prohibits* constraints.

Although all of these approaches propose a separation of concerns to decrease complexity issues, there is no consistency or coordination between them. Some of them lack a concrete representation that guides their practical use. Moreover, the mapping between models is still not formalized.

**Cloud Computing Variability Modeling.** García-Galán et al. [4] studied the decision process of migrating on-premise systems to the cloud. The approach was supported on an extended and cardinality-based feature model. They also searched for a solution based on a cost optimization function. Wittern et al. [13] presented Cloud Feature Models (CFMs) and defined a Cloud Service Selection Process (CSSP). CFMs contemplate the definition of a domain model that is instantiated in requirement models and service models. A cloud configuration is obtained through a CSP search. On the other hand, Quinton et al. [9] identified the complexity of selecting a PaaS or IaaS provider for the deployment of an application. They rely on the Domain Knowledge Model (DKM), an ontology model that represents a domain, a metamodel that represents cloud provider feature models, and a mapping metamodel that defines the relations between them. The resulting configuration is generated by a solver search with a cost objective function.

These approaches were considered in order to improve our modeling solution, especially when relating domain and alternative models. Furthermore, our searching strategy considers additional user preferences (*e.g.* hard limits and multi-variable optimization) that delivered a better cloud configuration. We unified these heterogeneous structures and concepts to obtain a consistent view.

## 7   Discussion

The proposed metamodel comprises multiple domain and implementation feature models. It also represents the cross-model and solution constraints that are used during the search for optimal solutions in the alternatives space. Our approach was applied to the selection of an IaaS provider configuration based on the set of functional and non-functional requirements of a JEE application. With this objective in mind, we modeled an independent set of IaaS services in the domain model, and a subset of AWS, GC, and Azure services in independent alternative models. We related the involved models through a set of cross-model and solution constraints. Finally, we automatically generated a CSP solver implementation to search for optimal solutions. The resulting cloud configuration is an AWS solution with an estimated monthly cost of $2.496 USD; it fulfills the requirements of the project, as well as three defined solutions constraints related to cost minimization, and compute and memory capacity assurance.

The presented processes are not a rule of thumb; they integrate different solutions to facilitate their applicability. The proposed metamodel, exhaustive search, user preferences, and even the solver implementation encoding could affect the resulting solutions. Therefore, our approach must be validated in multiple domains and variability scenarios to generalize its applicability. Moreover, we plan to test the performance and scalability of our solution when including more crosscutting models and a higher quantity of features.

# References

1. Chavarriaga, J., Noguera, C., Casallas, R., Jonckers, V.: Propagating decisions to detect and explain conflicts in a multi-step configuration process. In: Dingel, J., Schulte, W., Ramos, I., Abrahão, S., Insfran, E. (eds.) MODELS 2014. LNCS, vol. 8767, pp. 337–352. Springer, Heidelberg (2014). doi:10.1007/978-3-319-11653-2_21
2. Czarnecki, K., Eisenecker, U.W.: Generative Programming: Methods, Tools, and Applications. Addison-Wesley, New York (2000)
3. Czarnecki, K., Grünbacher, P., Rabiser, R., Schmid, K., Wasowski, A.: Cool features and tough decisions: a comparison of variability modeling approaches. In: Sixth International Workshop on Variability Modeling of Software-Intensive Systems, pp. 173–182. ACM, New York (2012)
4. García-Galán, J., Trinidad, P., Rana, O.F., Ruiz-Cortés, A.: Automated configuration support for infrastructure migration to the cloud. Future Gener. Comp. Sy. **55**, 200–212 (2016)
5. Holl, G., Thaller, D., Grünbacher, P., Elsner, C.: Managing emerging configuration dependencies in multi product lines. In: Sixth International Workshop on Variability Modeling of Software-Intensive Systems, pp. 3–10. ACM (2012)
6. Kang, K.C., Lee, H.: Systems and Software Variability Management. Concepts, Tools and Experiences, pp. 25–42. Springer, Heidelberg (2013)
7. Metzger, A., Pohl, K., Heymans, P., Schobbens, P.Y., Saval, G.: Disambiguating the documentation of variability in software product lines: a separation of concerns, formalization and automated analysis. In: 15th IEEE International Requirements Engineering Conference, pp. 243–253. IEEE Press, Delhi (2007)
8. Ochoa, L., Rojas, O.G., Thüm, T.: Using decision rules for solving conflicts in extended feature models. In: 8th International Conference on Software Language Engineering, pp. 149–160. ACM, Pittsburgh (2015)
9. Quinton, C., Romero, D., Duchien, L.: SALOON: a platform for selecting and configuring cloud environments. Softw. Pract. Exper. **46**, 55–78 (2016)
10. Rosenmüller, M., Siegmund, N., Thüm, T., Saake, G.: Multi-dimensional variability modeling. In: 5th Workshop on Variability Modeling of Software-Intensive Systems, pp. 11–20. ACM, New York (2011)
11. Schmid, K., Rabiser, R., Grünbacher, P.: A comparison of decision modeling approaches in product lines. In: 5th Workshop on Variability Modeling of Software-Intensive Systems, pp. 119–126. ACM, New York (2011)

12. Thüm, T., Kästner, C., Benduhn, F., Meinicke, J., Saake, G., Leich, T.: FeatureIDE: an éxtensible framework for feature-oriented software development. Sci. Comput. Program. **79**, 70–85 (2014)
13. Wittern, E., Kuhlenkamp, J., Menzel, M.: Cloud service selection based on variability modeling. In: Liu, C., Ludwig, H., Toumani, F., Yu, Q. (eds.) ICSOC 2012. LNCS, vol. 7636, pp. 127–141. Springer, Heidelberg (2012). doi:10.1007/978-3-642-34321-6_9

# A Link-Density-Based Algorithm
# for Finding Communities in Social Networks

Vladivy Poaka[1], Sven Hartmann[1(✉)], Hui Ma[2], and Dietrich Steinmetz[1]

[1] Clausthal University of Technology, Clausthal-Zellerfeld, Germany
`sven.hartmann@tu-clausthal.de`
[2] Victoria University of Wellington, Wellington, New Zealand

**Abstract.** Label propagation is a very popular, simple and fast algorithm for detecting communities in a graph such as a social network. However, it known to be non-deterministic, unstable and not very accurate. These shortcoming have attracted much attention by the research community, and many improvements have been suggested. In this paper we propose an new approach for computing preference to stabilize label propagation. The idea is to exploit the structure of the graph at study and use the link density to determine the preference of nodes. Our approach do not require any input parameter aside from the input graph itself. The complexity of propagation-based is slightly increased, but the stabilization and determinism are almost reached. Furthermore, we also propose a fuzzy version of our approach that allows one to detect overlapping communities as common in social networks. We have tested our algorithms with various real-world social networks.

**Keywords:** Network · Graph · Community · Cluster · Label propagation

## 1 Introduction

With the increasing volume of data collected in various domains, e.g., marketing, biology, economics, computer science and politics, analyzing data and networks, and detecting patterns in them to reveal valuable information can help with decision making and improving services, cf. [18]. For example, we might try to group people or customers of a shop depending on their habits, preferences and interests, in order to make a more efficient marketing by better recommendations of articles and products. This leads to the problem of finding communities in social networks.

In the last decade a range of methods has been proposed to compute communities (also called clusters) from collected data that are represented as graphs. However, existing methods often suffer some deficiencies that hamper their successful application in real-world situation. For example, some information about the social network at study might be needed that is unknown *a priori*, or too many input parameters are required that are hard to retrieve and maintain,

S. Link and J.C. Trujillo (Eds.): ER 2016 Workshops, LNCS 9975, pp. 76–85, 2016.
DOI: 10.1007/978-3-319-47717-6_7

or execution takes to much time or does not scale well for large networks, or the outcomes produced are of low quality or even meaningless for the particular application domain. For a thorough discussion we refer to survey papers [2,17,18] on the subject.

**Organization.** The remaining of the paper is organized as follows. We first assemble some preliminaries on social networks and their communities in Sect. 2. Then Sect. 3 recalls relevant related work on label propagation. In Sect. 4 we present a new variation of the label propagation approach to partition a network into communities without overlaps, and in Sect. 5 we extend our approach to the detection of overlapping communities. In Sect. 6 we present the results of an experimental evaluation of our approach. Section 7 provides a critical discussion of our approach. Finally, we conclude our work and suggest some future directions in Sect. 8.

## 2 Communities in Social Networks

Social networks are commonly represented as graphs, where nodes correspond to individuals or subjects, and edges correspond to links between them. We briefly introduce some graph notation to be used later on. A graph $G$ is a pair $(V, E)$ consisting of a finite set $V$ of nodes and a finite set $E$ of edges. Each edge connects a pair of nodes $u$ and $v$. The number of nodes and edges are denoted by $n = |V|$ and $m = |E|$, respectively. When nodes are connected by an edge we call them neighbors. The set of neighbors of a node $v$ is called its neighborhood and denoted by $\Gamma_v$. The number of neighbors of $v$ is called its degree and denoted by $deg_v = |\Gamma_v|$.

The successful application of computational methods to the problem of detecting *communities* in social networks requires some basic assumptions about the structure of a community. For a thorough discussion we refer the interested reader to [2,17,18]. A community could be regarded as a part of a (big) network system, which is more or less *"isolated"* from the others, i.e., with very few links to the rest of the system. Some people could also regard a community as a separate entity with its own autonomy. It is then natural to consider them independently of the graph as a whole. This gives rise to local criteria for defining a community which focus on the particular subgraph, including possibly its immediate neighborhood, but neglecting the rest of the graph. In a very strict sense, a community could even be defined as a subgroup whose members are all "friends" to each other, cf. [2].

On the other hand, a community could also be defined by taking into account the graph as a whole. This is more appropriate in those cases in which clusters are crucial parts of the graph, which cannot be removed without seriously impacting the functioning of the whole. The literature offers several global criteria for defining a community. Often they are indirect criteria, in which some global properties of the graph are used in an algorithm that outputs communities at the end. Many of these criteria are based on the idea that a network has a community structure if it is sufficiently different from a random graph, cf. [2].

The choice of a suitable definition of a community frequently depends on the application domain at hand. Once this assumption has been made, some methods are needed for detecting communities. In the literature two main approaches have been suggested for determining a good clustering of a graph into communities, cf. [2], namely

- *values-based* methods where some values are computed for the nodes, and then the nodes are assigned into clusters based on the values obtained; and
- *fitness-based* methods where a fitness measure is used over the set of possible clusters, and then one (or more) is selected among the set of cluster candidates whose fitness is good, if not best.

Graph databases show their advantages of storing, maintaining and analyzing graph data such as social networks. First, it has index-free adjacency property, which means each node stores information about its neighbors only and no global index of the connections between nodes exists. Secondly, graph databases stores data by means of multi-graph, or property graph, where each node and each edge is associated with a set of key-value pairs, called properties. Thirdly, data is queried using path traversal operations expressed in some graph-based query language, e.g., Cypher [1].

## 3    Related Work on Label Propagation

One of the most popular values-based methods for graph clustering is the Label Propagation Algorithm (LPA) [16]. Major advantages of LPA are its conceptual simplicity and its computational efficiency. It is merely based on the intrinsic structure of the graph, and does not require any advanced linear algebra, cf. [2,14]. As described in [11,16,18], LPA works with the following steps. First, each node $v_i$ is labeled with a unique label $\ell_i$. Then, at each iteration the node adopts the label that is shared by the majority of its neighbors. If there is no unique majority, one of the majority labels is selected *randomly*.

After a few iterations, this process converges quickly to form clusters that are just sets made up of nodes with the same label. The algorithm converges if during an iteration no label is changed anymore. All nodes with label $\ell_j$ will be assigned to the same cluster $C_j$. The advantage of this approach lies at its computational efficiency. Each iteration is processed in $O(m)$ time, and the number of iterations to convergence grows very slowly ($O(log(m))$ for many applications) or is even independent of the size of the graph, cf. [2,10,16,18].

Unfortunately, LPA has some severe disadvantages, too. As labels are selected randomly in case of ties between two or more majority labels, LPA turns out to be non-deterministic and very unstable. The communities obtained from different runs of LPA may differ considerably. It may even produce an output with one cluster made up of all nodes, which may not be adequate in practice. Much research has been devoted to investigate the disadvantages of the basic label propagation approach and to propose improved versions of LPA that overcome these shortcomings. For example, to avoid issues with the oscillation of labels,

[16] proposed to inspect nodes in each iteration in a random order when updating their labels. However, this encroaches on the robustness of the algorithm, and consequently also the stability of the detected community structure.

To avoid ties between multiple majority labels, one can assign a *preference* to each node to reflect its relevance and force the clustering process towards a more desirable partition. Preferences may be computed, for example, based on the degree centrality, betweenness centrality, or clustering coefficient centrality of a node, cf. [18]. In some of the cases, however, the computation of preferences may be expensive, thus affecting the overall efficiency of the label propagation approach.

## 4   Link-Density-Based Preferential Attachment

In this section we present a new approach for computing preferences that is relatively efficient and that may be used to avoid ties among multiple majority labels. Our approach, named *Link-Density-based Preferential Attachment (LDPA)*, is based on the assumption that a node "tends" more to belong to a cluster containing one or some of its neighbors with the most dense neighborhood.

More formally, for a subset $U$ of the node set $V$ of $G$ let $G_U$ denote the subgraph of $G$ spanned by $U$. Its node set is just $U$, and it contains all edges of $G$ that connect a pair of nodes in $U$. Let $m_U$ the number of edges in $G_U$. We define the *strength* $s_{uv}$ of link $uv$ as the number of edges within the neighborhood $\Gamma_v \setminus \{u\}$ of $v$, increased by 1 (accounting for the edge $uv$ itself), see Eq. (1a). It may be considered as the attraction strength of node $u$ towards node $v$. For technical reasons, our approach uses the normalized strength of link $uv$ within the neighborhood $\Gamma_u$, see Eq. (1b), as the *preference* of $u$ towards $v$.

$$s_{uv} = 1 + m_{\Gamma_v \setminus \{u\}}, \tag{1a}$$

$$b_{uv} = \frac{s_{uv}}{\sum_{w \in \Gamma_u \setminus \{u\}} s_{uw}} \tag{1b}$$

Note that the strengths of all links could be computed in the pre-processing phase of a label propagation methods such as LPA or its variations. For each node $u$ we have to consider the links to all its neighbors $v$. This pre-processing takes $O(n \cdot \overline{deg}_G)$ time where $\overline{deg}_G$ denotes the maximum degree of the nodes in $G$. Thus, for sparse graphs, it takes near-linear time. In fact, the computation could even be parallelized during implementation. Therefore, the global execution time of LDPA will be increased only slightly compared to the basic LPA.

## 5   Fuzzy Label Propagation for Detecting Overlapping Communities

Label propagation as discussed above results in a partition of the graph, that is, communities may not overlap. This may be meaningful in certain application domains, but in social networks overlapping communities are rather common. In this section we will present an extension of our proposed approach that is able to detect overlapping communities, too.

The main idea of LPA is that a node is assigned to the same cluster shared by the majority of its neighbors, while the others are grouped into different clusters. But the node at study may also belong to these clusters with a certain membership. That is the idea of the method that we called *Fuzzy LPA*. It allows each node to belong to all clusters detected within its neighborhood.

Note that a similar approach, called Community Overlap PRopagation Algorithm (COPRA) has been proposed in [5] which requires as input parameter the maximal number of clusters that each node may belong to. In practice, however, these numbers are unknown *a priori* and hard to estimate. We propose to overcome this limitation. In our algorithm the maximum number of clusters for each node is automatically obtained during runtime.

The extent to which a node $v_i$ belongs to a cluster $C_j$ is called its *membership* in this cluster and denoted by $m_{i,j}$. We want the membership to reflect the ratio $\gamma_{i,j}$ of the number of its neighbors sharing label $\ell_j$ by the total number of its neighbors plus 1 (for node $v_i$ itself), see Eq. (2a). The more neighbors of a node belong in the same cluster, the more probable this node should belong to this cluster. In this vein, we propose to consider at each iteration of LPA the probability of presence of each node, and to compute the membership $m_{i,j}$ as an ascending function in the ratio $\gamma_{i,j}$, as shown in Eq. (2b).

$$\gamma_{i,j} = \frac{|\Gamma_i \cap C_j|}{deg(v_i) + 1}, \tag{2a}$$

$$\mu_{i,j} = 1 - exp(-\lambda \cdot \gamma_{i,j}) \tag{2b}$$

Note that our algorithm requires a parameter $\lambda \in [1; +\infty[$ which may be seen as the *growth factor* of the membership of a node. Based on our experiments, we recommend to use $\lambda \in [1; 3]$.

The additional step to compute the memberships of each node $u$ takes $O(|\Gamma_u|)$ time. Thus, for each iteration an extra $O(n \cdot |\Gamma_u|)$ time is needed. The memberships need to be stored at each iteration. Consequently, the complexity is $O(n \cdot n_C)$, where $n_C$ is the number of clusters detected. Since the number of clusters decreases at each iteration as certain labels vanish due to the domination by others, the memory space occupied also decreases.

An extension of the proposed approach to link-density-based preferences is straightforward. In this case the ratio $\gamma_{i,j}$ is obtained by the normalization of the strengths of links within a detected cluster of its neighborhood. This gives rise to a fuzzy version of LDPA, too.

## 6   Experimental Evaluation

**Experimental Settings and Datasets.** To evaluate our proposed approach we have implemented the algorithms in a prototype systems, and tested them thoroughly. We conducted our experiments on a computer with x64 bits Windows

**Table 1.** Network datasets used for the experiments.

| Network | Description | Number of nodes (n) | Number of edges (m) |
|---|---|---|---|
| Zachary | Friendships [3] | 34 | 78 |
| Dolphins | Dolphins group [12] | 62 | 159 |
| Facebook | 'Circles' [9] | 4,039 | 88,234 |
| Jazz | Jazz musicians [4] | 198 | 5,484 |
| Science | Co-authorships [15] | 1,589 | 2,742 |
| Books | Politics books [8] | 105 | 441 |
| Power grid | US Power grid [19] | 4,941 | 6,594 |

8.1 operating system. The main specifications are: CPU Intel Pentium 2.40 GHz and 3.88 GB of RAM. For testing we used several popular network datasets such as *Zachary Karate club*, *Dolphins*, and *Facebook Anonymized*, *Network of Jazz Musicians*, *Co-authorship Network*, *Books about US Politics*, and *Power Grid*, see Table 1 for details. These real-world datasets have been used as benchmarks before and are publicly available at [7,9,13].

We imported all the datasets into a graph database. We use *Neo4j* [1] because it supports deep graph analytic and support for the Cypher declarative graph query language.

**Experimental Evaluation Results.** We have conducted 100 runs of each algorithm on each of the datasets. The average execution times till conversion are shown in Table 2. For the fuzzy versions of the algorithms the memberships of the nodes in the various clusters have been computed after each iteration. This contributed to the overhead of their execution times compared to the respective basic versions. But one could also choose to perform them only at the final step, and the execution times for Fuzzy LPA (in column 3) and Fuzzy LDPA (in column 5) would be quite smaller.

**Table 2.** Summary table showing the average execution times.

| Network | Average execution times (in ms) | | | |
|---|---|---|---|---|
| | LPA | Fuzzy LPA | LDPA | Fuzzy LDPA |
| Zachary | 4.65 | 13.71 | 108.1 | 112.33 |
| Dolphins | 11.4 | 17.91 | 112.67 | 125.66 |
| Facebook | 2016.47 | 5618.88 | 82034.15 | 82263.15 |
| Jazz | 49.55 | 368.85 | 368.85 | 481.24 |
| Science | 107.93 | 320.06 | 262.13 | 630.28 |
| Books | 12 | 30.47 | 117.63 | 144.24 |
| Power grid | 380.14 | 1406.52 | 944.7 | 3703.06 |

The Link-Density-based Preferential Attachment (LDPA) approach performs each node' preference attachment based only on the structure of the network, namely the density of edges. These values could be calculated once, since the graph's structure remains the same during the clustering. This improvement increases the global complexity time by $O(n \cdot m)$ in the worst case, i.e. on dense graphs. However, based on the inherent structure of the graph at study, the computation of independent parts, i.e. links and neighborhoods, could be parallelized during the implementation phase. Therefore, the global execution time of the whole clustering process would be slightly increased. Aside from keeping in memory labels during the execution of the basic LPA, this method needs also to store each link's strength computed, which is equal to twice the number of edges $m$ on undirected graphs. Similarly to the policy with labels storage, as this algorithm performs, less and less link's strengths are needed. They could be deleted and the memory space occupied will also decreases.

In addition to the execution time, we were also interested in accuracy and stability of the proposed approach. To study this question for LDPA we analyzed the community structure obtained as outcome of each of the 100 runs. Table 3 shows the smallest and largest number of communities detected.

**Table 3.** Minimum and maximum number of clusters detected during the 100 runs of LDPA on each network dataset.

| Network | Number of clusters detected | |
|---|---|---|
| | Minimum | Maximum |
| Zachary | 1 | 2 |
| Dolphins | 2 | 3 |
| Facebook | 6 | 9 |
| Jazz | 1 | 2 |
| Science | 412 | 420 |
| Books | 2 | 2 |
| Power grid | 419 | 450 |

The outcomes are more stable and more accurate, since the number of detected clusters is almost constant for each dataset. Apart from *Power grid*, the number of detected communities does not differ significantly. For example, with the *Zachary club*, 2 communities were detected in 94 % of all runs, and each of them partitioned the network into two disjoint subsets and assigned all the nodes correctly. For *Dolphins*, for example, we obtained 3 clusters in more than 75 % of the runs, always before reaching 10 iterations. For *Jazz* is split between two parts, as the inherent structure.

For the *Zachary club* the Fuzzy LPA detected 2 communities in most of the 100 runs. The only notable exception was one case where the algorithm converged already after four iterations and four communities were detected. Generally, the results obtained by our experiments are consistent with the logic of this dataset [3], as they show up the "fuzziness" of nodes 2, 8, 9, 19, 30 and 31, while the other nodes were assigned to their respective clusters with memberships greater than 0.9.

# 7   Discussion

In this section, we will compare the proposed approach against the existing ones. As first criteria, amongst the most important, is the *determinism* of method. The main idea of LPA approach allows to obtain several results, depending on the runtime. During the execution, a node may be swapped between different clusters before the convergence. Although adjunction of node preferences may reduce this effect, their precise values are hard to measure on real-world social networks. We proposed above how to compute these values only based on intrinsic characteristics of graph at study. Talking about spectral methods, due to the fact that they are mathematical laws-based, they can only be deterministic. However, social behavior does not always follow theoretical and mathematical laws. With regard to *overlaps* between clusters, this criteria depends strongly on the main idea of a method, even though extensions are allowed in many cases. For instance in the LPA, we kept tracks of changes during swapping of nodes between clusters, and evaluate corresponding *membership* values, as the proportion of the number of node's neighbors with the same label at a given iteration. This modification is essentially to view which clusters that nodes may belong to are wrongly assigned.

One more usage of the *fuzziness* in clustering, particularly in methods discussed above, is the detection of *mediator* or *super nodes* between communities. For example, nodes that all their memberships values are below to a certain threshold (0.1 for example) are connected to at least 5 different communities without belonging strongly to anyone. Such nodes may play an important role of mediation and lead the relationships and exchanges between different communities they are connected to. One the other hand, those with the greatest memberships values greater than a certain value (0.9) may be considered as *central nodes*. They may have an important function of control and stability within the community they belong to. These two features are very important. The former is useful when we want to know how a person may influence or have a certain impact within a subgroup, play a role as intermediate between communities or more, optimally reduce the search time that can be achieved by using them down to $O(log[log(n)])$ [6]. The latter, on the other hand, is worthwhile as well in social network ( *"person(s) you may know"* feature) as in business world ( *"content(s) you may like"*), just to mention few uses. This could also help to obtain a hierarchy of subgroups in an organization, from the top management down to interns.

Due to non-determinism of LPA, *accuracy* of the results it proposes could not be good. One way to improve it is to use node preference as mentioned above. We proposed a way to compute these preferences, LDPA, based only on the structure of the graph. The main idea of our improvement is that, a node is *attracted by* the most *link-dense* group within its neighborhood. Advantages are the accuracy and determinism of LPA are increased, highly dense groups are detected and the approach can be parallelized to minimize the increase of the global execution time in comparison to that of LPA. However, this enhancement suffers also from the random selection of the node from which to start the propagation. That leads (in some rare cases) to trivial results. Another drawback is that clusters with more or less same link-density and separated by only one – or few nodes –, are often merged together into only one (with nodes that are not strictly *"similar"* to each other). More generally, graphs without a community structure, like very dense ones may lead to trivial solution, since it is not easy to capture differences between preferences. That is the main reason why the number of detected clusters are sometimes less than expected.

With improvements we proposed, we can also obtain good and accurate clustering results with propagation-based methods and with a wise interpretation of them, more useful information become available, the axis of analysis of data depends on the application domain.

## 8    Conclusion and Future Work

Computational methods for clustering graphs and analyzing their community structure is a topic that is still attracting a lot of attention among researchers and practitioners. In this paper we proposed a variation of the basic label propagation that uses a new way of computing preferences of nodes based on the link density. In addition, we have studied fuzzy versions of our approach, to cope with overlapping communities. The accuracy of results obtained show that the increase of the global execution time is worthwhile. Thus it can be used on real-world network graphs with medium size or on large graphs with computation parallelization. We also show how our improvement could be used as pre-processing phase for many others existing algorithms. For instance in [10,18], preferences could be performed based on (local) link-densities of the network at study. To compare our approach to existing ones, we test it on some benchmark datasets. An analysis of results opens some inquisitiveness that worth the detour. First, the number of detected communities per graph varies slightly and the intrinsic structure is very well detected. The memberships computed during the fuzzy approach may help to classify the nodes either as *central, super* or *simple*. This function is till now mostly performed through linear algebra, which is characterized as computational demanding. The usefulness of the two former types of nodes is now well established in numerous domains such as business world, organizational studies, social networks, social capital, diffusion of innovations, economic sociology, just to mention a few.

## References

1. Neo4j graph database. http://www.neo4j.org
2. Fortunato, S.: Community detection in graphs. Phys. Rep. **486**(3), 75–174 (2010)

3.  Girvan, M., Newman, M.E.J.: Community structure in social and biological net-
    works. Proc. Natl Acad. Sci. **99**(12), 7821–7826 (2002)
4.  Gleiser, P., Danon, L.: Community structure in Jazz. eprint
    arXiv:cond-mat/0307434, July 2003
5.  Gregory, S.: Finding overlapping communities in networks by label propagation.
    New J. Phys. **12**(10), 103018 (2010)
6.  Hadaller, D., Regan, K., Russell, T.: Necessity of supernodes survey. Technical
    report, Technical Report 2005-1, Department of Computer Science, University of
    Toronto, vol. 67, p. 217 (2005)
7.  Heymann, S.: Gephi (2012). https://wiki.gephi.org/index.php/Datasets/
8.  Krebsl, V.: Social network analysis software & services for organizations, commu-
    nities, their consultants (2014). http://www.orgnet.com/
9.  Leskovec, J., Krevl, A.: Datasets: stanford large network dataset collection (2014).
    https://snap.stanford.edu/data/
10. Leung, I.X.Y., Hui, P., Liò, P., Crowcroft, J.: Towards real-time community detec-
    tion in large networks. Phys. Rev. E **79**, 066107 (2009)
11. Liu, X., Murata, T.: Advanced modularity-specialized label propagation algorithm
    for detecting communities in networks. Phys. A: Stat. Mech. Appl. **389**(7), 1493–
    1500 (2010)
12. Lusseau, D., Schneider, K., Boisseau, O.J., Haase, P., Slooten, E., Dawson, S.M.:
    The bottlenose dolphin community of doubtful sound features a large proportion
    of long-lasting associations. Behav. Ecol. Sociobiol. **54**(4), 396–405 (2003)
13. Newman, M.: Gephi (2013). http://www-personal.umich.edu/mejn/netdata/
14. Newman, M.E.: Detecting community structure in networks. Eur. Phys. J. B-
    Condens. Matter Complex Syst. **38**(2), 321–330 (2004)
15. Newman, M.E.: Finding community structure in networks using the eigenvectors
    of matrices. Phys. Rev. E **74**(3), 036104 (2006)
16. Raghavan, U.N., Albert, R., Kumara, S.: Near linear time algorithm to detect
    community structures in large-scale networks. Phys. Rev. E **76**(3), 036106 (2007)
17. Schaeffer, S.E.: Graph clustering. Comput. Sci. Rev. **1**(1), 27–64 (2007)
18. Šubelj, L., Bajec, M.: Group detection in complex networks: an algorithm and
    comparison of the state-of-the-art. Phys. A **397**, 144–156 (2014)
19. Watts, D.J., Strogatz, S.H.: Collective dynamics of small-world networks. Nature
    **393**(6684), 440–442 (1998)

# Modelling and Reasoning for Business Intelligence

## Preface to MORE-BI 2016

Corentin Burnay[1], Jennifer Horkoff[2], Ivan J. Jureta[1],
and Stéphane Faulkner[1,2]

[1] University of Namur, Namur, Belgium
[2] City University London, London, UK

The series of International Workshops on Modeling and Reasoning for Business Intelligence (MORE-BI) aims at advancing the engineering of Business Intelligence (BI) systems. The second edition of the workshop was collocated with the 35th International Conference on Conceptual Modeling (ER 2016), held in Gifu, Japon, in November 2016.

BI systems gather, store, and process data to turn it into information relevant for decision-making. Successful engineering, use, and evolution of BI systems require a deep understanding of the requirements of decision-making processes in organizations, of the kinds of information used and produced in these processes, of the ways in which information can be obtained through acquisition and reasoning on data, of the transformations and analyses of that information, of how the necessary data can be acquired, stored, and cleaned, of how its quality can be improved, and of how heterogeneous data can be used together. The fourth edition of MORE-BI focused on three topics: the search of patterns in sequential data, the design of spatial OLAP applications and the use of data mining techniques for security purposes.

We hope that the workshop has stimulated discussions and contributed to the research on the concepts and relations relevant for the various steps in the engineering of BI systems.We thank all authors who have submitted their research to MORE-BI 2016. We are grateful to our colleagues in the steering committee for helping us define the topics and scope of the workshop, our colleagues in the program committee for the time invested in carefully reviewing the submissions under a very tight schedule, the participants who have helped make this a relevant event, and the local organizers and workshop chairs of ER 2016. We hope that you find the workshop program and presentations of interest to research and practice of business intelligence, and that the workshop has allowed you to meet colleagues and practitioners focusing on modeling and reasoning for business intelligence. We look forward to receive your submissions and meet you at the next edition of the workshop.

## Accepted Papers

- Witold Andrzejewski, Bartosz Bebel, Szymon Klosowski, Bartosz Lukaszewski and Gastn Bakkalian. *Searching for Patterns in Sequential Data: Functionality and Performance Assessment of Commercial and Open-source Systems*
- Tatiana Penkova. *Analysis of Natural and Technogenic Safety of the Krasnoyarsk Region Based on Data Mining Techniques*
- Sandro Bimonte, Ali Hassan and Philippe Beaune. *From design to visualization of Spatial OLAP applications: A new prototyping methodology and tool*

## MORE-BI Organizing Committee

| | |
|---|---|
| Corentin Burnay | FNRS and University of Namur, Belgium |
| Ivan J. Jureta | FNRS and University of Namur, Belgium |
| Stéphane Faulkner | University of Namur, Belgium |

## MORE-BI Steering Committee

| | |
|---|---|
| Jennifer Horkoff | City University London, Belgium |
| Ivan J. Jureta | FNRS and University of Namur, Belgium |
| Stéphane Faulkner | University of Namur, Belgium |

## MORE-BI 2015 Program Committee

| | |
|---|---|
| Alberto Abello | Universitat Politcnica de Catalunya |
| Ladjel Bellatreche | Ecole Nationale Supérieure de Mécanique et d'Aérotechnique |
| Sandro Bimonte | Irstea Clermont Ferrand |
| Olivier Corby | Inria |
| Alfredo Cuzzocrea | ICAR-CNR and University of Calabria |
| Neil Ernst | University of British Columbia |
| Cécile Favre | Université Lyon 2 |
| Jennifer Horkoff | City University London |
| Dimitris Karagiannis | University of Vienna |
| Alexei Lapouchnian | University of Trento |
| Isabelle Linden | University of Namur |
| Patrick Marcel | Université Franois Rabelais de Tours |
| Jose-Norberto Mazon | University of Alicante |
| Catherine Roussey | Irstea Clermont Ferrand |

Monique Snoeck            Katholieke Universiteit Leuven
Thodoros Topaloglou       University of Toronto
Juan C. Trujillo          University of Alicante
Robert Wrembel            Pozna University of Technology

# Searching for Patterns in Sequential Data: Functionality and Performance Assessment of Commercial and Open-Source Systems

Witold Andrzejewski, Bartosz Bębel, Szymon Kłosowski, Bartosz Łukaszewski, Robert Wrembel, and Gastón Bakkalian[✉]

Institute of Computing Science, Poznan University of Technology, Poznań, Poland
{witold.andrzejewski,bartosz.bebel,robert.wrembel}@cs.put.poznan.pl,
bakka933@hotmail.com

**Abstract.** Ubiquitous devices and applications generate data that are naturally ordered by time. Thus elementary data items can form sequences. The most popular way of analyzing sequences is searching for patterns. To this end, sequential pattern discovery techniques were proposed in some research contributions and implemented in a few database systems, e.g., Oracle Database, Teradata Aster, Apache Hive. The goal of this work is to assess the functionality of the systems and to evaluate their performance with respect to pattern queries.

## 1 Introduction

Modern IT architectures include applications and devices that generate sequences of data items (events). The order that exists in sequences implies the existence of various patterns. By analyzing the patterns one can discover additional pieces of information of a business value. Some typical domains, where finding patterns in sequential data is of a business value include: stock exchange, energy management, public transportation, workflow systems, e-commerce.

**Example 1.** An example dataset comes from a public transportation network in the city of Poznań where commuters use intelligent cards. Card readers report simple records including: *cardID*, *stopID*, *tramNo*, *timestamp*, and *event_type* (in, out, travel). Based on such records, clustered for a given *cardID* and ordered by *timestamp*, one can represent passengers' travels as sequences of events. For example, the set of daily travels of a passenger identified by *cardID=1100* can be visualized as sequences shown in Fig. 1. In the example dataset, one may be interested in finding the number of commuters whose travels fall into the following pattern: getting in at stop 's7', traveling $n$ stops including 's10', and getting out at 's11'.

Sequential data are searched for patterns by means of pattern queries. Typically, the queries are expressed in SQL-like constructs that allow to form sequences and to define patterns. Such extensions were proposed in the research literature and implemented in a few database systems.

S. Link and J.C. Trujillo (Eds.): ER 2016 Workshops, LNCS 9975, pp. 91–101, 2016.
DOI: 10.1007/978-3-319-47717-6_8

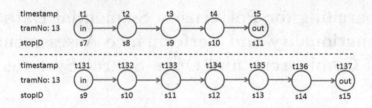

**Fig. 1.** An example sequential data set on travels in a public transportation network

**Example 2.** Let us consider data stored in table called *travels*. A query shown in Listing 1.1 searches for sequences (travels) that are composed of exactly 3 events, where attribute *stopID* of the first event (A) is equal to 's14'. Clause CLUSTER BY indicates which attribute of an event is used to cluster events to form sequences. SEQUENCE BY indicates an attribute used to order events within every sequence. AS defines the pattern of elements in a sequence (the syntax of SQL-TS [19]).

**Listing 1.1.** An example 3-element pattern query

```
SELECT A.stopID FROM travels
    CLUSTER BY cardID SEQUENCE BY timestamp AS (A, B, C)
WHERE A.stopID = 's14'
```

Based on the literature, we identified the two most popular query patterns in a transportation domain, namely: (1) an n-elements pattern query, and (2) at least n-elements pattern query (both discussed in Sect. 3). In this paper we asses the functionality of the most popular available database systems, i.e., Oracle Database 12c, Teradata Aster 6.00.01, Apache Hive 0.13.0, and evaluate their performance with respect to the aforementioned pattern queries (Section 4).

## 2    Related Work

Research on analyzing sequential data is focusing on: (1) mining sequential data for discovering patterns, (2) analyzing sequential data in a traditional SQL-like way and searching for given (known) patterns, (3) discovering patterns of events in data streams, (4) developing models and techniques for warehousing sequential data and analyzing them in an OLAP-like style. Only 4 production systems, i.e., Oracle, Teradata Aster, Hive, and Spark, implement pattern queries. Since mining sequential data is out of scope of this paper, we will not cover it here.

**SQL-like support for pattern search.** One of the first approaches to analyzing database-stored sequences used an object-relational data model with unary and aggregate operators [20]. The unary operators included a selection, projection, and offset within a sequence. The aggregate operators included aggregation (for aggregating in an n-elements window) and compose (for combining/joining two sequences). Another contribution, called the Sorted Relational Query Language (SRQL) [18], was based on an extended relational algebra with operators for: (1) creating sequences out of relational data, (2) matching two tuples at a given position in a sequence, (3) matching a tuple at a given position in a sequence with tuples within a sequence window, and (4) aggregating sequences within a given window. The extension of SRQL is Simple Query Language for Time Series (SQL-TS) proposed in [19]. SQL-TS introduced operators for: (1) clustering sequences, (2) sorting sequences, and (3) defining patterns. In [12], to represent ordered data a data model based on one-dimensional arrays (called arrables) was used. The proposed query language - AQuery offers selection, projection, join, grouping, and the possibility to apply a given function to an array cell. In [24], the authors proposed another array-based model and query language - SciQL that allows to manipulate arrays of sequences and perform SQL-like selects on the arrays.

**Discovering patterns in data streams**. In the area of Complex Event Processing [3,23], Stream Cube [9] and E-Cube [13,14] were developed to provide tools for OLAP analysis of stream data within a given time window. E-Cube includes: a query language (called SEQ) - to query events of a given pattern, a concept hierarchy - to compute coarser aggregates based on finer ones, a hierarchical storage with data sharing, and a query optimizer. SEQ enables grouping events by means of attributes and computing basic aggregate functions.

**Warehousing sequential data**. In S-OLAP [15], the concept of a Sequence Cuboid was proposed. It is based on the relational data model and storage. The cuboid represents answers to the so-called Pattern-Based Aggregate queries. The proposed data model defines a set of operators for the purpose of analyzing patterns. The model was further extended in [5,6] with an algorithm for supporting pattern-based aggregate queries.

[8] focused on warehousing RFID data. The authors proposed a few techniques for: (1) reducing the size of RFID cuboids and (2) computing higher level cuboids from lower level ones. They applied the relational data model to represent RFID data and their order. In [4], the authors provided a rough overview of their contribution to constructing an RFID warehouse.

[22] proposed a process cube to store process instances. The process cube is constructed based on: (1) a process cube structure that defines the "schema" of the cube, (2) a process cube view that is analogous to a relational view, and (3) a materialized process cube view that is the process cube view filled in with data coming from an event repository. The process cube is organized by dimensions that define the context of process mining. The author redefined typical OLAP operators (slice, dice, roll-up, and drill-down) to work on the process cube.

In [2,10], the authors presented a data model for storing and processing time point-based sequences. The model is based on the three fundamental components, namely: an event, a sequence, and a dimension. A sequence is created from events by clustering and ordering them. Sequences and events have measures that can be analyzed in an OLAP-like manner in contexts set up by dimensions. Based on the model, a query language implementation was presented in [1].

In [11], the authors proposed a whole data warehouse architecture for analyzing sequences of events in workflow logs. The sequences are stored in a data structure called Sequence Cube that organizes sequences by dimensions. The developed query language supports pattern matching and aggregations by dimensions.

[10] addresses the problem of analyzing sequences of intervals. It presents a formal model of Interval OLAP (I-OLAP) and the set of low-level operations. The sequences are organized by dimensions and are characterized by measures. The latter are expressed by user-defined functions. A follow-up I-OLAP architecture was discussed in [16], where the authors outlined their query language, called TidaQl, as an extension of SQL. Their roughly outlined select statement works in a multidimensional data model with measures and hierarchical dimensions.

**Production systems**. Oracle together with IBM defined an ANSI SQL standard for finding patterns within sequences stored in tables [17]. To this end, the MATCH_RECO-GNIZE clause was proposed and implemented in Oracle12c [7]. It allows to search for patterns, define patterns and pattern variables. Teradata Aster implemented the nPath clause (up to version 6.00.01) [21] for analyzing sequences and searching for patterns. Apache Hive (in versions from 0.11.0 to 0.13.0) also implemented the nPath clause. It was renamed as MATCHPATH and removed in version 0.14.0. Hive 0.13.0 was included as the component of Apache Spark 1.3.0. Microsoft StreamInsight is another system that allows to discover patterns in a data stream. However, the discovery has to be implemented in a procedural language.

## 3 Experimental Setup

In this section we present the prerequisites for the experimental evaluation, i.e.,: (1) the structure of data generated by intelligent card readers, (2) basic queries in the context of analyzing commuting patterns, and (3) the database systems under test.

**Data from card readers**. Card readers generate data of the following structure: (1) cardID (NUMBER) - a passenger's intelligent card ID, (2) stopID (STRING) - a tram stop at which a given event occurred (values: {'s1', ..., 's120'}), (3) tramNo (STRING) - the number of a tram, (4) timestamp (DATETIME) - a timestamp of an event, (5) card_type (NUMBER) - passenger's card type (values: {0, 1, 2, 3}), (6) cost (NUMBER) - a cumulative cost of a travel, (7) event_type (STRING) - a type of an event: 'in', 'out', null (commuting).

**Basic queries for analyzing commuting patterns**. Based on the literature, we identified the two most popular query patterns applicable to analyzing commuting patterns, namely: (1) an n-elements pattern query and (2) an at least n-elements pattern query.

The **n-elements pattern query** includes exactly $n$ elements in its pattern, where an element represents a tram stop. An example of such a query, for $n=5$, is shown in Listing 1.2. It searches for travels of every passenger identified by *cardID* (CLUSTER BY *cardID*) that started at tram stop 's14', went through stop 's15', went through 2 other stops, and finished at the 5-th stop ($E.event\_type$ = 'out').

**Listing 1.2.** An example 5-element pattern query

```
SELECT A.stopID, B.stopID, C.stopID, D.stopID, E.stopID
FROM travels
   CLUSTER BY cardID SEQUENCE BY timestamp AS (A, B, C, D, E)
WHERE A.stopID = 's14' AND B.stopID = 's15' AND A.event_type = 'in' AND E.event_type = 'out'
```

The **at least n-elements pattern query** includes at least $n$ pattern elements in its AS clause. An example query that searches for sequences composed of at least 3 elements, defined as A, B, and C, is shown in Listing 1.3. *B in the AS clause denotes that element B may appear in the pattern one or more times, whereas elements A and C must appear exactly once. The WHERE clause allows to define conditions that must be fulfilled by the values of: attribute *cost* (of elements A and C) as well as attribute *event_type* (of element A).

**Listing 1.3.** An example pattern query of at least 3 elements

```
SELECT A.stopID, B.stopID, C.stopID
FROM travels
   CLUSTER BY cardID SEQUENCE BY timestamp AS (A, *B, C)
WHERE C.cost − A.cost > 3 AND C.cost − A.cost < 10 AND A.event_type = 'in'
```

**Systems under test.** Initially, we considered assessing the functionality and performance of: Oracle Database 12c, Teradata Aster 6.00.01, Apache Hive 0.13.0, and Apache Spark 1.3.0. After a thorough investigation it turned out that Apache Spark 1.3.0 couldn't execute any pattern query due to a bug. Pattern search in Oracle 12c and Teradata Aster 6.00.1 is supported by the MATCH_RECOGNIZE and NPATH clauses, respectively. Apache Hive 0.13.0 implements the NPATH clause, whose syntax is similar to the one of Teradata Aster. NPATH was available in Hive version 0.11.0, in version 0.12.0 it was renamed to MATCHPATH, and became unavailable starting from version 0.14.0. Due to space limits, we refer to technical documentations of the aforementioned systems for further information on the clauses.

## 4  Experimental Evaluation

The goal of the experimental evaluation was twofold. First, to verify the functionality of pattern queries offered by Oracle, Aster, and Hive. Second, to test the performance of these systems w.r.t.: (1) the n-elements pattern query, (2) the at least n-elements pattern query, and (3) pattern search for queries of various selectivities.

In the experiments we used artificially generated sequential data, representing passenger travels in the public transportation network of the city of Poznań, which includes 120 tram stops. Artificial sequential data were obtained from a generator that we implemented in C++. The generator allowed to parameterize the distribution of travel lengths (the number of stops traveled) and card types.

In the experiments, we used the Poisson distribution of travel lengths (median equal to 7.6) and card types.

Elementary data items, from which sequences were built, were stored in a table whose structure was outlined in Sect. 3. The average row size in this table was equal to 30B. The number of data items stored in our database was equal to: 24,055,341 (1 GB), 121,020,658 (5GB), 240,543,617 (10GB), and 480,057,689 (20 GB). Each experiment was repeated 6 times, and the charts discussed below show average values and standard deviations. The experiments were conducted on two workstations (equipped with Intel R CoreTM i7-4700MQ, 16GB DDR3 1600MHz CL9 RAM, HDD Seagate ST1000LM014-1EJ164), under Linux Ubuntu 14.10.

## 4.1  n-Elements Pattern Query

In this experiment, queries were formulated to find sequences of 3, 5, 7, 9, and 11 elements. To prevent from retrieving sequences being sub-sequences of other sequences, additional conditions were defined on: (1) the first element in the sequence (i.e., $event\_type$ = '$in$') and (2) the last element in the sequence (i.e., $event\_type$ = '$out$'). An example Oracle query finding 5-elements sequences is shown in Listing 1.4.

**Listing 1.4.** An example 5-elements pattern query

```
SELECT stA, stB, stC, stD, stE, count(*)
FROM (SELECT * FROM travels
    MATCH_RECOGNIZE
      (PARTITION BY cardID ORDER BY timestamp ASC
      MEASURES a.stopID as stA, b.stopID as stB, c.stopID as stC, d.stopID as stD, e.stopID as stE
      ONE ROW PER MATCH AFTER MATCH SKIP TO NEXT ROW PATTERN(a b c d e)
      DEFINE a as a.event_type = 'in', e as e.event_type = 'out'))
GROUP BY stA, stB, stC, stD, stE
ORDER BY 6 DESC
```

The obtained performance characteristics for 7, 9, and 11-elements queries are shown in Fig. 2 (for 3- and 5-elements pattern queries, the characteristics are similar). The chart reveals that: (1) in Teradata Aster, query execution times are linearly dependent on a sequence length and on a data volume and (2) in Oracle Database and Apache Hive, query execution times are linearly dependent on a data volume and they do not depend much on a sequence length.

## 4.2  At Least n-Elements Pattern Query

In this experiment, the following three queries were executed. The first query (labeled as $A_{s8} * B_{s5} * C_{s11}$) retrieves sequences (travels) that started, went through, and ended at given tram stops. The following conditions are defined for this query: (1) $stopID$ = '$s8$' for the first element, (2) $stopID$ = '$s11$' for the last element, and (3) $stopID$ = '$s5$' for at least one element between the first and the last one. For this query, sequence length is undefined. The second query (labeled as $A * B_{length \leq 11}$) searches for sequences with at most 11 elements. The third query (labeled as $A_{in} * B_{s8} * C_{out}$) searches for sequences (travels) of any

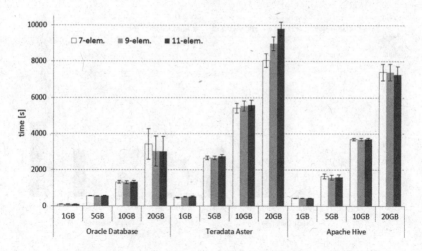

**Fig. 2.** Execution times of n-elements pattern queries

length that went through a given tram stop. The following conditions are defined for this query: (1) *event_type* = *'in'* for the first element, (2) *event_type* = *'out'* for the last element, and (3) *stopID* = *'s8'* for at least one element between the first and the last one.

Query $A_{s8} * B_{s5} * C_{s11}$ - finding at least 5-elements sequences, in the Oracle and Aster syntax is shown in Listing 1.5 and Listing 1.6, respectively.

**Listing 1.5.** An example at least 5-element pattern query $A_{s8} * B_{s5} * C_{s11}$ - Oracle syntax

```
SELECT count(*)
FROM
(SELECT * FROM travels
    MATCH_RECOGNIZE
      (PARTITION BY cardID ORDER BY timestamp ASC
        ONE ROW PER MATCH AFTER MATCH SKIP TO NEXT ROW PATTERN(a b* c d* e)
         DEFINE a as stopID LIKE 's8', c as stopID LIKE 's5', e as stopID LIKE 's11'))
ORDER BY 1 DESC
```

**Listing 1.6.** An example at least 5-element pattern query $A_{s8} * B_{s5} * C_{s11}$ - Aster syntax

```
SELECT count(*)
FROM
  NPATH (ON travels
        PARTITION BY cardID ORDER BY timestamp ASC MODE(OVERLAPPING)
        PATTERN('a.b*.c.b*.d')
        SYMBOLS (stopID='s8' as a, stopID='s5' as c, stopID='s11' as d, true as b)
        RESULT ( ACCUMULATE (station OF ANY(a,b,c,d)) AS path))
GROUP BY path
```

It turned out that Apache Hive does not allow to define queries with at least n-elements patterns. Therefore, Fig. 3 presents time performance characteristics for Oracle and Aster only. For both systems, the characteristics show a linear dependency of the execution time on a data volume. We can also observe that

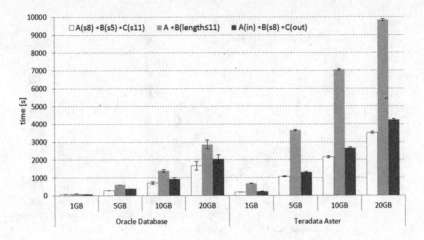

**Fig. 3.** Execution times of at least n-elements pattern queries

the execution time of query $A * B_{length \leq 11}$ is much higher than the other two queries. It is because the systems under test had to first compute all possible sequences and next eliminated sequences whose length was greater than 11.

### 4.3   Variable Selectivities of Pattern Queries

This experiment investigated the impact of query selectivity on the query execution time. Query selectivity is defined as $RetSeq/AllSeq$, where $RetSeq$ is the number of sequences returned by a test query and $AllSeq$ is the total number of sequences returned by a reference query. In our case, the reference query returned

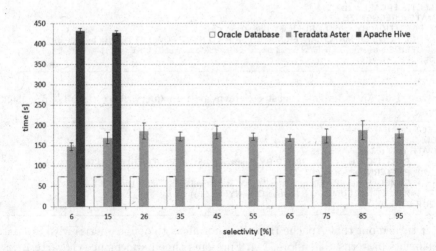

**Fig. 4.** The performance of sequence searching under variable selectivities of pattern queries

all sequences composed of at least 2 elements where the first element fulfilled condition *event_type* = *'in'* and the last element fulfilled condition *event_type* = *'out'*, i.e., all at least 2-stops travels were included in the reference set.

The time performance characteristics of queries of selectivities from 6 % to 95 % are shown in Fig. 4. Unfortunately, it turned out that Hive does not allow to define regular expressions with complex conjunction and alternatives. Therefore, we were not able to express other selectivities than 6 % and 15 %. As we can observe from the chart, a query selectivity has a minor impact on the query execution time. The reason for this behavior is that in order to construct sequences, for each query, the systems under test had to perform a full table scan. Having constructed the sequences, those that fulfilled the conditions were included into the query result.

# 5    Conclusions and Future Work

Techniques for analyzing sequential data have been of interest of research and business for several years. Multiple data models, algorithms, SQL-like languages, and prototypes have been proposed by researchers. A few commercial and open-source database systems included tools for sequential data analysis as well. In this paper, we assessed the functionality of the most popular database systems available on the market (Oracle 12c, Teradata Aster 6.00.01, and Apache Hive 0.13.0) and evaluated their performance with respect to sequential pattern queries.

The functionality assessment reveals that only Oracle and Aster offer SQL syntax and implementation that are complex enough to support real pattern queries. Apache Hive (in the evaluated version) revealed inability to define queries with at least n-elements patterns and use regular expressions with complex conjunction and alternatives.

The performance evaluation shows that typical pattern queries perform linearly w.r.t. a data volume, although the difference in performance can be substantial between the systems under test. Queries that cluster sequences based on their length are typically costly in all the systems under test, since such queries require full table scans. From our experiments, Oracle turned out to offer the best performance.

This paper presents a piece of broader work leading to assessing languages, systems, and architectures for storing and analyzing sequential data. Currently we are experimenting with storage techniques for sequences (e.g., NoSQL, relational, graph, arrays). The next step will focus on analyzing the applicability and performance of Spark and Hadoop as well as novel sequence databases (e.g., TSDB, InfluxDB).

**Acknowledgement.** The research of G. Bakkalian has been funded by the European Commission through the "Erasmus Mundus Joint Doctorate Information Technologies for Business Intelligence Doctoral College (IT4BI-DC)". The research of W. Andrzejewski, B. Bębel, and R. Wrembel has been funded by the Polish National Science Center, grant "Analytical processing and mining of sequential data: models, algorithms, and data structures".

# References

1. Bebel, B., Cichowicz, T., Morzy, T., Rytwiński, F., Wrembel, R., Koncilia, C.: Sequential data analytics by means of Seq-SQL language. In: Chen, Q., Hameurlain, A., Toumani, F., Wagner, R., Decker, H. (eds.) DEXA 2015. LNCS, vol. 9261, pp. 416–431. Springer, Heidelberg (2015). doi:10.1007/978-3-319-22849-5_28

2. Bębel, B., Morzy, M., Morzy, T., Królikowski, Z., Wrembel, R.: OLAP-like analysis of time point-based sequential data. In: Castano, S., Vassiliadis, P., Lakshmanan, L.V., Lee, M.L. (eds.) ER 2012. LNCS, vol. 7518, pp. 153–161. Springer, Heidelberg (2012). doi:10.1007/978-3-642-33999-8_19

3. Buchmann, A.P., Koldehofe, B.: Complex event processing. Inf. Technol. **51**(5), 241–242 (2009)

4. Chawathe, S.S., Krishnamurthy, V., Ramachandran, S., Sarma, S.: Managing RFID data. In: Proceedings of International Conference on Very Large Data Bases (VLDB), pp. 1189–1195 (2004)

5. Chui, C.K., Kao, B., Lo, E., Cheung, D.: S-OLAP: an OLAP system for analyzing sequence data. In: Proceedings of ACM SIGMOD International Conference on Management of Data, pp. 1131–1134 (2010)

6. Chui, C.K., Lo, E., Kao, B., Ho, W.-S.: Supporting ranking pattern-based aggregate queries in sequence data cubes. In: Proceedings of ACM Conference on Information and Knowledge Management (CIKM), pp. 997–1006 (2009)

7. Fred Zemke, F., Witkowski, A., Cherniak, M., Colby, L.: Pattern matching in sequences of rows, 2007. Accessed 2 Mar 2016. http://web.cs.ucla.edu/classes/fall15/cs240A/notes/temporal/row-pattern-recogniton-11.pdf

8. Gonzalez, H., Han, J., Li, X.: FlowCube: constructing RFID flowcubes for multidimensional analysis of commodity flows. In: Proceedings of International Conference on Very Large Data Bases (VLDB), pp. 834–845 (2006)

9. Han, J., Chen, Y., Dong, G., Pei, J., Wah, B.W., Wang, J., Cai, Y.D.: Stream Cube: an architecture for multi-dimensional analysis of data streams. Distrib. Parallel Databases **18**(2), 173–197 (2005)

10. Koncilia, C., Morzy, T., Wrembel, R., Eder, J.: Interval OLAP: analyzing interval data. In: Bellatreche, L., Mohania, M.K. (eds.) DaWaK 2014. LNCS, vol. 8646, pp. 233–244. Springer, Heidelberg (2014). doi:10.1007/978-3-319-10160-6_21

11. Koncilia, C., Pichler, H., Wrembel, R.: A generic data warehouse architecture for analyzing workflow logs. In: Morzy, T., Valduriez, P., Bellatreche, L. (eds.) ADBIS 2015. LNCS, vol. 9282, pp. 106–119. Springer, Heidelberg (2015). doi:10.1007/978-3-319-23135-8_8

12. Lerner, A., Shasha, D.: AQuery: query language for ordered data, optimization techniques, and experiments. In: Proceedings of International Conference on Very Large Data Bases (VLDB), pp. 345–356 (2003)

13. Liu, M., Rundensteiner, E., Greenfield, K., Gupta, C., Wang, S., Ari, I., Mehta, A.: E-Cube: multi-dimensional event sequence analysis using hierarchical pattern query sharing. In: Proceedings of ACM SIGMOD International Conference on Management of Data, pp. 889–900 (2011)

14. Liu, M., Rundensteiner, E.A.: Event sequence processing: new models and optimization techniques. In: Proceedings of SIGMOD PhD Workshop on Innovative Database Research (IDAR), pp. 7–12 (2010)

15. Lo, E., Kao, B., Ho, W.-S., Lee, S.D., Chui, C.K., Cheung, D.W.: OLAP on sequence data. In: Proceedings of ACM SIGMOD International Conference on Management of Data, pp. 649–660 (2008)

16. Meisen, P., Kenig, D., Meisen, T., Recchioni, M., Jeschke, S.: TidaQL: a query language enabling on-line analytical processing of time interval data. In: Proceedings of International Conference on Enterprise Information Systems (ICEIS), pp. 54–66 (2015)

17. Melton, J. (ed.): Working Draft Database Language SQL - Part 15: Row Pattern Recognition (SQL/RPR). ANSI INCITS DM32.2-2011-00005 (2011)

18. Ramakrishnan, R., Donjerkovic, D., Ranganathan, A., Beyer, K.S., Krishnaprasad, M.: SRQL: Sorted relational query language. In: Proceedings of International Conference on Scientific and Statistical Database Management (SSDBM), pp. 84–95 (1998)

19. Sadri, R., Zaniolo, C., Zarkesh, A.M., Adibi, J.: A sequential pattern query language for supporting instant data mining for e-services. In: Proceedings of International Conference on Very Large Data Bases (VLDB), pp. 653–656 (2001)

20. Seshadri, P., Livny, M., Ramakrishnan, R.: Sequence query processing. SIGMOD Rec. **23**(2), 430–441 (1994)

21. Aster nPath. http://developer.teradata.com/aster/articles/aster-npath-guide. Accessed 13 Mar 2014

22. Aalst, W.M.P.: Process cubes: slicing, dicing, rolling up and drilling down event data for process mining. In: Song, M., Wynn, M.T., Liu, J. (eds.) AP-BPM 2013. LNBIP, vol. 159, pp. 1–22. Springer, Heidelberg (2013). doi:10.1007/978-3-319-02922-1_1

23. Wu, E., Diao, Y., Rizvi, S.: High-performance complex event processing over streams. In: Procedings of ACM SIGMOD International Conference on Management of Data, pp. 407–418 (2006)

24. Zhang, Y., Kersten, M., Manegold, S.: SciQL: Array data processing inside an RDBMS. In: Proceedings of ACM SIGMOD International Conference on Management of Data, pp. 1049–1052 (2013)

# Analysis of Natural and Technogenic Safety of the Krasnoyarsk Region Based on Data Mining Techniques

Tatiana Penkova[(⊠)]

Institute of Computational Modelling SB RAS, Krasnoyarsk, Russia
penkova_t@icm.krasn.ru

**Abstract.** This paper presents a comprehensive analysis of natural and technogenic safety indicators of the Krasnoyarsk region in order to explore geographical variations and patterns in occurrence of emergencies by applying the multidimensional analysis techniques – principal component analysis and cluster analysis – to data of the Territory Safety Passports. For data modelling, two principal components are selected and interpreted taking account of the contribution of the data attributes to the principal components. Data distribution on the principal components is analysed at different levels of the territory detail: municipal areas and settlements. Two- and three- cluster structures are constructed in multidimensional data space; the main clusters features are analyzed. The results of this analysis have allowed to identify the high-risk municipal areas and rank the territories according to danger degree of occurrence of the natural and technogenic emergencies. It gives the basis for decision making and makes it possible for authorities to allocate the forces and means for territory protection more efficiently and develop a system of measures to prevent and mitigate the consequences of emergencies in the large region.

**Keywords:** Comprehensive data analysis · Data mining · Principal component analysis · Cluster analysis · Prevention of emergencies · Territorial management · Decision making support

## 1 Introduction

Prevention of natural and technogenic emergencies is a one of the major tasks of the territory management. Analytical support of decision-making processes based on modern technologies and efficient methods of data analysis is a necessary condition for improving the territorial safety system and management quality.

The Krasnoyarsk region is the second largest federal subject of Russia and the third largest subnational governing body by area in the world. The Krasnoyarsk region lies in the middle of Siberia and occupies an area of 2,339,700 km$^2$, which is 13 % of the country's total territory. This territory is characterised by heightened level of natural and technogenic emergencies which is determined by social-economic aspects, large resource potential, geographical location and climatic conditions [1]. In order to improve the population and territory safety, a lot of monitoring systems and control tools for on-line observation and strategic planning are being actively introduced within

© Springer International Publishing AG 2016
S. Link and J.C. Trujillo (Eds.): ER 2016 Workshops, LNCS 9975, pp. 102–112, 2016.
DOI: 10.1007/978-3-319-47717-6_9

the region [2–6]. The Ministry of Emergency has enacted the structure and order of conducting the Territory Safety Passport, which defines a system of indicators to assess the state of territory safety, the risk of emergencies and possible damages to create efficient prevention and mitigation actions [7]. At present, there are massive data collections about the state of controlled objects, occurred events and sources of emergencies. However, we have to admit that the processing stored data, aimed at obtaining the new and useful knowledge, is insufficient. The local databases remain unused, while the reasonable decisions, comprehensive analysis and emergencies prediction are sorely needed. Thus, identification of risk factors of emergencies based on monitoring data and investigation of their impact on key indicators of human safety are topical and important tasks in territorial management.

Data Mining, as the extraction of hidden predictive information from large databases, is a powerful modern technology of intelligent data processing. Data mining techniques provide the effective tool for discovering previously unknown, nontrivial, practically useful and interpreted knowledge needed to make decisions [8, 9]. This paper presents a comprehensive analysis of natural and technogenic safety indicators of the Krasnoyarsk region in order to explore geographical variations and patterns in occurrence of emergencies by applying the data mining techniques – principal component analysis and cluster analysis – to data of the Territory Safety Passports.

The outline of this paper is as follows: Sect. 1 contains introduction. Section 2 describes the initial data. Section 3 presents the principal component analysis: identification and interpretation of principal components; analysis of data distribution on the principal components at different levels of the territory detail. Section 4 presents the cluster analysis: construction of two- and three-cluster structures in multidimensional data space and analysis of their main features. Section 5 draws the conclusion.

## 2 Data Description

Analysis of natural and technogenic safety indicators is based on data of the Territory Safety Passports of the Krasnoyarsk region for 2014 collected in Center of Emergency Monitoring and Prediction (CEMP). Original dataset contains 1,690 objects, essentially discrete settlements-level geographical entities of the Krasnoyarsk region, each with 12 measured attributes. Data attributes are listed in Table 1. One part of attributes characterizes the sensitivity of the territory to the risk factors effects (e.g. population density, the presence of industrial and engineering facilities) that is determined by the number of objects located on the territory (i.e. number of potential sources of emergencies), it is so-called "object attributes". The other part of attributes characterizes the presence of potential factor that can damage the health of people, can cause irreversible damage to the environment that is determined by the statistic of events occurred in the territory (i.e. number of emergencies), it is so-called "event attributes".

The preliminary analysis of original data has shown a fairly strong correlation between "object" and "event" attributes, therefore for further analysis we will consider the attributes that characterize events and population. In addition, some reference characteristics and identifiers are used for data visualization and interpretation.

**Table 1.** List of the data attributes of territory safety passports

| No | Attributes | Description |
|----|------------|-------------|
| 1 | Pop | Population |
| 2 | Soc_object | Number of important social facilities (e.g. educational, health, social, cultural and sports facilities) |
| 3 | Water_object | Number of dangerous water bodies |
| 4 | Indust_object | Number of potentially dangerous industrial objects (e.g. plants, factories, mines) |
| 5 | Oil_line | Number of pipeline sectors in 5 km. radius from borders of settlement |
| 6 | Munic_object | Number of municipal facilities (e.g. power supply, water supply and heating facilities) |
| 7 | Flood_event | Number of floods |
| 8 | NFire_event | Number of natural fires |
| 9 | TFire_event | Number of technogenic fires |
| 10 | Munic_event | Number of accidents at municipal facilities |
| 11 | Nat_event | Number of natural events (excluding natural fires and floods) |
| 12 | Tech_event | Number of technogenic events (excluding technogenic fires and accidents at municipal facilities) |

Within this research, the analysis and visualisation of multidimensional data are conducted using the ViDaExpert [10]. Data visualization on geographical maps is performed by applying the mapping tools «ArcGIS» [11].

## 3   Principal Component Analysis

Principal Component Analysis (PCA) is one of the most common techniques used to describe patterns of variation within a multi-dimensional dataset, and is one of the simplest and robust ways of doing dimensionality reduction. PCA is a mathematical procedure that uses an orthogonal transformation to convert a set of observations of possibly correlated variables into a set of values of linearly uncorrelated variables called principal components [12]. The number of principal components is always less than or equal to the number of original variables. This transformation is defined in such a way that the first principal component has the largest possible variance and each subsequent component, respectively, has the highest variance possible under the constraint that it is orthogonal to the preceding components.

### 3.1   Contribution of the Data Attributes to the Principal Components

In general, the method allows to identify $k$ components based on $k$ initial attributes. Table 2 shows the results of calculating the eigenvectors of the covariance matrix arranged in order of descending eigenvalues.

**Table 2.** Results of principal components calculation

| Components | 1 | 2 | 3 | 4 | 5 | 6 | 7 |
|---|---|---|---|---|---|---|---|
| Eigenvalues | 0.404 | 0.249 | 0.141 | 0.116 | 0.075 | 0.010 | 0.005 |
| Accumulated dispersion | **0.504** | **0.652** | 0.793 | 0.909 | 0.985 | 0.995 | 1 |
| Pop | **0.509** | 0.109 | 0.111 | 0.113 | 0.227 | 0.182 | 0.787 |
| TFire_event | **0.513** | 0.083 | 0.061 | 0.088 | 0.171 | 0.616 | −0.557 |
| NFire_event | 0.060 | **0.439** | −0.876 | 0.186 | −0.022 | −0.033 | 0.012 |
| Munic_event | **0.503** | 0.096 | 0.120 | 0.084 | 0.251 | −0.764 | −0.263 |
| Flood_event | 0.235 | −0.314 | −0.325 | −0.853 | 0.109 | −0.004 | 0.029 |
| Nat_event | 0.086 | **−0.822** | −0.311 | 0.458 | 0.103 | −0.015 | 0.010 |
| Tech_event | **0.397** | −0.072 | 0.019 | 0.013 | −0.913 | −0.051 | 0.024 |

Based on combination of Kaiser's rule and the Broken-stick model [14], two principal components were identified (PC1 и PC2). The contribution of the reduced data attributes to principal components is presented in Fig. 1.

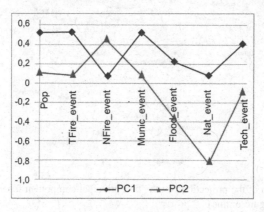

**Fig. 1.** Contribution of the data attributes to the first (PC1) and second (PC2) principal components

From Fig. 1 we can see that the first principal component (PC1) is characterised by the following attributes: a high level of population, high proportions of technogenic fires, accidents at municipal facilities and other technogenic events, a low percentage of natural events including natural fires and floods. In combination, these characteristics present the big settlements (e.g. cities) with high levels of technogenic hazards. The second principal component (PC2) is characterised by the following attributes: a low level of population, high proportion of natural fires, strong negative correlation with the percentage of natural events including floods and technogenic events including fires and accidents at municipal facilities. In combination, these characteristics present relatively small settlements (e.g. villages) with high levels of natural fires. This means that in comparison with other types of emergencies the technogenic and natural fires are the greatest threat for the Krasnoyarsk region.

## 3.2    Data Distribution on the Principal Components

The visualisation of the projections on the first and second principal components on the geographic map is displayed in Figs. 2 and 3. On these figures, the negative values in range [−1, 0] correspond to Group 1 (blue), the highest positive values in range (0.5; 1] correspond to Group 2 (red). The color intensity of municipal areas correspond to the number of settlements in the group.

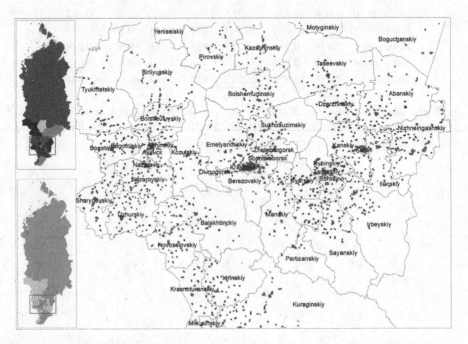

**Fig. 2.** Visualisation of the projections on the first principal component for municipal areas and settlements (Color figure online)

The lowest values of projections on the first principal component (Fig. 2, blue points) are observed for such settlements as: Ust-Kamo, Shigashet, Kasovo, Verhnekemskoe, Srednya Shilka, Komorowskiy, Noviy Satysh, Angutiha, Lebed. It can be explained by the fact that these settlements are very small villages and, at present, in these settlements there are no any socially significant objects and residents. The complete absence of the economic activity in these settlements leads to the lowest level (or absence) of technogenic fires. The highest values of the projections on the first principal component (Fig. 2, red points) are observed for such large settlements as Krasnoyarsk, Norilsk, Achinsk, Kansk, Minusinsk Lesosibirsk, Nazarovo, Emelya-novo, Aban, Yeniseiysk, Berezovka. These settlements present the big cities of the Krasnoyarsk region where the population and number of socially significant and industrial facilities are above average level in region.

The lowest values of projections for the second principal component (Fig. 3, blue points) are observed for such settlements as: Turuhansk, Cheremshanka, Tanzybey,

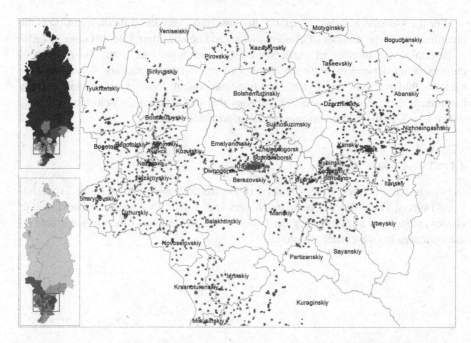

**Fig. 3.** Visualisation of the projections on the second principal component for municipal areas and settlements (Color figure online)

Emelyanovo, Ermakovskoe, Nizhniy Ingash, Velmo, Kuragino and Uzhur. Low levels of natural fires can be explained by the following facts: the absence of vegetation as a source of emergency in steppe areas (e.g. Western and Southern groups) and the absence of settlements in forest zone (e.g. Evenk Autonomous Okrug, Yeniseiysk and Turukhansky areas). The highest values of projections for the second principal component (Fig. 3, red points) are observed for such settlements as: Startsevo, Tilichet, Kuray, Baikal, Glinniy, Udzhey, Abalakovo and Protochniy. The high risk of natural fires is observed in the large settlements that are located close to the forest zones. In addition, there is probability of natural fires in the big cities where the forests constitute the part of their territories.

## 4  Cluster Analysis

Cluster analysis is a tool for discovering and identifying associations and structure within the data and typology development. Cluster analysis provides insight into the data by dividing the dataset of objects into groups (clusters) of objects, such that objects in a cluster are more similar to each other than to objects in other clusters. At present, there are many various clustering algorithms which are categorized based on their cluster model [13]. In this research, the centroid-based clustering method is used. *K*-means is a well-known and widely used clustering method which aims to partition objects based on attributes into *k* clusters. The *k*-means clustering is done by minimizing the sum of squares of distances between data and the corresponding cluster centroid.

For the k-means clustering method the most important and difficult question is the identification of the number of clusters that should be considered. In this case, in order to determine the number of clusters the PCA technique was used: the number of clusters being dependent upon the number of principal components. Thus, referring back to the previous discussion, the first component forms two clusters, second component forms three clusters. This means that the data has 2–3-cluster structures, where k = 3, is the maximum number of informative clusters.

## 4.1    Two-Cluster Structure

In two-cluster structure ($k = 2$) Cluster 1 (blue) has 352 objects and Cluster 2 (red) has 1,338 objects. The difference between clusters is identified by the standard deviation of cluster averages of attributes. Figure 4 shows the distribution of the clustered data on the attributes in two-cluster structure.

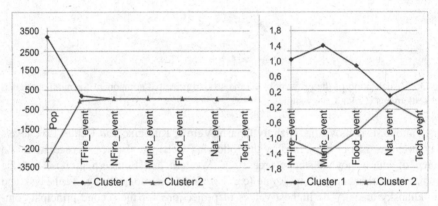

**Fig. 4.** Distribution of the clustered data on the attributes in two-cluster structure in small-scale (left) and large-scale (right) presentations (Color figure online)

As can be seen from Fig. 4, the two clusters differ significantly on such characteristics as population and number of technogenic fires. In addition, Cluster 1 is characterized by high proportions of accidents at municipal facilities, natural fires and floods. Therefore Cluster 1 covers both large settlements with well-developed infrastructure that increases the risk of technogenic emergencies and large settlements with rich natural environment (e.g. forests, water bodies etc.) that increases the risk of natural emergencies. Cluster 2 combines small settlements with low risk of natural and technogenic emergencies. The distribution of the clustered data on the territories in two-cluster structure is represented in Fig. 5.

Representatives of Cluster 1 are the following biggest settlements: Krasnoyarsk, Norilsk, Achinsk, Kansk, Zheleznogorsk, Zelenogorsk, Minusinsk, Lesosibirsk, Sosnovoborsk and Nazarovo. Representatives of Cluster 2 are the following biggest settlements: Novohayskiy, Solnechniy, Kozulka, Podgorniy, Krasnoturansk, Zykovo and Krasnokamensk. A lot of industrial facilities and municipal facilities with high

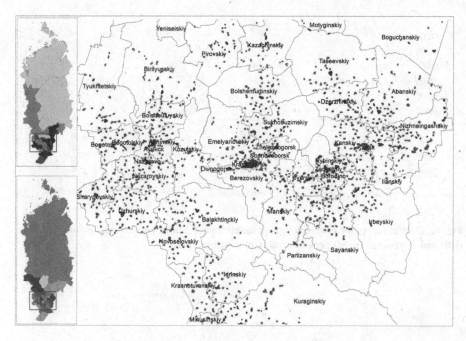

**Fig. 5.** Two-cluster structure on the geographic coordinates

level of operation time in the big settlements lead to the high risk of technogenic emergencies; a lot of water bodies on these territories lead to the high risk of floods.

## 4.2    Three-Cluster Structure

In the three-cluster structure (k = 3) Cluster 1 (blue) has 80 objects, Cluster 2 (red) has 720 objects and Cluster 3 (green) has 890 objects. Figure 6 shows the distribution of the clustered data on the attributes in three-cluster structure.

As can be seen from Fig. 6, the Cluster 1 differs significantly from Cluster 2 and Cluster 3 on such characteristics as population, number of technogenic fires, accidents at municipal facilities and other technogenic events. In contrast, Cluster 2 and Cluster 3 are characterized by low level of population and low proportions of natural and technogenic events in general but Cluster 3 demonstrates a trend to higher level of natural fires. Therefore, Cluster 1 combines the large settlements with well-developed infrastructure that increases the risk of technogenic emergencies. Cluster 2 combines the settlements with minimal risk of natural emergencies. Cluster 3 combines settlements where the basic threat is a natural fire.

The distribution of the clustered data on the territories in three-cluster structure is represented in Fig. 7.

Representatives of Cluster 1 are the following biggest settlements: Achinsk, Kansk Zelenogorsk Lesosibirsk, Minusinsk, Sharypovo, Nazarovo, Norilsk; representatives of Cluster 2 are the following biggest settlements: Divnogorsk Kozulka, Severo-Yeniseisk,

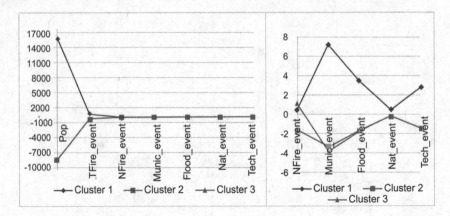

**Fig. 6.** Distribution of the clustered data on the attributes in three-cluster structure in small-scale (left) and large-scale (right) presentations (Color figure online)

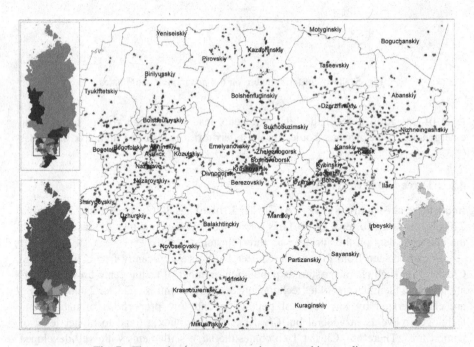

**Fig. 7.** Three-cluster structure on the geographic coordinates

Podgorny, Krasnoturansk, Kedroviy, Koshurnikova, Verhnepashino, Baykit; representatives of Cluster 3 are the following biggest settlements: Krasnoyarsk, Zheleznogorsk, Sosnovoborsk, Borodino, Shushenskoye, Kodinsk, Aginskoe. The high risk of natural fires is observed in the small settlements that are located close to the forest zones and in the large settlements where the forests are integral part of their territory.

# 5  Conclusion

The comprehensive analysis of natural and technogenic safety of the Krasnoyarsk region in the context of settlements is carried out in this paper by applying the data mining techniques – principal component analysis and cluster analysis – to data of the Territory Safety Passports. The data analysis results show that the technogenic and natural fires are the greatest threat for territory of the Krasnoyarsk region. The explored geographical variations and patterns allow to identify the high-risk municipal areas and particular settlements, rank the territories according to danger degree of occurrence of the natural and technogenic emergencies. The results of this research make it possible for specialists of CEMP to develop a system of measures to prevent and mitigate the consequences of emergencies in the Krasnoyarsk region.

The reported study was funded by RFBR according to the research project No. 16-37-00014.

# References

1. Report of the State of Natural and Anthropogenic Emergencies Protection of Territory and Population in the Krasnoyarsk Region: Annual Report of Ministry of Emergency, Krasnoyarsk, p. 254 (2014) (in Russian)
2. Regional Organizational System of Emergency Monitoring and Prediction: The Regulation of the Krasnoyarsk Region, p. 80 (2011) (in Russian)
3. Penkova, T.G., Korobko, A.V., Nicheporchuk, V.V., Nozhenkova, L.F.: On-line modelling and assessment of the state of technosphere and environment objects based on monitoring data. Procedia Comput. Sci. **35**, 156–165 (2014)
4. Yronen, Y.P., Yronen, E.A., Ivanov, V.V., Kovalev, I.V., Zelenkov, P.V.: The concept of creation of information system for environmental monitoring based on modern gis-technologies and earth remote sensing data. In: IOP Conference Series: Materials Science and Engineering, vol. 94, 012023 (2015). doi:10.1088/1757-899X/94/1/012023
5. Shaparev, N.Y.: Environmental monitoring of the krasnoyarsk region in terms of sustainable environmental management. Inf. Anal. Bull. (Scientific and Technical Journal) **18**(12), 110–113 (2009). (in Russian)
6. Bryukhanova, E.A., Kobalinskiy, M.V., Shishatskiy, N.G., Sibgatulin, V.G.: Improvement of environmental monitoring information maintenance as an instrument for sustainable social and economic development (on the example of the Krasnoyarsk Region). Inf. Commun. **1**, 43–47 (2014) (in Russian)
7. The Standard Territory Passport of Regions and Municipal Areas: The Regulation of Ministry of Emergency, no. 484 (2004) (in Russian)
8. Giudici, P.: Applied Data Mining: Statistical Methods for Business and Industry, p. 376. Wiley, Chichester (2005)
9. Williams, G.J., Simoff, S.J.: Data Mining: Theory, Methodology, Techniques, and Applications. LNAI, vol. 3755, p. 331. Springer, Heidelberg (2006)
10. Gorban A., Pitenko A., Zinovyev A.: ViDaExpert: User-friendly Tool for Nonlinear Visualization and Analysis of Multidimensional Vectorial Data. Cornell University Library. http://arxiv.org/abs/1406.5550

11. Using ArcViewGIS: The Geographic Information System of Everyone. ESRI Press, p. 350 (1996)

12. Abdi, H., Williams, L.: Principal components analysis. Wiley Interdisc. Rev. Comput. Stat. **2**(4), 439–459 (2010)

13. Jain, A., Dubes, R.: Algorithms for Clustering Data, p. 320. Michigan State University, Prentice Hall, East Lansing, Englewood Cliffs (1988)

14. Peres-Neto, P., Jackson, D., Somers, K.: How many principal components? stopping rules for determining the number of non-trivial axes revisited. Comput. Stat. Data Anal. **49**(4), 974–997 (2005)

# From Design to Visualization of Spatial OLAP Applications: A First Prototyping Methodology

Sandro Bimonte[1(✉)], Ali Hassan[1], and Philippe Beaune[2]

[1] TSCF, Irstea, 9 Avenue Blaise Pascal, 63178 Aubiere, France
{sandro.bimonte,ali.hassan}@irstea.fr
[2] Agaetis, 10 Rue Evariste Galois, 63000 Clermont-Ferrand, France
pbeaune@agaetis.fr

**Abstract.** The design of Spatial OLAP (SOLAP) applications consists of (i) Spatial Data Warehouse (SDW) model design and (ii) SOLAP visualization definition because a specific set of understandable and readable cartographic visualizations corresponds to a particular type of SOLAP query. Unfortunately few works investigate geovisualization issues in SOLAP systems and propose new methodologies to visualize spatio-temporal data, and no works investigate tools for readable SOLAP cartographic displays. Moreover, some works propose ad-hoc methodologies for DWs and SDWs exclusively based on data and user analysis requirements. Therefore, we present in this paper (i) a new geovisualization methodology for SOLAP queries that yields readable maps and (ii) a new prototyping design methodology for SOLAP applications that accounts for geovisualization requirements.

**Keywords:** Spatial data warehouse · Spatial OLAP · Geovisualization

## 1 Introduction

Spatial Data Warehouse (SDW) and Spatial OLAP (SOLAP) systems are first citizens of GeoBusiness Intelligence technologies. A SOLAP system has been defined as "*A visual platform built especially to support rapid and easy spatio-temporal analysis and exploration of data. It follows a multidimensional approach that is available in carto-graphic displays, as well as in tabular and diagram displays*" [1]. SOLAP systems allow for the analysis of huge volumes of geo-referenced data by simple interactive and online data exploration operators (i.e., SOLAP operators). Decision-makers trigger SOLAP operators through simple interactions with the visual components of SOLAP clients (pivot tables and graphical and cartographic displays). Therefore, they can easily and interactively explore spatial data, looking for unknown and/or unexpected spatial patterns. The success of SOLAP rests on the geovisualization analytic paradigm. Geovisualization "*integrates the techniques of scientific visualization, cartography, image analysis, and data mining to provide a theory of methods and tools for the representation and discovery of spatial knowledge*" [14]. Semiology rules allow the good readability of (spatial and alphanumeric) information displayed on a map. In the context of GISs, several works provide semiology tools and frameworks for readable maps [4, 19]. These

© Springer International Publishing AG 2016
S. Link and J.C. Trujillo (Eds.): ER 2016 Workshops, LNCS 9975, pp. 113–123, 2016.
DOI: 10.1007/978-3-319-47717-6_10

rules depend on several factors, such as the number and type (i.e., numerical, ordinal, etc.) of variables (i.e., represented information elements), and the type of geometry (points, lines, etc.). An adequate visual variable must be used for each variable, for example, for one numerical variable (e.g., the total products sold), the color visual variable (cloropeth map) can be safely used [13]. Contrary to GISs, SOLAP cartographic displays are represented by interactive maps that are created online using SOLAP operators. The choice of the correct visual variable is manually performed by decision-makers during the analysis process, which represents an important limitation on effective visual analysis for two reasons: it can delay the exploration process, and decision-makers have to be geovisualization experts to choose the right visualization for the right data. Therefore, *we present in this paper a framework for the correct (readable) visualization of the results of SOLAP queries.*

Moreover, we have *integrated it in a SOLAP prototyping methodology.* The design of SOLAP applications consists of (i) SDW model design [16] and (ii) SOLAP visualization configuration. Indeed, a set of understandable and readable cartographic visualizations is needed for each particular spatial data set. Unluckily, some works propose ad-hoc methodologies for SDWs based exclusively on data and user analysis requirements [9, 16]. Therefore, we present a new prototyping design and implementation methodology for SOLAP applications that takes into account (i) user analysis requirements and (ii) geovisualization requirements. The proposed design methodology allows decision-makers to rapidly implement their SDW model and deploy it on a web-based SOLAP system [5] with well-suited cartographic visualizations. It extends the ProtOLAP DW methodology [6] that allows for the prototyping of DW models using the ICSOLAP UML profile for SDW [7]. Therefore, motivated by the relevance of conceptual representations of complex data models in prototyping tools [16], we extend ICSOLAP with various new conceptual representations of the geovisualization methods for SOLAP, and we integrate it in the ProtOLAP methodology. Finally, we implement our approach by extending our previous SOLAP tool presented in [5].

## 2    Related Work

Integration of spatial data in DW and OLAP systems leads to the concept of Spatial OLAP (SOLAP) [1]. SOLAP introduces the concept of spatial dimension, which is a classical dimension with geometrical attributes. Typically, SOLAP architectures are multi-tier systems composed of a Spatial DBMS (database management system) to store (spatial) data; a SOLAP server, which implements the SOLAP operators; and a SOLAP client, which combines and synchronizes tabular, graphical, and interactive maps. Existing academic and industrial systems propose the use of simple geographic visualization methods, such as cloropeth maps, thematic maps, and multimaps [5, 10, 15]. Indeed, only a few works suggest particular geovisualization methods (a survey can be found in [5]). For example, [13] studied a new geovisualization method for trajectory DWs. [3] added multimedia elements, such as photos, videos, etc., to spatial data warehouse data. Finally, [12] studied the usage of chorems to enrich visual variables of SOLAP displays. To best of our knowledge, only [18] has investigated the readability of SOLAP maps, which it accomplished by providing clustering-based SOLAP visualization methods to avoid visual cluttering.

Several works provide frameworks for the creation of readable thematic maps [1, 4]. However, apart from some simple rules based on "1 or more variables", the existing SOLAP systems do not implement these frameworks. Therefore, they still provide decision-makers with unreadable maps and leave them to select the correct visualization for each SOLAP query. Moreover, visual variable configuration (i.e., the association of measures with visual variables) is usually conducted manually by the SDW expert using wizards. These tools do not allow for the specification of configurations based on dimensions (for example, using animated maps on the temporal dimension), and their use is quite long and tedious. Therefore, although visualization plays a fundamental role in SOLAP visual analytics and consequently in SOLAP application design, the configuration of the visual variables of SOLAP maps has yet to be included in SDW prototyping methodologies. This represents an important limitation because the success of a SOLAP project is usually related to the definition of a spatio-multidimensional model that fits users' needs. For that reasons, several works propose DW design methodologies based on data sources and/or user requirements [16]. Among them, some rapid prototyping approaches, based on standard (e.g., ER, UML, etc.) and ad-hoc formalisms, have been developed because they yield time and economic gains [6, 8]. Finally, dashboard design and prototyping have also been investigated in some works, such as [17].

## 3   Motivation

In this section, using a SOLAP application developed in [12], we describe the motivation of our work. The SDW is loaded using open-data of FAO (Food and Agriculture Organization of the United Nations). It allows for analysis of the total agricultural cultivated surface and the total production per year, country and crop. It presents a spatial hierarchy grouping countries in areas and years by decade. In the remainder of the paper, we use *"nb"* to denote the maximum number of cells (pieces of information) of the resulting pivot table associated with each spatial member. For example, for the pivot table of Fig. 1d, nb is 2. Using this SDW, it is possible to answer queries such as *"What was the total surface of wheat per country in 1990?"* (**Q1**). The SOLAP query is visualized using the cloropeth map shown in Fig. 1a.

Consider the following query, *"What was the total production of wheat per country per year (over the last 15 years)?"* (**Q2**). The result counts 15 variables (the production per year) per country (i.e., nb = 15). Therefore, a classical bar chart thematic map as shown in Fig. 1b appears unreadable because it conveys too much information [4]. Therefore, some other geovisualization method, such as a dynamic map [11], should be used. This problem exists because the number of visual variables that can be shown in a map is smaller than the amount of readable information shown in a pivot table. Finally, we consider another query *"What was the total production of wheat and cultivated surface per country in 1990?"* (**Q3**). The results of this query can be shown using a bar chart with two bars (left side of Fig. 1c). Although the map is readable in terms of visual

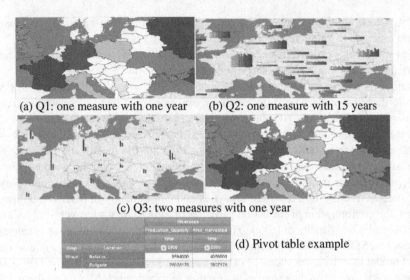

(a) Q1: one measure with one year     (b) Q2: one measure with 15 years

(c) Q3: two measures with one year

(d) Pivot table example

**Fig. 1.** SOLAP maps (Color figure online)

variable number, it is not adequate for representing two different measures with different numerical domains (hectares and tons). Therefore, the use of different visual variables for different measures is recommended [12], as shown on the right side of Fig. 1c. This means that decision-makers should be able to configure their cartographic displays according to the semantics of the warehoused data [12].

## 4   Framework SOLAP Visualization

To avoid the manual configuration of SOLAP cartographic displays and to avoid readability issues related to the number of visual variables (nb), we propose a new geovisualization framework based on the "display rules". First, it is necessary to define the maximum number of pieces of information to display for one spatial member ($nb_{max}$). Then, a set of rules can be specified. For each rule, we must define:

**Preference:** determines what rule must be used if several rules are applicable.

**Conditions:** determines when the rule should be utilized depending on nb. Several conditions could specify:

- Range of nb: $nb = [x_1, x_2]$,
- Range of the number of measures used in the SOLAP query: $n_{Measure} = [x_{1M}, x_{2M}]$,
- Range of the number of members of each dimension (except the spatial dimension) to which the rule will be applied: $n_{di} = [x_{1di}, x_{2di}]$

**Actions:** determines how information will be visualized on the map (cloropeth, bar chart, dynamic map, etc.) if all conditions are achieved.

**Example:** In the context of the FAO example, to avoid unreadable (see Fig. 1b) or unsuitable (see the left side of Fig. 1c) geovisualization methods, we can define the rules of Table 1. R1 imposes the use of a cloropeth map when only one piece of information is to be displayed in a spatial member, which corresponds to Fig. 1a (nb = 1). If there are two pieces of information, each for a different measure, then R2 imposes the display of the 'Production' measure by cloropeth and the 'Surface' measure by circles, which corresponds to the right side of Fig. 1c. If nb is between two and six, the information can be displayed by bars (R3). R2 is preferred to R3 to prevent the geovisualization method of the left side of Fig. 1c. If one measure is to be displayed for one crop over several years, a dynamic map is used (R4); if several measures and/or several crops are used, then multi-dynamic maps should be used (R5). Using '*' in the condition means that there is no limit. Let us note that these rules have been defined by SDW experts in collaboration with decision-makers.

**Table 1.** Display rules for the FAO example

| R1 | R2 | R3 | R4 | R5 |
|---|---|---|---|---|
| **Preference** = 1 | **Preference** = 2 | **Preference** = 3 | **Preference** = 2 | **Preference** = 4 |
| **Conditions** | **Conditions** | **Conditions** | **Conditions** | **Conditions** |
| nb = [1] | nb = [2] | nb = [2, 6] | nb = [2, *] | nb = [2, *] |
| **Actions:** | $n_{Measure}$ = [2] | **Actions:** | $n_{Measure}$ = [1] | $n_{Time}$ = [2, *] |
| Cloropeth map | **Actions:** | Bars | $n_{Time}$ = [2, *] | **Actions:** |
| | Production: clor- | | $n_{Crops}$ = [1] | Multi-dynamic |
| | opeth | | **Actions:** | maps |
| | Surface: circles | | Dynamic map | |

Once the rules have been defined, taking into account the number of visual variables to displays, the system has to guarantee that one visual display exists for each possible pivot table display. In other words, we have to define a way to verify that the defined rules allow for displaying all possible pivot tables. Therefore, for example, considering that an $nb_{max}$ of 15 is chosen, display rules should cover all possible analyses that correspond to this number. By using a multidimensional matrix (Fig. 2a), we can present the number of pieces of information to display (nb) for each analysis according to the number of measures and members of each non-spatial dimension. In our example, $nb = n_{Measure} \times n_{Time} \times n_{Crops}$. In Fig. 2a, red cells correspond to the number of pieces of information greater than $nb_{max}$, and therefore the display rules do not concern these cases of analysis; contrariwise, they should cover all green cells that have a number smaller than $nb_{max}$. To verify this, we use the algorithm below.

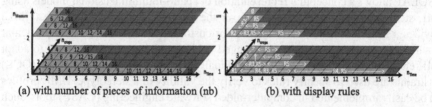

(a) with number of pieces of information (nb)          (b) with display rules

**Fig. 2.** Multidimensional matrix. (Color figure online)

This algorithm takes as input the display rules (Table 1) and the multidimensional matrix (Fig. 2a). It gives as results (i) a Boolean value indicating if the rules cover all required cases or not and (ii) the multidimensional matrix with the display rules (Fig. 2b). To accomplish this, the algorithm checks if each green cell (line 2) attains all conditions (lines 5–7) for each rule (line 4). If so, the rule is added to the result table (T) (lines 8–9). If the algorithm cannot find a rule to apply for a cell, the resulting Boolean value becomes 'false' (line 10), indicating that the rules do not cover all required cases.

The result of the application of this algorithm to our example (i.e., the display rules of Table 1 and the multidimensional matrix of Fig. 2a) is shown in Fig. 2b. This result shows that there is a case of analysis (grey cell) with $n_{Measure} = 2$, $n_{Time} = 1$ and $n_{Crops} = 4$ that is not covered by the rules. This requires either the addition of a new rule to cover this case or a modification of the conditions of an existing rule to cover it.

```
Algorithm verification
Input: Display Rules, the multidimensional matrix T
Output:T with rules, result
1: result = true
2: for each green cell C_i in T:
3:    found_rule = false
4:    for each Rule R_j in Display Rules:
5:       If (C_i.nb < nb_max and C_i.nb  R_j.nb) then applicable_rule = true;
6:       for each dimension D_k of T:
7:             If (C_i.n_Dk  R_j.n_Dk) then applicable_rule = false;
8:             found_rule = (found_rule OR applicable_rule)
9:             If applicable_rule then C_i.add(R_j);
10: result = (result and found_rule);
```

## 5  Prototyping Methodology

### 5.1  Background

ProtOLAP has already been successfully applied in some real DW projects. ProtOLAP allows for rapid DW prototyping [6]. With ProtOLAP, decision-makers' analysis requirements are translated by DW experts into a UML model presented in [7]. Then, this model is automatically translated into a relational model and its corresponding OLAP server model. Then, ProtOLAP allows decision-makers to feed the DW some sample data. Finally, decision-makers interact with a real OLAP client to validate the multidimensional model.

Encouraged by time and important economic gains associated with the usage of conceptual models (UML, ER, etc.), ProtOLAP is based on the ICSOLAP UML profile. ICSOLAP allows a conceptual representation of spatio-multidimensional models using UML stereotypes [7]. Indeed, a profile in the Unified Modeling Language (UML) provides a generic extension mechanism for customizing UML models for particular domains and platforms. Stereotypes, tagged values, and constraints are used to adapt UML elements to a specific application. Finally, Object Constraint Language (OCL) constraints are used to specify rules to verify the validity of a stereotype. UML profiles can be easily implemented in computer-aided software engineering (CASE) tools, such as MagicDraw or Eclipse. ICSOLAP contains stereotypes for each spatio-multidimensional element. A ≪Fact≫ is composed of ≪Measure≫. An ≪AggLevel≫ is composed of dimensional attributes and can be thematic, spatial or temporal. Moreover, the stereotype ≪BasicIndicator≫ defines aggregation rules for a given measure (i.e., "aggregatedAttribute"). It indicates the functions used in the aggregation process along dimensional hierarchies. ICSOLAP has been implemented in the commercial CASE tool MagicDraw, and a tool for its automatic implementation in Postgres/Oracle and Mondrian has also been developed. An example of ICSOLAP for our case study is shown in Fig. 3.

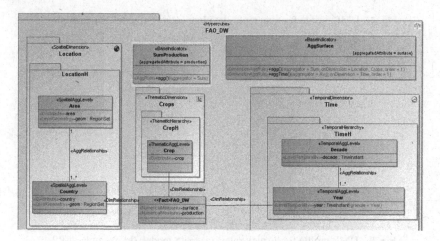

**Fig. 3.** FAO Spatial Data Warehouse

## 5.2  SOLAP Prototyping Methodology

To take SOLAP geovisualization issues into account in a prototyping methodology, we propose the following methodology *extending ProtOLAP with steps 3, 4, 6 and 9.*

1. *Informal definition of indicators*: Decision-makers define the analysis needs in terms of dimensions and measures.
2. *Conceptual design*: DW experts translate decision-makers' spatio-multidimensional needs from step 1 using ICSOLAP [7] (e.g., Fig. 3).
3. *Informal definition of geovisualization methods*: Decision-makers define how to visualize their data using cartographic displays.
4. *Extending the conceptual design*: DW experts translate decision-makers' geovisualization needs from step 3 into a UML model extending [7] (e.g., Figs. 4 and 5).
5. *SDW implementation*: The system automatically creates the DBMS and the OLAP server schemata.
6. *SOLAP visualization implementation*: The system automatically creates the geovisualization schemata.
7. *Domain feeding data*: Decision-makers feed the SDW with sample data.

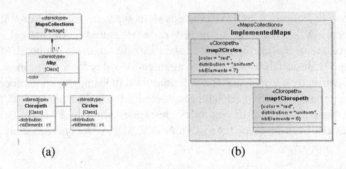

**Fig. 4.** UML profile for map representation: (a) meta-model, (b) example

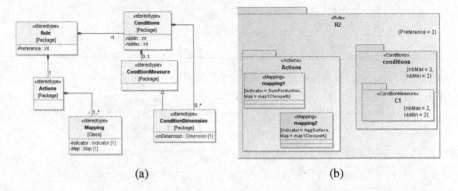

**Fig. 5.** UML profile for display rules: (a) meta-model, (b) example of R2

8. *OLAP-based indicator validation*: Decision-makers validate the dimensions and measures of the SDW. If the spatio-multidimensional model has not been validated, go to step 1.
9. *SOLAP-based geovisualization validation*: Decision-makers validate the geovisualization methods for SOLAP query results. If the geovisualization methods have not been validated, go to step 3.
10. *ETL implementation:* During this last step, the ETL is implemented to load the SDW defined in step 5.

As described in step 4, our methodology uses an extension of ICSOLAP to conceptually represent geovisualization methods and rules. This extension is described in the remainder of the section.

A map (≪Map≫) is defined as an abstract class, and its implementations represent the geovisualization methods implemented in the SOLAP system, as shown in Fig. 4a. Here, the two stereotypes ≪Cloropeth≫ and ≪Circles≫ have been defined to represent cloropeth and thematic maps with circles in a generic manner. A cloropeth map is described by a color range ("color"), a number of color classes ("nbElements") and a distribution function. An example is shown in Fig. 4b, where a cloropeth map (i.e., *map1Cloropeth*) that uses 5 classes of the color red with a uniform distribution (e.g., Fig. 1a) is implemented.

To define display rules as defined in Sect. 4, we define some new stereotypes as shown in Fig. 5a. A rule (defined as a ≪Rule≫ package) is composed of a set of conditions (≪Conditions≫) and actions (≪Actions≫). A condition is defined as a package and presents the minimum and maximum number of elements ("nbMin" and "nbMax"); a condition can be defined on measures (≪ConditionMeasures≫) and on dimensions (≪ConditionDimension≫ presents a tagged value with the ICSOLAP ≪Dimension≫ type). An example for rule R2 of Table 1 is shown in Fig. 5b. An action is defined as a package containing a set of ≪mapping≫ classes (Fig. 5b). A mapping is a class that contains two tagged values representing an ≪Indicator≫ ICSOLAP and a ≪Map≫, and it is used to define what geovisualization method is used for each indicator. For example Fig. 5b indicates that, when the conditions are verified, the two indicators *SumProduction* and *AggSurface* of Fig. 3 are visualized with cloropeth maps. Our profile has been implemented in MagicDraw.

# 6   Implementation

In this section, we present the implementation of our proposal.

Based on our previous work [5], the architecture of our prototype consists of three tiers: the SDW tier, SOLAP Server and SOLAP Client. The SDW tier is implemented using PostGIS, which is a spatial DBMS. This tier is responsible for storing alphanumeric and spatial multidimensional data. The OLAP server used is Mondrian. The SOLAP client tier is composed of the Pivot4 J OLAP client and OpenLayers GIS client. OpenLayers has been integrated in the ProtOLAP architecture [6]. For the implementation of the geovisualization methods represented by the ≪Map≫ stereotype, we have defined a set of SLD (Styled Layer Descriptor) and GML (Geography Markup Language) templates (more details in [5]). GML and SLD are XML-based representations of spatial data with visualization. SLD and GML templates provide an implementation of the geovisualization methods that is not dependent on the SOLAP client used. Therefore, according to our prototyping methodology, the SLD and GML templates can be automatically generated from UML diagrams.

Because [5] does not support display rules, we extend it by adding an XML representation of displays rules as described in Sect. 4. These rules have been integrated in the SOLAP client and are automatically triggered during each SOLAP query. These XML files correspond to the ≪Rule≫ packages previously described.

A video example of a SOLAP application with display rules is shown at https://www.youtube.com/watch?v=ZHUTqVRtKu8. Decision-makers visualize their pivot table and their associated bar thematic maps. Then, changing the pivot table by 2 measures and one year, the cartographic visualization is automatically adapted using rule R2 as previously described.

# 7  Conclusion

Motivated by the importance of geovisualization tools in SOLAP analysis, we present a methodology for prototyping SOLAP applications. Our current work involves the automatic implementation of the UML profile and the evaluation of the methodology using the Goal Question Metric framework. Moreover, because decision-makers are not always GIS experts, we will define a methodology to automatically derive maps and display rules from the SDW schema.

**Acknowledgement.**  This work is supported by the CAPTIVEN project of the ANR 11-CNRT-0003 program "investissements d'Avenir - valorisation PME".

# References

1. Andrienko, G., Andrienko, N.: Interactive maps for visual data exploration. Int. J. Geogr. Inf. Sci. **13**(4), 355–374 (1999)
2. Bédard, Y., Han, J.: Fundamentals of spatial data warehousing for geographic knowledge discovery. In: Geographic Data Mining and Knowledge Discovery (2001)
3. Bédard, Y., Proulx, M., Rivest, S., Badard, T.: Merging hypermedia gis with spatial on-line analytical processing: towards hypermedia SOLAP. In: Stefanakis, E. (ed.) Geographic Hypermedia, pp. 167–187. Springer, Heidelberg (2006)
4. Bertin, J.: The Semiology of Graphics. University of Wisconsin Press, New York (1983)
5. Bimonte, S.: A generic geovisualization model for spatial OLAP and its implementation in a standards-based architecture. ISI **19**(5), 97–118 (2014)
6. Bimonte, S., Edoh-Alove, E., Nazih, H., Kang, M., Rizzi, S.: ProtOLAP: rapid OLAP prototyping with on-demand data supply. DOLAP **2013**, 61–66 (2013)
7. Boulil, K., Bimonte, S., Pinet, F.: Conceptual model for spatial data cubes: A UML profile and its automatic implementation. Comput. Stand. Interfaces **38**, 113–132 (2015)
8. Corr, L., Stagnitto, J.: Agile Data Warehouse Design: Collaborative Dimensional Modeling, from Whiteboard to Star Schema. DecisionOne Press, Leeds (2011). ISBN: 9780956817204
9. Ezzedine, S., Turki, Y., Faïz, S.: An approach based on the clustering of spatial requirements' models and MDA to design spatial data warehouses. IJDMMM **7**(4), 276–292 (2015)
10. Golfarelli, M., Mantovani, M., Ravaldi, F., Rizzi, S.: Lily: a geo-enhanced library for location intelligence. In: Bellatreche, L., Mohania, M.K. (eds.) DaWaK 2013. LNCS, vol. 8057, pp. 72–83. Springer, Heidelberg (2013). doi:10.1007/978-3-642-40131-2_7
11. Harrower, M., Fabrikant, S.: The role of map animation in geographic visualization. Geographic Visualization: Concepts, Tools and Applications, 49–65 (2008)
12. Johany, F., Bimonte, S.: A framework for spatio-multidimensional analysis improved by chorems: application to agricultural data. In: Helfert, M., et al. (eds.) DATA 2015. CCIS, vol. 584, pp. 59–80. Springer, Heidelberg (2016). doi:10.1007/978-3-319-30162-4_5
13. Leonardi, L., Orlando, S., Raffaetà, A., Roncato, A., Silvestri, C., Andrienko, G., Andrienko, N.: A general framework for trajectory data warehousing and visual OLAP. GeoInformatica **18**(2), 273–312 (2014)
14. MacEachren, A., Gahegan, M., Pike, W.: Geovisualization for knowledge construction and decision support. IEEE Comput. Graph. Appl. **24**(1), 13–17 (2004)
15. Malinowski, E.: GeoBI Architecture Based on Free Software. Geographical Information Systems Trends and Technologies. Elaheh Pourabbas CRC Press, New York (2014)

16. Malinowski, E., Zimányi, E.: Advanced Data Warehouse Design From Conventional to Spatial and Temporal Applications. Springer, Heidelberg (2008)
17. Palpanas, T., Chowdhary, P., Mihaila, G., Pinel, F.: Integrated model-driven dashboard development. Inf. Syst. Front. **9**(2–3), 195–208 (2007)
18. Silva, R., Moura-Pires, J., Santos, M.: Spatial clustering in SOLAP systems to enhance map visualization. IJDWM **8**(2), 23–43 (2012)
19. Southall, H.: Visualization, data sharing and metadata, in geographic visualization: concepts, tools and applications. In: Dodge, M., McDerby, M., Turner, M. (eds.) (2008)

# Conceptual Modeling in Requirements and Business Analysis

## Preface to MReBA 2016

Requirements Engineering (RE) aims to capture intended system functionality and qualities. In practice, requirements activities often fall under the heading of Business Analysis (BA), determining how a business can make use of technology in order to improve its operations, meet targets, and thrive in a competitive economy. Use of models in RE and BA allows for a shared perception of requirements and an explicit consideration of business strategy. Models can ease the transformation towards design, specification, and code, operationalizing strategies through socio-technical systems.

The third MReBA (Modelling in Requirements and Business Analysis) workshop aims to provide a forum for discussing the interplay between requirements engineering, business analysis and conceptual modeling. Of course, more than ever, we investigate how goal approaches help in conceptualising purposeful systems. But also, we are interested in all conceptual modelling issues in RE and BA contexts. What are the unresolved open questions? What lessons are there to be learnt from industrial experiences? What empirical data are there to support the cost-benefit analysis when modelling requirements? Are there applications domains or types of project settings for which conceptual modelling is particularly suitable or not suitable? What degree of formalization, automation or interactivity is feasible and appropriate for what types of participants during requirements engineering and business analysis?

MReBA builds on the success of the first and the second workshop with the International Conference on Conceptual Modeling - 2014 in Atlanta and 2015 in Stockholm, as well as an evolution of the previous RIGiM (Requirements Intentions and Goals in Conceptual Modeling) Workshop (2007-9, 12–13). While RIGiM was specifically dedicated to goal modelling and the use of intentional concepts in RE, MReBa handles any kind of modelling notation or activity in the context of RE or BA.

This year, MReBA includes a keynote by Prof. Oscar Pastor on A Capability-Driven Development Approach for Requirements and Business Process Modeling. In addition, three high-quality full papers are presented.

Each of the eight submitted papers went through a thorough review process with at least three reviews from our program committee. We thank authors and reviewers for their valuable contributions.

November 2016

Takako Nakatani
Jelena Zdravkovic
Jennifer Horkoff

## Organization

### Workshop Organizers

Takako Nakatani     The Open University of Japan, Japan
Jelena Zdravkovic   Stockholm University, Sweden
Jennifer Horkoff    City University London, UK

### Steering Committee

Colette Rolland     Université Paris 1 Panthéon - Sorbonne, France
Eric Yu             University of Toronto, Canada
Renata Guizzardi    Universidade Federal do Espírito Santo (UFES), Brazil

### Table of Contents

### Full Papers

# Bridging User Story Sets
# with the Use Case Model

Yves Wautelet[1(✉)], Samedi Heng[2], Diana Hintea[3],
Manuel Kolp[2], and Stephan Poelmans[1]

[1] KU Leuven, Leuven, Belgium
{yves.wautelet,stephan.poelmans}@kuleuven.be
[2] Université catholique de Louvain, Louvain-la-neuve, Belgium
{samedi.heng,manuel.kolp}@uclouvain.be
[3] Coventry University, Coventry, UK
diana.hintea@coventry.ac.uk

**Abstract.** User Stories (US) are mostly used as basis for representing requirements in agile development. Written in a direct manner, US fail in producing a visual representation of the main system-to-be functions. A Use-Case Diagram (UCD), on the other hand, intends to provide such a view. Approaches that map US sets to a UCD have been proposed; they however consider every US as a Use Case (UC). Nevertheless, a valid UC should not be an atomic task or a sub-process but enclose an entire scenario of the system use instead. A unified model of US templates to tag US sets was previously build. Within functional elements, it notably distinguishes granularity levels. In this paper, we propose to transform specific elements of a US set into a UCD using the granularity information obtained through tagging. In practice, such a transformation involves continuous round-tripping between the US and UC views; a CASE-tool supports this.

**Keywords:** User Story · UML · Agile development · XP · SCRUM

## 1 Introduction

Following [3], *User stories are short, simple descriptions of a feature told from the perspective of the person who desires the new capability, usually a user or customer of the system.* [19] acknowledged that no unification is provided in *User Story* (*US*) templates. Indeed, the general pattern relates a WHO, a WHAT and possibly a WHY dimension (examples are provided in Sect. 4), but in practice different keywords are used to describe these dimensions (e.g. Mike Cohn's *As a < type of user >, I want < some goal > so that < some reason >* [3]). Moreover, in the literature, no semantics are ever associated to these keywords. This is why, [19] conducted research to find the majority of templates used in practice, sort them and associate semantics to each keyword. These semantics were derived from several sources and frameworks (by order of importance [5,11,17,23]); some of these are derived from Goal-Oriented Requirements Engineering (GORE, see [8]).

© Springer International Publishing AG 2016
S. Link and J.C. Trujillo (Eds.): ER 2016 Workshops, LNCS 9975, pp. 127–138, 2016.
DOI: 10.1007/978-3-319-47717-6_11

After performing a redundancy analysis, a first selection of keywords with associated semantics was performed. Then, applying them on large test sets led to a sub-selection of keywords forming a unified model. In the end, most of the semantics adopted for the remaining keywords were selected from the i* framework (i-star [4,22,24]); this is due to the research design that favored adopting elements of i* to higher the internal consistency of the unified US templates model (see [19]). Note that it is not the i* framework that is fully rebuilt for tagging US since concepts like the resource, the agent, etc. are not included in the unified model. The capability, a concept non-existent in i*, has been included in the unified model (see [19] and Sect. 3).

One may question the utility of such a model; why should US be "tagged" to a certain template and not simply be expressed using the WHO/WHAT and WHY pattern. The main advantage is that, if the tagging respects the semantics associated to the concepts, it provides information about both the nature and the granularity of the US element. Such information could possibly be used at a further stage for software analysis: structuring the problem and its solution, identifying missing requirements, etc. [9]. Visual GORE models were envisaged for graphical representation in [20]; the paper showed that GORE models are very well adapted for the purpose of US sets representation. Nevertheless, since GORE models are not an industry adopted practice, we explore in this paper an independent representation with the far more used *Unified Modeling Language* (*UML* [12]), *Use Case Model*. An instance of the latter produces a *Use Case Diagram* (*UCD*). A *Use Case* (*UC*) is a list of actions or event steps, typically defining the interactions between a role and a system in order to achieve a goal.

Facing the definition of US and UC, we can notice that there is a possible mismatch between the two concepts - the US can indeed include (very) fine-grained elements and the UC should be a coarse-grained element describing the software problem encompassing a set of fine-grained actions. When sorting is applied within US elements, a transformation process can generate a UCD. This is why, in this paper, **we envisage the representation of problem domain coarse-grained US elements as UC**. To this end, we map the elements defined in the UCM – i.e. the *Actor*, the *UC* and the relationships between use cases – with the elements defined in the unified US template model of [19].

In practice it is sometimes discouraged to use US and UCD concurrently because if not kept mutually up to date they can be inconsistent (see e.g. [6]). We therefore propose keeping US sets and the UCD consistent by auto-updating each change performed to one in the other through the use of a CASE-tool. They are considered here as two complementary views. We identify three primary benefits of our transformation approach: (1) a graphical high-level (coarse-grained) representation of requirements through the UCD; (2) multi-dimensional structuring of requirements and US dependencies at UCD level (not possible with US Maps); (3) identification of missing requirements (not expressed in the current US set) and the elimination of redundant US.

## 2   Related Work and Positioning

The CASE-Tool *Visual Paradigm* [13] (VP) already proposes to transform US into a UCD. In their approach, the actor expressed in the WHO dimension becomes an actor of the UCD and the element in the WHAT dimension becomes a UC without any selection based on granularity. The rule is simple - a US with a WHAT element becomes a UC in the UC diagram. Nevertheless, UML points to the use of UC as elements representing an entire process rather than fine-grained (or atomic) elements as US can be. This does not mean that a US cannot include elements adequately describing UC, but that a sorting process is required in order to only include relevant elements as UC. The approach of VP can thus be said to be "naive" because including elements not relevant as UC.

Structuring US is often performed using the *User Story Mapping (USM)* technique (see [14]); the latter uses *Story Maps* which are difficult to maintain and read. Building a UCD from a set of US could be compared to USM. In our approach, we split a US in 2 or 3 dimensions and we use the graphical representation of the UCD for relevant elements. Our aim is to obtain:

- an easy to read graphical representation of requirements. Story Maps remain limited to post-its on a board or even on the ground;
- an advanced structuring of requirements where we can overview the dependencies of coarse-grained elements to one another with the use of $<<include>>$ and $<<extend>>$ relationships. Fine-grained elements are not part of the UCD but can be represented under the scope of particular UC for example in workflows (UML activity diagrams or BPMN Diagrams, etc.). The latter is outside the present scope;
- an identification of gaps in requirements and elimination of redundant US elements from the graphical representation. By limiting the graphical UCD representation to solely coarse-grained elements we can obtain a high-level representation of the system-to-be. This allows to overview if, at an operational level, all aspects required to solve the software problem have been taken into account; if not they can be added to the US set. Similarly, elements appearing to be redundant because appearing in several US of the US set can lead to remove US from the set.

AgileModeling [2] emphasizes the usage of models for better understanding of the system-to-be and argues that it is useful to produce at least some models including a UML UCD and class diagram for the very first iteration called *iteration zero*. No transformation process is nevertheless provided.

## 3   Unified-Model of User Stories' Descriptive Concepts

As evoked, [19] propose to build a unified model for designing US templates. The overall approach is further structured in [20]; this structure is also valid for the present research. Figure 1 represents the meta-model of US templates in the form of a class diagram. The instance of one of these classes is a US element in itself from a concrete US. A US template can be designed taking an element from the WHO, WHAT and possibly WHY dimensions. The link between the classes conceptually represents the link from one dimension to the other. Specifically, the unidirectional association from the *Role* to one of the *Capability*, *Task* or *Goal* classes implies that the target class instantiates an element of the WHAT dimension (always tagged as *wants/wants to/needs/can/would like* in the model). Then, the unidirectional association from one of these classes instantiating the WHAT dimension to one of the classes instantiating the WHY dimension (always tagged as *so that* into the model) implies that the target class can instantiate an element of the WHY dimension. The following is a US template supported by our model: *As a <Role>, I would like <Task> so that <Hard-goal>*.

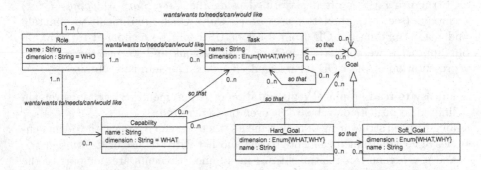

**Fig. 1.** Unified model for user story descriptive concepts

Each concept is associated with a particular syntax (identical to the name of the class in Fig. 1) and a semantic. Due to a lack of space we do not depict the semantic associated to each of the concepts here; it can be found in [19,20].

For granularity evaluation for functional elements, a few more explanations are required to distinguish the *Hard-goal*, *Task* and *Capability* elements.

The *Hard-goal* is the most abstract element; there is no defined way to attain it and several ways could be followed in practice. It is indeed part of the problem domain. The *Task* represents an operational way to attain a *Hard-goal*. It is thus part of the solution domain. An example of a *Hard-goal* could be to *Be transported from Brussels to Paris*; it can be the *Hard-goal* of a traveler but there are several ways to attain this *Hard-goal* (by train, by car, etc.).

The *Task* and the *Capability* represent more concrete and operational elements but these two need to be distinguished. The *Capability* does in fact represent a *Task* but the *Capability* has more properties than the former since it is expressed as a direct intention from a role. In order to avoid ambiguities in interpretation, we point to the use of the *Capability* element only for *an atomic Task* (i.e., a task that is not refined into other elements but is located at the lowest level of hierarchy). A *Task* could then be *Move from Brussels to Paris by car* and a *Capability* would be *Sit in the car*.

## 4    Running Example

Our proposal will be illustrated using a running example about carpooling. Carpooling deals with sharing car journeys so that more than one person travels within a car. In this context, it becomes increasingly important to save gas, reduce traffic, save driving time and control pollution. *ClubCar* [15] is a multichannel application available as an Android application, SMS service and IVR system. Users of ClubCar are riders and/or drivers that can register by SMS, voice or through an Android app. Roughly speaking, the software allows drivers to propose rides and submit their details with *dates, times, sources* and *destinations* while riders can search for available rides.

As shown in Table 1, we have taken a sample of the US of the ClubCar application to illustrate the research developed in this paper. Some of these US contain elements to be transformed in UC and elements that are not relevant as UC (see Sect. 5). The first column depicts the *Dimension* of US *Descriptive_Concept* (*D_C*), the second column describes the element itself and the last column provides the type of the *D_C*[1].

**Table 1.** US sample of the ClubCar application development

| Dimension | Element | D_C Type |
|-----------|---------|----------|
| WHO | *As a DRIVER* | Role |
| WHAT | *I want to register to the service* | Task |
| WHY | *So that I can propose a ride to go from A to B* | Hard-goal |
| WHO | *As a DRIVER* | Role |
| WHAT | *I want to propose a ride from A to B with the price location and time of departure, and number of seats available* | Task |
| WHO | *As a DRIVER* | Role |
| WHAT | *I want to log in to the platform* | Capability |
| WHY | *So that I can register to the service* | Task |
| WHO | *As a RIDER* | Role |
| WHAT | *I want to be transported from A to B* | Hard-goal |
| WHO | *As a DRIVER* | Role |
| WHAT | *I want to confirm the proposal* | Capability |
| WHO | *As a DRIVER* | Role |
| WHAT | *I want the RIDER to be satisfied of my service* | Soft-goal |

---

[1] Note that, when there were several possibilities, a choice ensuring the consistency of the entire set has been made.

# 5    User Stories Integration Through a Use-Case Diagram

## 5.1    The Role

A Role within a US can be forwarded to an Actor in the UCD. The UCD Actor is indeed the only structure defined to represent the WHO dimension (see Fig. 2).

## 5.2    Hard-Goal, Task and Capability

Three functional elements – the *Hard-goal*, the *Task* and the *Capability* – can be found in the unified model. The *Capability* is located on a fine level of granularity and thus non relevant for inclusion in the UCD. The Hard-goal and the Task elements are aimed to contain coarse-grained elements thus relevant for inclusion as UC.

Hard-goal and Task elements can be distinguished by their nature (i.e. their formulation) rather than by their grain level. Both are indeed intended to represent coarse-grained elements. The Hard-goal is the most abstract element and the Task is its counterpart expressed in an operational manner. This means that the Task represents a way of fulfilling the Hard-goal (entirely or parts of it); the Task is thus the counterpart of the Hard-goal in the solution domain while the Hard-goal belongs to the problem domain.

In line with UML, the use case does not necessarily explicit HOW the problem should be solved (this can be documented within on a workflow containing fine-grained elements) but rather WHAT should be achieved. **US elements tagged as Hard-goals should thus necessarily be represented as use cases** since they depict WHAT problem should be solved. The tricky question is then to determine if Task elements must also be represented as UC. Since Tasks are part of the solution domain, if they are represented as UC they should be linked to the Hard-goals they furnish part of a solution to; this means that we can make their relationship explicit. This is something useful when different US elements represented as Hard-goals make use of the same US elements represented as Tasks. It indeed allows to show that some behavior can be reused in several situations. This is what $<<include>>$ and $<<extend>>$ dependency relationships are intended to model in a UCD. We can then link the UC corresponding to a Hard-goal element with the one corresponding to a Task element using an $<<include>>$ and $<<extend>>$ dependency in function of the particular situation. If no behavior is recycled, we do not point to the representation of the US element tagged as Task in the UCD because this would lead to several UC that do not need to be externalized (leading to lots of $<<include>>$ and $<<extend>>$ dependencies) and are only sub-processes of the UC. Moreover, we want to make clear that we do not point to use these dependencies to depict means-end relationships between Hard-goals and Tasks. We point to keep the UCD as simple as possible and leave the description of solutions to the Hard-goal in other views (e.g. workflows). In a phrase, only decompositions of Hard-goals in Tasks where the Tasks are used in multiple Hard-goals are represented as UC in the UCD.

There is thus no universal answer to the representation of US elements tagged as Tasks in the UCD; as evoked it may be interesting to highlight the reuse of more special behavior but some Tasks are just subprocesses of the Hard-goal elements and should then not be represented as UC. These need to be documented for example in workflows depicting the realization scenario(s) of the Hard-goal (thus UC).

Let's finally note that UC transformed from Hard-goal elements can also be linked with other UC transformed from Hard-goal elements through an << include >> relationship. In our context this shows that some Hard-goals are possibly needed for the realization of other Hard-goals. We do not consider <<extend>> relationships among Hard-goals because such elements do have a possible stand-alone realization.

Concretely, in Fig. 2, the Task is linked with the UC representing the Hard-goal with an << include >> dependency relationship from the Hard-goal to the Task. This is illustrated in the left side of Fig. 2 in a canonical form and instantiated on the Carpooling example in the right side of the same figure.

Representing both elements in the UCD is thus in some cases a way of explicitly linking the problem and solution domains where system behavior can be recycled in multiple use cases (thus Hard-goals).

## 5.3   The Soft-Goal

*A Soft-goal is a condition or state of affairs in the world that the actor would like to achieve* [22]. For a Soft-goal *there are no clear-cut criteria for whether the condition is achieved*; it cannot be represented as such into an element of a standard UCD. In a standard UML UCD there is no element for the representation of softgoals but a refinement of the UCD is included in the *Rational Unified Process* (*RUP*, see [7]) and known as the RUP/UML Business Use Case Model (see [16]). A representation in the UCD would allow us to trace which functional requirement (in the form of a Hard-goal or a Task) *supports* the realization of a Soft-goal. [21] suggests to map the Soft-goal with the RUP/UML Goal because a semantic analysis of both definitions concludes that those represent the same type (or at least closely related) elements. This solution is relevant for us since it allows a graphical representation of Soft-goals in the UCD as well as a potential support analysis (by highlighting which UC contributes to the satisfaction of the represented Soft-goal). Consequently and even though it is not standard UML, we map the Soft-goal elements from the US set to the graphical representation of the business Goal element. As shown in Fig. 2, we can have:

- The Soft-goal in the WHAT dimension. Then, in the UCD, we immediately relate the Actor (Role in the US WHO dimension) to a Business Goal (Soft-goal in the US WHAT dimension) and a simple link is used;
- The Soft-goal in the WHY dimension. Then, in the UCD, if the element in the WHAT dimension leads to a UC (Hard-goal or a Task in the US), it can be linked to the Business Goal (Soft-goal in the US WHAT dimension) using a << support >> dependency relationship. This link visually expresses that

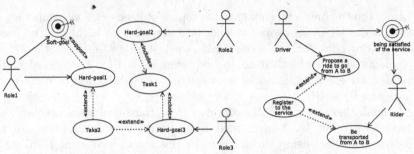

(a) Use-Case Model Forwarded on the Basis of Stereotyped User Stories

(b) Partial Use-Case Diagram for the
Carpooling Example

**Fig. 2.** Use case diagram: Canonical Form and Carpooling Example

the functional element contributes to the realization of the Soft-goal within
the software implementation.

# 6   Automating the Approach and Round-Tripping Between Views

In order to support the approach, we have built an add-on to the cloud version
of the Descartes Architect CASE-Tool [1] that, for the present purpose, allows
multiple views:

- the *User Story View (USV)* to edit US through virtual US cards. Each US
  element in a dimension must be tagged with a concept of the unified model;
- the *Use-Case View (UCV)* to edit a UCD. The UCD is automatically transformed from the US set defined in the USV. When changes are made to UC or
  Actors in the UCV, the corresponding elements are automatically updated in
  the USV and vice-versa. These indeed are the same logical element represented
  in multiple views;
- the *Class, Sequence and Activity Diagram Views* (outside the scope of this
  paper).

The CASE-Tool immediately build elements in the UCV, when elements are
built in the USV following the rules given in this paper and summarized in
Table 2.

The editing process is continuous over the requirements analysis stage and
over the entire project life cycle. In practice, US elements are re-tagged several
times when they analyzed and structured. Consistency among views is ensured
by separating the conceptual element in the CASE-tool memory from its representation in a view (Fig. 3).

**Table 2.** Mapping a US set with the UCD

| US Set Element | UCD Element |
|---|---|
| Role | Actor |
| Hard-goal | Use Case; several Use Cases transformed from Hard-goals can be linked through $<<include>>$ dependencies |
| Task | (Possible) Use Case; the Use Case transformed form a Task should be linked through $<<include>>$ or $<<extend>>$ dependencies with Use Cases transformed from Hard-goals |
| Capability | No possible transformation |
| Soft-goal | RUP/UML Business Goal |

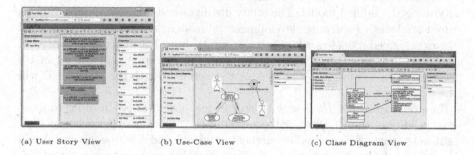

(a) User Story View          (b) Use-Case View          (c) Class Diagram View

**Fig. 3.** The supporting CASE-Tool.

# 7 Impact on Produced Software: Future Work

Two types of impacts will be evaluated in future work:

– *What is the impact on the software design of using our approach versus using another one?* Since we aim to transform coarse-grained US elements in UC, the produced UC are likely to become the scope elements for which realization scenarios will be build. Also, sets of US are expressed in a fined-grained way only or parts of the requirements are not expressed. In order to fill the gap, one or more UC can then be added; US are then automatically generated accordingly. Fine-grained elements can also be omitted from the US set and be identified through the approach. Finally, identifying and representing soft-goals in the UCD may lead to better take them into account in the design. These aspects need further investigation;

– *What will be the variability in the UCD produced from the same US set by different modelers?* Various modelers applying the transformation will not produce exactly the same model. They are indeed likely to interpret elements differently and consequently tag them differently. Analysis activities occurring after the initial transformation often lead to reconsider some of the associated tags (granularity of US elements is thus not set once and for all but refined through the requirements elicitation). This variability needs to be studied and evaluated.

## 8    Validity and Threats to the Validity: Future Work

As already evoked, the prerequisite to the use of our approach is to tag the US when setting them up. In terms of time, the investment for disposing of first input models is limited to the tagging and encoding in the CASE-tool. A few threats to the validity will also be highlighted; these should be clarified in later validation of the work:

- *The accuracy in US tags.* [18] studies the perception of US elements' granularity using the unified model. The study distinguished different groups of users from students to software development professionals. The models produced by experienced modelers where more accurate, but identifying granularity did not lead to major issues in any group with the condition that the set of US was taken as a consistent whole. A new experiment with the UML UCD will be performed;
- *The accuracy of the UCD with respect to the system-to-be.* In order to asses the validity of the UCD, we will proceed to the following experience. At first, subjects (part of 3 groups: researchers, students and business analysts) will be informed about a case and asked to carefully read and tag a set of US. Secondly, these same subjects will be asked to rank their perceived relevancy of 3 UCD: (UCD1) generated from their own US set tagging (from the first part); (UCD2) generated from an internally validated solution; and (UCD3) randomly generated out of the US set. The perceived relevancy of the UCD will then be evaluated by the subjects.

Future work also includes the application of the full validation of the technique on real-life projects. We will notably proceed to a statistical analysis of the stakeholders perception of the relevancy of the UC model for a project they have worked on in the past. Moreover, they will be interviewed about the value of a consistent UCD complimentary to the US sets. Finally, the application of the technique on large sets of US will allow us to precisely determine the contribution of the method in terms of scalability. Other metrics for the evaluation of UCD will also be envisaged in line with quality elements for US defined by [10].

## 9    Conclusion

Agile methods use very simple requirements descriptions in the form of US. These are easy to read but difficult to structure leading to the need of visual requirements representations to sort them, understand the system-to-be, dialogue with stakeholders, etc. We have consequently suggested to structure coarse-grained elements found in US sets in a UML UCD. The UCD view is aimed to remain consistent with the set of US, encompassing changing requirements to furnish the possibility of UC driven development in methods where US sets are the firstly expressed requirement artifact. This work is complementary to previous work focusing on the representation of US sets with GORE models; further work includes the evaluation of the benefits of the integrated use of the UCD and GORE views.

# References

1. The descartes architect case-tool (2016). http://www.isys.ucl.ac.be/descartes/
2. Ambler, S.: Agile Modeling: Effective Practices for eXtreme Programming and the Unified Process. Wiley, New York (2002)
3. Cohn, M.: Succeeding with Agile: Software Development Using Scrum, vol. 1. Addison-Wesley Professional, Boston (2009)
4. Dalpiaz, F., Franch, X., Horkoff, J.: iStar 2.0 language guide. CoRR abs/1605.07767 (2016)
5. Glinz, M.: A glossary of requirements engineering terminology, version 1.4 (2012)
6. Hastie, S., Wick, A.: User stories and use case - don't use both! (2014). http://www.batimes.com/articles/user-stories-and-use-cases-dont-use-both.html
7. Kruchten, P.: The Rational Unified Process: An Introduction. Addison-Wesley, Boston (2003)
8. van Lamsweerde, A.: Goal-oriented requirements enginering: a roundtrip from research to practice. In: 12th IEEE International Conference on Requirements Engineering (RE 2004), 6–10 September 2004, Kyoto, Japan, pp. 4–7. IEEE Computer Society (2004)
9. Liskin, O., Pham, R., Kiesling, S., Schneider, K.: Why we need a granularity concept for user stories. In: Cantone, G., Marchesi, M. (eds.) XP 2014. LNBIP, vol. 179, pp. 110–125. Springer, Heidelberg (2014). doi:10.1007/978-3-319-06862-6_8
10. Lucassen, G., Dalpiaz, F., van der Werf, J.M.E.M., Brinkkemper, S.: Improving agile requirements: the quality user story framework and tool. Requir. Eng. **21**(3), 383–403 (2016)
11. OMG: Business process model and notation (bpmn). version 2.0.1. Technical report, Object Management Group (2013)
12. OMG: Omg unified modeling language$^{TM}$(omg uml). version 2.5. Technical report, Object Management Group (2015)
13. Oscar, S.: Visual Paradigm for UML. International Book Market Service Limited (2013)
14. Patton, J., Economy, P.: User Story Mapping: Discover the Whole Story, Build the Right Product. 1st edn. O'Reilly Media Inc. (2014)
15. Shergill, M.P.K., Scharff, C.: Developing multi-channel mobile solutions for a global audience: the case of a smarter energy solution. In: SARNOFF 2012 (2012)
16. Shuja, A., Krebs, J.: IBM; Rational Unified Process; Reference and Certification Guide: Solution Designer, 1st edn. IBM Press, Upper Saddle River (2007)
17. Van Lamsweerde, A.: Requirements engineering: From System Goals to UML Models to Software Specifications. Wiley, Hoboken (2009)
18. Velghe, M.: Requirements engineering in agile methods: contributions on user story models. Master's thesis, KU Leuven, Belgium (2015)
19. Wautelet, Y., Heng, S., Kolp, M., Mirbel, I.: Unifying and extending user story models. In: Jarke, M., Mylopoulos, J., Quix, C., Rolland, C., Manolopoulos, Y., Mouratidis, H., Horkoff, J. (eds.) CAiSE 2014. LNCS, vol. 8484, pp. 211–225. Springer, Heidelberg (2014). doi:10.1007/978-3-319-07881-6_15

20. Wautelet, Y., Heng, S., Kolp, M., Mirbel, I., Poelmans, S.: Building a rationale diagram for evaluating user story sets. In: 10th IEEE International Conference on Research Challenges in Information Science, RCIS 2016, Grenoble, France, 1–3 June 2016, pp. 477–488 (2016)
21. Wautelet, Y., Kolp, M.: Mapping i* within UML for business modeling. In: Doerr, J., Opdahl, A.L. (eds.) REFSQ 2013. LNCS, vol. 7830, pp. 237–252. Springer, Heidelberg (2013). doi:10.1007/978-3-642-37422-7_17
22. Yu, E.: Modeling Strategic Relationships for Process Reengineering (Chap. 1–2), pp. 1–153. MIT Press, Cambridge (2011)
23. Yu, E., Giorgini, P., Maiden, N., Mylopoulos, J.: Social Modeling for Requirements Engineering. MIT Press, Cambridge (2011)
24. Yu, E.S.: Social Modeling and i*. In: Borgida, A.T., Chaudhri, V.K., Giorgini, P., Yu, E.S. (eds.) Conceptual Modeling: Foundations and Applications - Essays in Honor of John Mylopoulos. LNCS, vol. 5600, pp. 99–121. Springer, Heidelberg (2009). doi:10.1007/978-3-642-02463-4_7

# A Study on Tangible Participative Enterprise Modelling

Dan Ionita[3]([⊠]), Julia Kaidalova[1,2], Alexandr Vasenev[3], and Roel Wieringa[3]

[1] School of Engineering, University of Jönköping,
P.O. Box 1026, 55111 Jönköping, Sweden
Julia.Kaidalova@ju.se
[2] School of Informatics, University of Skövde,
Högskolevägen, Box 408, 541 28 Skövde, Sweden
[3] University of Twente, Services, Cybersecurity and Safety Group,
Drienerlolaan 5, 7522 Enschede, NB, The Netherlands
{d.ionita,a.vasenev,r.j.wieringa}@utwente.nl
http://scs.ewi.utwente.nl/

**Abstract.** Enterprise modelling (EM) is concerned with discovering, structuring and representing domain knowledge pertaining to different aspects of an organization. Participative EM, in particular, is a useful approach to eliciting this knowledge from domain experts with different backgrounds. In related work, tangible modelling – modelling with physical objects – has been identified as beneficial for group modelling.

This study investigates effects of introducing tangible modelling as part of participative enterprise modelling sessions. Our findings suggest that tangible modelling facilitates participation. While this can make reaching an agreement more time-consuming, the resulting models tend to be of higher quality than those created using a computer. Also, tangible models are easier to use and promote learnability. We discuss possible explanations of and generalizations from these observations.

**Keywords:** Enterprise modelling · Tangible modelling · Participative modelling · Empirical study

## 1 Introduction

Enterprise modelling (EM) may serve a variety of purposes: developing or improving the organizational strategy, (re-)structuring business processes, eliciting requirements for information systems, promoting awareness of procedures and commitment to goals and decisions, etc. [16]. All these application scenarios require the involvement of a multitude of domain experts with different background knowledge [22]. It is therefore a challenge to express an enterprise model in a way equally well understood by all domain experts [11]. Limited understanding of the EM by stakeholders may result in low quality of the model and low commitment by stakeholders.

© Springer International Publishing AG 2016
S. Link and J.C. Trujillo (Eds.): ER 2016 Workshops, LNCS 9975, pp. 139–148, 2016.
DOI: 10.1007/978-3-319-47717-6_12

Traditional EM approaches involve an enterprise modelling expert who constructs an EM by interviewing domain experts, analyzing documentation and observing current practice, and validates the resulting model with stakeholders. Models constructed by such a *consultative* approach tend to exhibit low quality and poor commitment [21].

Recently, practitioners and researchers have advocated the potential of *participative* EM approaches, both in terms of promoting stakeholder agreement and commitment, as well as in producing higher quality models [1,4] In other studies, *tangible modelling* approaches – in which physical tokens represent conceptual models – were found to be faster, easier and more interactive compared to a computer-supported approaches, where diagrams on a screen were manipulated [5,8,10]. In this paper we extend studies on tangible modelling to the EM domain by combining participative EM and tangible modeling in a hybrid approach.

We report on an empirical study in a graduate EM course in which we compared the effect of using a tangible modelling set with the use of computerized tools. The results were encouraging, as the tangible modelling groups showed a higher level of collaboration, produced better results, and scored higher on posttests. On the other hand, they felt that it took longer to produce models and reported slightly lower levels of agreement. We discuss possible explanations and implications of these results. and indicate several avenues for further research.

In the next section, we summarize background and related work on enterprise modeling. Section 3 describes our research design; Sect. 4 presents our observations and measurements, and discusses possible explanations and generalizations; Sect. 5 discusses implications for practice and for research.

## 2   Background

In our experiment we use **4EM**, which consists of an EM language, as well as guidelines regarding the EM process and recommendations for involving stakeholders in moderated workshops. [19]. 4EM sub-models includes Goals, Business Rules, Concepts, Business Process, Actors and Resources and Technical Components and Requirements models.

**Participative EM**, where modeling sessions in groups are led by EM practitioners, has been established as a practical approach to deal with organizational design problems. This relies on dedicated sessions where stakeholders create models collaboratively [21]. Participative EM process includes three general activities that can be performed iteratively: (1) extracting information about the enterprise, (2) transforming information into models, (3) using enterprise models (after mutual agreement on models is achieved) [11]. Participative EM attempts to alleviate the burden of analyzing numerous intra and inter-organizational processes, which makes the traditional consultative approach hard to apply [22].

With the EM practitioner serving as a facilitator during participative modelling sessions, the way participants interact is a crucial factor for EM success. Stirna et al. [21] claim that active involvement of workshop participants into modelling allows to generate models of a better quality and also increase understanding and commitment to the created models among the participants. Barjis [1] provides evidence that participation and interaction among stakeholders enables more effective and efficient model derivation and increases the validity of models. Front et al. [6] points out that a participative approach enables more efficient data acquisition and better understanding of enterprise processes.

**Tangible modelling** is a modelling process where components of the model can be grasped and moved by the participants [10]. Tangible modelling implies synchronicity: participants can perform changes to the model in parallel [9], making it suitable for participative modelling sessions [20]. In this way, tangible modelling is different from computer-based modelling, where models are often created by one person operating the modelling tool. There is evidence that tangible modelling sessions with domain experts can produce more accurate models and result in higher levels of collaboration as well as increased stakeholder engagement and agreement [5,8,10]. Related work has also found that the interactive nature of tangible modelling increases usability [20], while its resemblance to board games can make the modelling activity more fun [7]. Tangible *process* modelling, for instance, was found to provide better engagement [13], increase comprehensibility of the result [26] and promote higher consensus and more self-corrections while helping stakeholders involved in the tangible modelling sessions remember more details [3]. Similarly, some *EM* practitioners recommend using plastic cards as a means of improving the quality of models resulting from participative sessions [15,19]. Advantages of tangible modelling can be related to evolutionary capabilities of human beings with regard to interacting with their physical surroundings. Psychological research has shown that by reducing cognitive load [14,23] and improving cognitive fit [25], physical representations are easier to understand and manipulate [1]. This agrees with constructivist theories of learning, which maintain that learning takes place in project-based learning rather than in one-way communication, and that this is most effective when people create tangible objects in the real world [2].

## 3   Research Design

The research goal of this paper is to study effects of employing a tangible approach to EM compared to conducting computer-based modelling sessions. This section describes our research design following the checklist provided by Wieringa [27]. We translate our research goal in the following research question:

> What are the effects of introducing tangible modelling as part of participative EM sessions?

The effects we concentrate on are the *quality* of the models, as well as the *difficulty, degree of collaboration*, and *efficiency* of the modelling process. Furthermore, we are interested in the educational value, namely the relative *learnability* with regard to 4EM. Measurement design is presented later in Table 1.

## 3.1  Object of Study (OoS)

Our experiment with tangible enterprise modeling was carried out with graduate students of an enterprise modeling course at Jönköping University. Students were asked to form groups no larger than five members. Although all sessions were supervised, the supervisor did not lead the sessions (as an EM practitioner would do), but just observed and provided feedback with regard to the correct application of the 4EM method. Therefore, *objects of study*, i.e. the entities about which we collect data, are EM sessions performed by students. The *population* to which we wish to generalize, consists of enterprise modeling sessions carried out by domain experts.

**OoS validity.** The objects of study have both similarities and differences to the target of generalization. Similarities include general cognitive and social mechanisms that are present in both our objects of study and in the population, such as evolutionary capabilities of grasping physical objects and the role of construction and participation in group work in learning. We also recognize several differences: the students have no shared experience in the organization being modeled and the supervisor did not lead the modeling session as a real-world enterprise modeling facilitator would do. Furthermore, the student groups were self-formed and so, while some groups may consist of very conscientious students, others could contain uninterested ones. Besides, some students may be shy and thus could collaborate less with their group. Nevertheless, as all of these phenomena may exist in the real world as well, these aspects (arguably) also make our lab experiment more realistic in terms of external validity. To take these possible confounding factors into account, we tried to make the presence of these phenomena visible by performing most measurements on an individuals instead of on groups and by observing group behavior, dynamics and outliers.

## 3.2  Treatment Design

Participants were first presented with a description of a real-world anonymized case of a sports retailer company. Each group was then given five weeks to perform a business diagnosis of the retailer by constructing three out of the six 4EM sub-models, namely the goal, concepts and business process viewpoints. The groups were instructed to perform as much of the modelling as possible together, during weekly, dedicated modelling sessions (4 h session a week). Treatment was self-allocated: Groups were allowed to choose between tangible or computer-based modelling sessions, as long as there was an even split. The tangible modelling groups were given a large plastic sheet, colored paper cards and pens to create the models. Different colors of paper cards were representing different types of elements—goals, problems, concepts and processes, similar to Fig. 5.1 of [19]. Cards could be easily attached to the plastic sheet and moved if necessary. These groups were instructed to make use of the cards when collaboratively building the models, and create digital versions of models after that. By contrast, the computer-based modelling groups (allowed to use a diagram tool of their choice) started working directly on a computer.

**Treatment validity.** While in real-life situations, the modelling technique might sometimes be prescribed, it was noted that free choice of the preferred notation to be used in EM activities and its effects on ease-of-use and understandability is desirable and worth investigating [26]. Our experiment is similar to situations where modellers have the freedom to choose their tools, and dissimilar to situations where the modelling technique is prescribed to them. Noticeably, the choosing of tools may hamper external validity of this study. In addition, internal validity may be threatened by the fact that participants were informed about both available treatments. This may cause an observer-expectancy effect, where participants change their behavior based on what they think the expectations of the experimenter are. In an attempt to mitigate this, we did not inform participants about the goal of the research nor of the measurements.

## 3.3    Measurement Design

We are interested in comparing the effects of tangible modelling versus computer-supported modelling on the quality of the result, on the modelling process, and in connection to their educational potential.

**Table 1.** Operationalized indicators and measurement scales

|         | Factor          | Indicator                | Type       | Scale                          |
|---------|-----------------|--------------------------|------------|--------------------------------|
| Result  | Model quality   | Semantic quality         | Group      | 1(poor) - 5 (excellent)        |
|         |                 | Syntactic quality        | Group      | 1(poor) - 5 (excellent)        |
| Process | Difficulty      | Perceived difficulty     | Individual | 1(very easy) - 5(very dif-lt)  |
|         | Collaboration   | Observed collaboration   | Group      | 1(very low) - 5 (very high)    |
|         |                 | Perceived agreement      | Individual | 1(none) - 5 (very much)        |
|         | Task efficiency | Observed pace            | Group      | 1(very slow) - 5 (very fast)   |
|         |                 | Perceived duration       | Individual | 5/10/15/20/>20 h               |
| Edu.value | Learnabilty   | Exam questions on 4EM    | Individual | 0-15                           |
|         |                 | Final report grade       | Group      | F (fail) - A (excellent)       |

The quality of a conceptual model is commonly defined on three dimensions: syntax (adhering to language rules), semantics (meaning, completeness, and representing the domain) and aesthetics (or comprehensibility) [12,24]. In this study we measured the *semantic quality* and *syntactic quality* of the resulting model and omitted measuring aesthetics due to its highly subjective nature. Both semantic and syntactic quality were estimated by the supervisor on a 5-point semantic difference scale by comparing the final models with the case description and 4EM syntax, respectively.

With regard to the modelling process, relevant factors are difficulty, amount of collaboration, as well as the overall task efficiency. Difficulty is a purely subjective measure [18] and was therefore measured as *perceived difficulty* via individual online questionnaires distributed at the end of the course. The questions (available at https://surfdrive.surf.nl/files/index.php/s/ixW4JlmtXma6OlE) were linked to a semantic difference scale, and provided room for optional free-text explanations. Collaboration—the amount in interaction between group members—is crucial for creating a shared understanding of a representation [17]. We indirectly measured collaboration by means of two indicators: *observed collaboration* (estimated by the supervisor throughout the five sessions) and *perceived agreement* (measured the same on-line questionnaire). Task efficiency is the amount of time to produce the final, digital model. In our case, because the task was spread across several weeks and groups may have worked at home, we could not directly measure the time groups spent. Therefore, we operationalize task efficiency in terms of *perceived duration* (measured via the online questionnaire) and *observed pace* (progress achieved during the dedicated modelling sessions, as estimated by the supervisor).

Finally, to evaluate the educational value of a tangible modelling approach, we looked at the final results of the students. As indicators we use *final report grades* and students' performance on two *exam questions on 4EM*. The final report grade was decided by the supervisors and lecturer together, while exams were graded by the course lecturer, who otherwise did not take part in this study.

**Measurement validity.** Potential issues with measurement validity might occur due to the qualitative and self-reported nature of the data (internal causes), as well as the loosely controlled environment (contextual causes). Potentially, different in scales (e.g. '1' can correspond to 'poor' in one case on 'very easy' in another) could confuse the respondents. The fact that model quality, collaboration (observed collaboration), task efficiency (observed pace) and learnability (final report grade) were assessed by one of the authors of the paper, who was one also the supervisor of the modelling sessions, is related to the self-reported nature of data and might influence validity. The person aimed at doing the assessments objectively, however still could have been biased or made mistakes. The way students formed groups (not randomly) and that they were allowed to choose a diagram tool might also be noted. To preserve construct validity, we tried to reduce mono-operation bias by operationalizing each concept in terms of two different indicators (where possible). We also attempted to minimize mono-method bias by using both self-reported and observed values where possible.

## 4   Results

**Measurements** included data on work of 38 students from Information Engineering and Management (School of Engineering) and IT, Management and Innovation (School of Business), who formed eight groups of three to five students. Although self-assigned, exactly half of the groups opted for "physical" (i.e. tangible) modelling. Every group submitted a report containing final, digital versions of their model (constructed in a tool of their choice), as well as justifications of their design decisions. No student dropped out of the modelling sessions, but only 23 filled in the questionnaire and 26 were in the exam[1].

---

[1] Full anonymized results available at: https://docs.google.com/spreadsheets/d/ 1RB74Gk1O-G43Wv2WdR4c3a-XCwb1E8-5KqhCqRlcKQo

**Table 2.** Group measurements, aggregated per group type

| Group type | Count | MEASURED | | | OBSERVED | |
|---|---|---|---|---|---|---|
| | | Semantic quality | Syntactic quality | Final report grade | Pace | Collaboration |
| Tangible | 4 | 4($\sigma$0.82) | 3.75($\sigma$0.5) | see Fig.1(a) | 4($\sigma$2) | 4($\sigma$1.41) |
| Non-tang | 4 | 3.5($\sigma$0.57) | 4.25($\sigma$0.5) | see Fig.1(a) | 3 ($\sigma$0.8) | 2.75($\sigma$1.25) |

**Table 3.** Individual measurements, aggregated respondent group type

| Respondent group type | Count | MEASURED | SELF REPORTED | | |
|---|---|---|---|---|---|
| | | Exam questions on 4EM | Perceived difficulty | Perceived agreement | Perceived duration |
| Tangible | 12 | 8.76($\sigma$4) | 3.08($\sigma$1.08) | 3.83($\sigma$1.03) | see Fig.1(b) |
| Non-tang | 11 | 8.15 ($\sigma$3.86) | 3.55 ($\sigma$0.82) | 3.91 ($\sigma$0.54) | see Fig.1(b) |

*Results per group* (Table 2) show a higher degree of collaboration and a faster pace of the tangible groups. We observed that these groups tended to communicate more and make better use of the dedicated modelling sessions, while computer-based groups tended to divide tasks and occasionally skip sessions. Also, tangible groups produced models with slightly less syntactic quality but with a higher level of content correctness. *Individually* (Table 3), participants from tangible groups reported slightly lower perceived agreement (by 2%) and lower difficulty (down 13%). Furthermore, such participants sometimes reported of longer durations than their peers from groups using only a computer. Figure 1(b) shows that more tangible modelling participants than computer-based modelling participants perceived duration as being more than 20 h. Regarding the educational effect of using tangible models, we have noticed a significant improvement on both measured indicators of learnability. The reports submitted tangible groups were scored consistently higher than others (see Figure 1(a)). Furthermore, tangible modelling students obtained, on average, 7.5% higher on questions related to the 4EM method and its application.

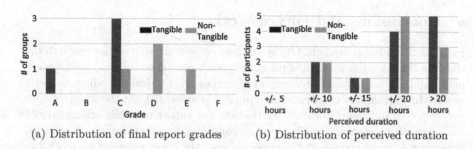

(a) Distribution of final report grades    (b) Distribution of perceived duration

**Fig. 1.** Final report grades and perceived duration

**Discussion.** We cannot exclude the possibility that all differences between tangible and computer-based groups are random fluctuations explained by chance alone. Also, since our sample and treatments were not formed and allocated randomly, we refrain from using statistical inference to generalize. However, plausible explanations to interpret the noted differences can be offered.

First, the reduced syntactic quality of tangible models can be explained by the fact that tangible modelling does not constrain the syntax of models as strictly as computers do. Thus, some students might have used this freedom to construct models that are not syntactically correct.

Second, our explanation for the higher semantic quality of tangible models is that the tangible groups interacted more (without dividing tasks) and seemed to work harder (higher pace and longer perceived duration). This can be that tangible modelling supported participation by providing the fun-factor. The perceived duration might have also been influenced by the fact that after completion of tangible models, the students had to enter them into a software tool.

Third, the lower perception of difficulty and better exam results of tangible groups can be explained by the theory of constructivism, which says that learning is most effective when people jointly create tangible objects in groups.

Finally, the slightly lower perceived agreement within tangible groups may be explained by higher levels of collaboration. Due to less subdivision of tasks, tangible modelling forced groups to promptly discuss disagreements. It is also possible that the computer-based groups had lower *actual* levels of agreement without noticing this. Since they divided tasks among members and discussed less than the tangible groups, they may have overlooked some disagreements or misinterpretations. While our data do not exclude this possibility, it do not support it either. More research is needed to test this hypothesis.

**Generalizability.** Given available data, this study employs generalization by analogy: "If an observation is explained by a general theory, then this observation may also occur in other cases where this general theory is applicable" [27]. Since social or psychological mechanisms can explain the observed phenomena using constructs such as synchronicity, cognitive load, cognitive fit, gamification, and constructive learning (see Sect. 2), we can expect similarities in practice.

## 5    Conclusions and Future Work

**Implications for research.** Our results are consistent with earlier research that showing that tangible modelling promotes collaboration because of synchronicity, manipulability of physical tokens, and increased fun, while leading to better results due to the joint construction of physical models [10]. At the same time, the perception of increased duration contradicts our earlier research, where tangible modelling was observed to be faster than computer-based modelling. Results also show that collaborative modelling may increase the effort required for modelling, contrary to [1,6]. One explanation of this is that our earlier results [10] used iconic physical tokens, i.e. objects that resemble the entities being modelled, which made them easier to understand. To test this explanation, we need to compare tangible modelling with iconic tokens and with plastic cards in future research. Also needed is a similar real-world experiment with EM practitioners, to verify the external validity of our results. Another interesting direction for further investigation are computer-based participative modelling tools (such as using smart boards and touch screens).

**Implications for practice.** Our results suggest that tangible enterprise modelling could be a useful tool for building consensus of stakeholders with diverse backgrounds and little EM experience. This is particularly useful on the early stages of enterprise modelling, when the goal is to improve the quality of the business [10,21]. Our results also suggest that tangible EM has a positive educational effect by providing higher understandability and improved learnability.

**Acknowledgments.** The authors would like to thank Anders Carstensen for adapting his EM course at Jönköping University to accommodate our study. The research has received funding from the European Union Seventh Framework Programme (FP7/2007-2013) under grant agreement ICT-318003 (TREsPASS) and from the Joint Program Initiative (JPI) Urban Europe via the IRENE project.

# References

1. Barjis, J.: Collaborative, participative and interactive enterprisemodeling. In: Filipe, J., Cordeiro, J. (eds.) ICEIS 2009. LNBIP, vol. 24. Springer, Heidelberg (2009)
2. Cakir, M.: Constructivist approaches to learning in science andtheir impolications for science pedagogy: a literature review. Int. J. Environ. Sci. Educ. **3**(4), 193–206 (2008)
3. Edelman, J., Grosskopf, A., Weske, M., Leifer, L.: Tangible businessprocess modeling: a new approach. In: Proceedings of the 17th International Conference on Engineering Design, ICED, vol. 9, pp. 153–168, August 2009
4. F3-Consortium: F3 reference manual. Technical report MSU-CSE-00-2, SISU, Stockholm (1994). eSPRIT III Project 6612
5. Fleischmann, A., Schmidt, W., Stary, C.: Tangible or not tangible - a comparative study of interaction types for process modeling support. In: Kurosu, M. (ed.) HCI 2014. LNCS, vol. 8511. Springer, Heidelberg (2014)
6. Front, A., Rieu, D., Santorum, M.: A participative end-user modeling approach for business process requirements. In: Bider, I., Gaaloul, K., Krogstie, J., Nurcan, S., Proper, H.A., Schmidt, R., Soffer, P. (eds.) BPMDS/EMMSAD -2014. LNBIP, vol. 175, pp. 33–47. Springer, Heidelberg (2014). doi:10.1007/978-3-662-43745-2_3
7. Garde, J., van der Voort, M.: The procedure usability game: a participatory game for development of complex medical procedures & products. In: Proceedings of the CIRP IPS2 Conference 2009 (2009)
8. Grosskopf, A., Edelman, J., Weske, M.: Tangible business process modeling - methodology and experiment design. In: Rinderle-Ma, S., Sadiq, S., Leymann, F. (eds.) ER-BPM 2009. LNBIP, vol. 43. Springer, Heidelberg (2009)
9. Hinckley, K.: Synchronous gestures for multiple persons andcomputers. In: Proceedings of the 16th Annual ACM Symposium on User Interface Software and Technology, UIST 2003, pp. 149–158. ACM, New York (2003)
10. Ionita, D., Wieringa, R., Bullee, J.-W., Vasenev, A.: Tangible modelling to elicit domain knowledge: an experiment and focus group. In: Johannesson, P., Lee, M.L., Liddle, S.W., Opdahl, A.L., López, Ó.P. (eds.) ER 2015. LNCS, vol. 9381, pp. 558–565. Springer, Heidelberg (2015). doi:10.1007/978-3-319-25264-3_42

11. Kaidalova, J., Siegerroth, U., Bukowska, E., Shilov, N.: Enterprise modeling for business and it alignment: Challenges and recommendations. Int. J. IT Bus. Alignment Gov. **5**(2), 44–69 (2014)
12. Lindland, O.I., Sindre, G., Solvberg, A.: Understanding quality in conceptual modeling. IEEE Software **11**(2), 42–49 (1994)
13. Lübbe, A.: tangible business process modeling: design and evaluation of a process model elicitation technique. Ph.D. thesis, Universitt Potsdam (2011)
14. Miller, G.: The magical number seven, plus or minus two: some limits on our capacity for processing information. Psychol. Rev. **63**, 81–97 (1956)
15. Nurcan, S., Rolland, C.: Using EKD-CMM electronic guide book formanaging change in organisations. In: Proceedings of the 9th European-Japanese Conference on Information Modelling and Knowledge Bases, pp. 105–123 (1999)
16. Persson, A., Stirna, J.: An explorative study into the influence ofbusiness goals on the practical use of enterprise modelling methods and tools. In:Proceedings of the 10th International Conference on Information Systems Development (ISD). Kluwer, London (2001)
17. Renger, M., Kolfschoten, G.L., Vreede, G.J.D.: Challenges in collaborative modelling: a literature review and research agenda. Int. J. Simul. Process Model. **4**(3–4), 248–263 (2008)
18. Robinson, P.: Task complexity, task difficulty, and task production: exploring interactions in a componential framework. Appl. Linguist. **22**(1), 27–57 (2001)
19. Sandkuhl, K., Stirna, J., Persson, A., Wißotzki, M.: Enterprise Modeling: Tackling Business Challenges with the 4EM Method. Springer, Heidelberg (2014)
20. Scholtz, B., Calitz, A., Snyman, I.: The usability of collaborativetools: Application to business process modelling. In: Proceedings ofthe South African Institute for Computer Scientists and Information Technologists Conference. ACM (2013)
21. Stirna, J., Persson, A.: Ten Years Plus with EKD: reflections from using an enterprise modeling method in practice. In: Proceedings ofthe 11th International Workshop on Exploring Modeling Methods in Systems Analysis and Design (EMMSAD 2007). Springer, Heidelberg (2007)
22. Stirna, J., Persson, A., Sandkuhl, K.: Participative enterprise modeling: experiences and recommendations. In: Krogstie, J., Opdahl, A., Sindre, G. (eds.) CAiSE 2007. LNCS, vol. 4495, pp. 546–560. Springer, Heidelberg (2007). doi:10.1007/978-3-540-72988-4_38
23. Sweller, J.: Cognitive load during problem solving: effects on learning. Cogn. Sci. **12**(2), 257–285 (1988)
24. Unhelkar, B.: The Quality Strategy for UML, pp. 1–26. Wiley, Hoboken (2005)
25. Vessey, I., Galletta, D.: Cognitive fit: an empirical study of information acquisition. Inf. Syst. Res. **2**(1), 63–84 (1991)
26. Weitlaner, D., Guettinger, A., Kohlbacher, M.: Intuitive comprehensibility of process models. In: Fischer, H., Schneeberger, J. (eds.) S-BPM ONE 2013. CCIS, vol. 360, pp. 52–71. Springer, Heidelberg (2013). doi:10.1007/978-3-642-36754-0_4
27. Wieringa, R.J.: Design Science Methodology for Information Systems and Software Engineering. Springer, Heidelberg (2014)

# Bridging the Requirements Engineering and Business Analysis Toward a Unified Knowledge Framework

Mikio Aoyama(✉)

Department of Software Engineering, School of Science and Engineering,
Nanzan University, 18 Yamazato Showa-Ku, Nagoya 466-8673, Japan
mikio.aoyama@nifty.com

**Abstract.** Several similar but different disciplines have evolved in the arena of requirements engineering and business analysis, including business analysis, BPM (Business Process Management), and business architecture. Yet, they are forming bodies of knowledges in each discipline. Each discipline has its raison d'etre. However, such diversity of the bodies of knowledge causes a confusion. This article is intended to review the bodies of knowledge, and proposes a unified knowledge framework of the bodies of knowledge across the disciplines.

**Keywords:** Requirements engineering · Business analysis · Business process management · Business architecture · Body of knowledge

## 1 Introduction

The motivation for writing this article is an apparent confusion of similar, but might be different, concepts related to business analysis: business process management, business architecture management, business model generation/innovation. These concepts evolved from different communities, gaining momentum, and forming a body of knowledge. We can see several BOK(Body Of Knowledge)s including BABOK (Business Analysis Body Of Knowledge) [16], BIZBOK (Business Architecture Body of Knowledge) [5], BPM CBOK (Business Process Management Common Body Of Knowledge) [3]. On requirements engineering, Software Requirements in SWEBOK (Software Engineering Body Of Knowledge) [4] and REBOK (Requirements Engineering Body Of Knowledge) [19] provide the foundation. Besides those BOKs, there are many books which provide techniques from the authors' own viewpoints.

This article is intended to review the literature on the RE (Requirements Engineering), BA (Business Analysis), and related disciplines, and propose a unified framework to understand the techniques of them. To meet the goal, the author sets the following research questions.

RQ1: Which scope spanning from the business to software those disciplines deal with?

RQ2: What are the commonality and variability in terms of the process and techniques those disciplines employ?

RQ3: How to visualize the scope and process/techniques in a uniform framework?

S. Link and J.C. Trujillo (Eds.): ER 2016 Workshops, LNCS 9975, pp. 149–160, 2016.
DOI: 10.1007/978-3-319-47717-6_13

## 2 Related Works

There is a large number of literature on the techniques within each discipline. However, very few works on the analysis of knowledge between different disciplines and bodies of knowledges. Each discipline differs by the techniques, scope of subject, and scope of lifecycle to be covered. However, the things become more complicated by introducing the roles of professions. For example, from the business analyst's perspective, Haas and Rubin argued the similarity in the techniques, but the difference in the roles, that is requirements engineer and business analyst, between RE and BA [14, 33].

To establish a common ground among the disciplines, REO (Requirements Engineering Ontology) proposed a common ontology of REBOK, SWEBOK, and BABOK, and analyzed the differences of those BOKs [34]. However, the analysis is limited to three BOKs, and did not discuss the relationships to other related disciplines.

There are some works to bridge the different disciplines. For example, Decreus, et al. proposed an alignment of the RE lifecycle and the BPM lifecycle [8]. However, the proposed technique is limited to transforming an artifact of RE to BPM, say RE2BPM, and does not discuss the commonality and difference between the two disciplines. An experience of integrating RE and BA suggested that the integration level is higher if the project team had a clear view to of the use of business analysis [12].

## 3 Approach

The author takes an approach which we call "perspective-based review of BOKs". It consists of the following two ideas.

(1)  Use BOKs and Major Textbooks as the Source of Knowledge of the Disciplines

The author use BOKs or textbooks as the source of the review since, in each discipline, there are certain accumulation of knowledge in the form of either BOK or text books. We are interested in to explore the similarity and difference of techniques between the different disciplines. Therefore, it is necessary to review the techniques at a certain depth, which is different from the approach taken by systematic literature review. To avoid the potential bias of the knowledge source, the author set a policy to refer at least two documents of high reputation on a discipline.

(2)  Perspective-Based Review

To analyze the literature, the author employs perspective-based reading, a technique used for code inspection [35], to identify certain knowledge through common perspective across the multiple disciplines. Perspective-based approach is necessary since BOKs and textbooks generally compile diverse knowledge and techniques interwoven.

In this article, we set the following two orthogonal perspectives for review:

(1)  Scope: Which Part of the business requirements should be dealt with
(2)  Technique/Process Perspective: What should be done in the discipline with which techniques at the process

From reading the BOKs and documents based on the two perspectives, we can generate a *knowledge framework* across the disciplines.

# 4   Perspective-Based Review of BOKs and Literature

## 4.1   Summary of Review

The author conducted the perspective-based review of the BOKs and textbooks listed in Table 1. In the followings, the author describes a summary of findings.

**Table 1.**   List of documents reviewed

| Discipline | Documents |
| --- | --- |
| RE (Requirements Engineering) | REBOK [19], SWEBOK [4], ISO/IEC/IEEE 29148 [17] |
| BA (Business Analysis) | BABOK [16], BCS BA Text Book [26] |
| BPM (Business Process Management) | BPM CBOK [3], BPM Text Book [10, 18, 32] |
| Business Architecture and BAM | BIZBOK [5], Business Architecture Text Book [36, 37] |

## 4.2   RE (Requirements Engineering)

(1)   Summary of the State of RE

RE evolved from software engineering. The body of knowledge of RE has been developed by the software engineering community. The SWEBOK (Software Engineering Body Of Knowledge) is a BOK of software engineering [4], and its Chapter 1 defined BOK of software requirements, that is, RE in software engineering context. REBOK (Requirements Engineering Body Ok Knowledge) is a BOK dedicated to RE [2, 19]. As illustrated in Fig. 1, the knowledge structure of REBOK is an extension of that of "Software Requirements" in SWEBOK. REBOK adds a new KA of "Requirements Planning and Management". The knowledge structure of REBOK is also consistent with ISO/IEC/IEEE 29148 [17].

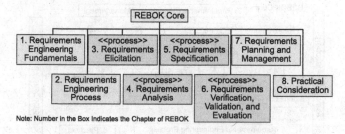

**Fig. 1.**   Structure of knowledge areas of REBOK [19]

(2)  Scope of RE

A well-known survey on requirements engineering states that RE is "discovering the purpose, by identifying stakeholders and their needs", and "documenting these in a form that is amenable to analysis, communication, and subsequent implementation" [24].

The design of REBOK is intended to cover all three layers of requirements from business requirements, system requirements, and software requirements as illustrated in Fig. 2. The requirements scope model of three layers indicates that the system requirements should be derived from the business requirements, and the software requirements from the system requirements. Therefore, REBOK is a common BOK across the three layers of requirements. However, techniques employed at each layer might be different.

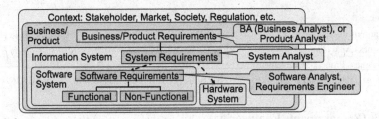

**Fig. 2.**  Three layers of requirements scope of REBOK [19]

(3)  Techniques/Processes of RE

Figure 3 illustrates the basic RE process defined by REBOK. The process is structured in an iterative way from elicitation, analysis, specification, verification, validation, and evaluation. The whole process is incrementally conducted to three layers of requirements from business, system, and software, which are illustrated in as Fig. 2. The incremental and iterative structure of the RE process conforms closely to ISO/IEC/IEEE 29148:2011, which is an international standard of the RE process [17]. Therefore, the process in Fig. 3 is considered as a generic process model of RE.

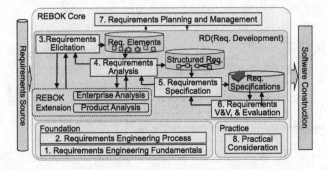

**Fig. 3.**  RE process of REBOK [19]

### 4.3 BA (Business Analysis)

(1) Summary of the State of BA

BA has been used as an umbrella term to cover a wide range of techniques to "analyze" business [6, 14]. One of the well-received BOK for BA is BABOK (Business Analysis Body Of Knowledge), which has been developed by IIBA (The International Institute of Business Analysis) founded in 2003. Since its first version published in 2005, the BABOK has evolved to the latest BABOK V3.0 published in 2015 [16].

The knowledge structure of BABOK is illustrated in Fig. 4. Comparing BABOK with REBOK, "Strategy Analysis" is unique to business analysis.

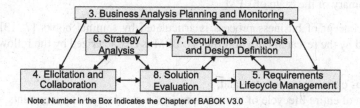

Note: Number in the Box Indicates the Chapter of BABOK V3.0

**Fig. 4.** Structure of knowledge areas of BABOK [16]

There is a textbook on BA compiled by the British Informatics Society, BCS Book hereafter, first published in 2006. It was revised for the second edition in 2010 [26]. As illustrated in Fig. 5, the BCS Book defines BA with a bit more concrete activities of "investigating business situations", "identifying and evaluating options for improving business systems", and "defining requirements and ensuring the effective use of information systems in meeting the needs of the business".

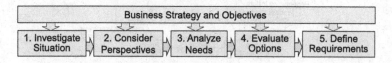

**Fig. 5.** Structure of knowledge areas of BA in the BCS book [26]

(2) Scope of BA

BABOK 3.0 defines BA with two activities of "defining needs" and "recommending solutions that deliver value to stakeholders" [16], which is intended to enable change of the enterprise. It is clear that the similar but slightly different definitions on BA are essentially same to that of RE. It might be said that BA is a part of RE at the level of business requirements. However, as BABOK and BCS Book illustrate their own set of KA (Knowledge Area), BA include some unique techniques due to the wide scope and its diverse characteristics of business requirements.

(3)  Techniques/Processes of BA

The representation methods of the BABOK and part of BCS Book, are both process-oriented in the sense that each process is defined with input, detailed processes, and output. The descriptive style of BABOK and BCS Book is different from that of SWEBOK and REBOK, which defined knowledge in a declarative way. However, the fundamental techniques in both BABOK and BCS Book are same to those of REBOK, and textbooks on the requirements engineering [21, 28, 39, 40].

### 4.4  BPM (Business Process Management)

(1)  Summary of the State of BPM

The concept of business process is articulated by seminal books [7, 13], and is supported by the research on workflow [1]. BPM is characterized by the following two aspects:

(1)  Focus on business process, and,
(2)  Span of entire lifecycle of business process, instead of just requirements.

BPM lifecycle is a foundation of BPM, as illustrated in Fig. 6 [10, 20, 31]. It encompasses its technical scope from modeling, analysis, design, performance measurement, and transformation of business identification, discovery, analysis, redesign, implementation, monitoring and controlling of business process. Therefore, technical scope of BPM is similar to software engineering, if the business process is considered as software, and is beyond RE.

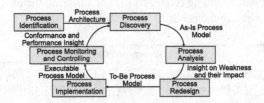

**Fig. 6.**  BPM lifecycle model [10]

ABPMP (Association of Business Process management Professionals) published the BPM CBOK (Common Body Of Knowledge) in 2009, which evolved to version 3.0 in 2013 [3]. Figure 7 illustrates the structure of knowledge areas of BPM CBOK. However, it is not as popular as BABOK yet. There are many textbooks, which offer a slightly different set of techniques [10, 18]. For example, a comprehensive framework of BPM is represented as "BPM house" [18].

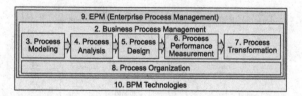

**Fig. 7.** Structure of knowledge areas of BPM CBOK [3]

(2)  Scope of BPM

Scope of BPM is mainly limited to business process. However, to improve business process, it is naturally extended to business strategy upwardly, and to information system, namely BPMS (BPM Systems), downwardly.

(3)  Techniques/Processes of BPM

As stated BPM covers the entire lifecycle of business process. Therefore, the techniques of BPM include not only of requirements to business process, but also (re)design, implementation, and monitoring/controlling.

## 4.5  Business Architecture and BAM (Business Architecture Management)

(1)  Summary of the State of Business Architecture

Business architecture is not a new term. It is the application of the concept of architecture to business, where business is considered as a system comprised of process, technology, and people [29]. It is also known as the top layer of EA (Enterprise Architecture), and bridge the business strategy/business model for information systems [22, 38]. However, it emerged as a sub-discipline in the BA arena as the BIZBOK (Business Architecture Body Ok Knowledge) is newly developed by the Business Architecture Guild, which is founded in 2010 [5].

According to BIZBOK, business architecture is "a blueprint of the enterprise and is used to align strategic objectives and tactical demands" [5].

BIZBOK defines four fundamental perspectives, including capability, information, organization, and value stream. Figure 8 illustrates part of the value stream. It represents a process to create and deliver the value to the stakeholders. Therefore, the value stream is considered as a process in the context of business architecture.

BAM (Business Architecture Management) is similar, but a slightly different discipline [36]. It is based on the Business Motivation, Business Model, and Business Execution developed by OMG.

(2)  Scope of Business Architecture and BAM

Although the term Business Architecture is very generic, the BIZBOK claims that the primary blueprint is value stream, which is a higher abstraction to business process [9]. This definition might not be generally accepted. BAM claims three entities. One of them, Business Execution includes business process and organizational units, which are subject of BPM. Therefore, at this moment, the notion of business architecture is not yet

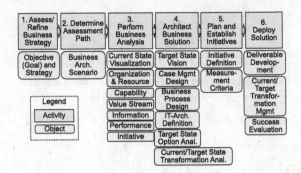

**Fig. 8.** Business architecture value stream of BIZBOK (Part)

commonly defined. However, since the BIZBOK, the primary knowledge source of this discipline, claims, the author employ the definition of business architecture from BIZBOK.

(3)  Techniques/Processes of Business Architecture and BAM

As illustrated in Fig. 8, the range of value stream processes defined by BIZBOK covers similar to those of BPM in Fig. 7. It also includes activities on the implementation level, e.g. "Business-Driven IT Architecture Definition". It is not intended to encompass to entire software solution, but emphasizes the importance of alignment of business to IT architecture [5, 30].

# 5   A Unified Knowledge Framework

From the perspective-based review of BOKs and literatures in four disciplines, the author generated two instances of unified knowledge framework according to the two perspectives of scope and techniques/processes. The Unified Knowledge Framework proposed here is a simple table illustrating the distribution and dependencies of the knowledge areas with respect to specific perspective.

(1)  Unified Knowledge Framework for Scope

Figure 9 illustrates the scope of five disciplines with respect to the levels of abstractions of business and the span in lifecycle processes. The six rows define hierarchical levels from business strategy to software systems. It extends the business requirements layer into three layers, which reflects the recent advancement of research and practice in BA, Business Architecture and BMI (Business Model Innovation)/BMD (Business Model Design) [11, 25]. However, there is no agreed model of the hierarchical classification of the business requirements. Therefore, the author adopted a coarse grained layer for the purpose of scoping the disciplines.

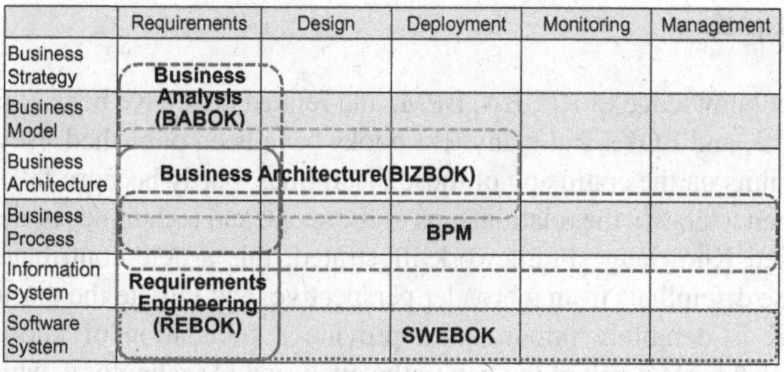

| | Requirements | Design | Deployment | Monitoring | Management |
|---|---|---|---|---|---|
| Business Strategy | **Business Analysis (BABOK)** | | | | |
| Business Model | | | | | |
| Business Architecture | **Business Architecture(BIZBOK)** | | | | |
| Business Process | | | **BPM** | | |
| Information System | **Requirements Engineering (REBOK)** | | | | |
| Software System | | | **SWEBOK** | | |

**Fig. 9.** A unified knowledge framework: scope perspective

Figure 9 gives a holistic view to the span of the scope of the five disciplines. Although it is not so precise, it can help to understand the position of the each discipline with respect to related disciplines.

(2)  Unified Knowledge Framework on Techniques and Processes

Figure 10 illustrates the Unified Knowledge Framework on the techniques and processes with respect to six BOKs and textbooks. The framework illustrates a refinement of Fig. 9 with the distribution of knowledge units of each discipline. The framework indicates that the process and techniques of BA, BPM, and business architecture are very analogous and overlapping in their scopes, which causes some confusions to especially practitioners [6, 8]. Similarly, there is also discussion on the confusion between RE and BA, and how to integrate them [12, 33].

| BOKs and Text Books | Requirements | | | | Design | Imple./Monitor | Mgmt |
|---|---|---|---|---|---|---|---|
| | Elicitation | Analysis | Specification | V&V | --- | --- | |
| RE REBOK[19] | Req. Elicitation | Req. Analysis | Req. Specification | Req. V&V and Eval. | --- | --- | RE Plan & Mgmt |
| Business Analysis BABOK[16] | Elicitation & Collaboration | Strategy Analysis / Req. Analysis | | Solution Evaluation | Design Def. | --- | Req. Life-Cycle Mgmt |
| Business Analysis BCS Book [26] | Situation & Perspective | Analysis Needs, Evaluation Options | Define Req. | Performance | --- | --- | --- |
| BPM CBOK[3] | Process Modeling | Process Analysis | | | Process Design | Performance Measurement, Transformation | Enterprise Process Mgmt |
| BPM Book [10] | Identification, Discovery | Analysis | | | Redesign | Implementation Mnitor&Control | --- |
| Business Architecture BIZBOK[5] | Assess/Refine Business Strategy Determine Assessment Path | Business Analysis including Performane | | | Architect Business Solution | Plan & Establish Initiatives Deploy Solution | --- |

**Fig. 10.** A unified knowledge framework: techniques/process perspective

## 6  Discussions

The bodies of knowledge of RE, BA, BPM, and related area have been evolved within each discipline, and BOKs and many text books have been published. However, there have been claims on the confusion of those disciplines, partly because few works have been conducted to clarify the relationships of the scope and techniques of the discipline. As the Unified Knowledge Framework illustrated, this article contributes to understanding those disciplines from a broader perspective, and initiate the discussions.

The BOK is definitely important to provide a foundation of knowledge [27]. However, it also faces a risk of the gap to the evolution of technology, which is particularly notable in IT. For example, BMI (Business Model Innovation) is an emerging discipline on top of business architecture and processes [11, 25]. It may bring another confusion to the RE and BA arena. However, it is also necessary to align the business process and information system to its business model [15]. Further research is necessary.

## 7  Conclusions

This article contributes to clarify the relationship of RE, BA, BPM, and business architecture by reviewing their BOKs and literatures with a common perspective, and create a uniform knowledge framework to understand the related disciplines. The proposed framework is still in its early stage. Further research is necessary.

## References

1. van der Aalst, W.M.: Business Process Management Demystified: A Tutorial on Models, Systems and Standards for Workflow Management. In: Desel, J., Reisig, W., Rozenberg, G. (eds.) Lectures on Concurrency and Petri Nets. LNCS, vol. 3098, pp. 1–65. Springer, Heidelberg (2004)
2. Aoyama, M., Nakatani, T., Saito, S., Suzuki, M., Fujita, K., Nakazaki, H., Suzuki, R.: A model and architecture of REBOK(Requirements Engineering Body Of Knowledge) and its evaluation. In: Proceeding of APSEC 2010, IEEE Compute Society, November-December 2010, pp. 50–59 (2010)
3. Benedict, T., et al.: BPM CBOK Version 3.0: guide to the business process management common body of knowledge, In: ABPMP International/Createspace (2013). http://www.abpmp.org/
4. Bourque, P., Fairley, R.E. (eds.) SWEBOK 3.0: Guide to the Software Engineering Body of Knowledge. IEEE Computer Society (2014)
5. Business Architecture Guild, A Guide to the Business Architecture Body of Knowledge (BIZBOK Guide), V. 4.5 (2015). http://www.businessarchitectureguild.org/
6. Darwish, A.: Business Process Analysis versus Business Analysis: Why Most Organizations Confuse Them? August 2015. http://www.at-turjuman.com/files/BABPA%20Article_R015.pdf
7. Davenport, T.H.: Process Innovation: Reengineering Work Through Information Technology. Harvard Business School Press, Boston (1993)
8. Decreus, K., et al.: Bridging requirements engineering and business process management., In: Proceeding of the REBPM 2009, Gesellschaft für Informatik e.V., pp. 215–222, March 2009

9. Dugan, L., et al.: Business Architecture and BPM, Business Architecture Group Whitepaper, September 2014. http://c.ymcdn.com/sites/www.businessarchitectureguild.org/resource/resmgr/bpmwhitepaper.pdf

10. Dumas, M., et al. (eds.): Fundamentals Business Process Management. Springer, Heidelberg (2013)

11. Foss, N.J., Saebi, T. (eds.): Business Model Innovation. Oxford University Press, Oxford (2015)

12. Haglind, M., Johansson, L.: Experiences integrating requirements engineering and business analysis. In: Proceeding of RE 1998, pp. 108–117. IEEE Computer Society, April 1998

13. Hammer, M., Champy, J.: Reengineering the Corporation. Harper Collins, New York (1993)

14. Hass, K.B.: Professionalizing Business Analysis. Management Concepts Inc, Vienna (2008)

15. Ide, M., et al.: An IT-driven business model design methodology and its evaluation. In: Proceeding of REBPM 2014, pp. 1–10. IEEE Computer Society, August 2014

16. IIBA, A Guide to the Business Analysis Body of Knowledge (BABOK Guide), Version 3.0, IIBA (2015). http://www.iiba.org/

17. ISO/IEC/IEEE 29148:2011 Software and Systems Engineering – Life Cycle Processes – Requirements Engineering, ISO (2011)

18. Jeston, J., Nelis, J.: Business Process Management, 3rd edn. Routledge, Abingdon (2014)

19. Jisa Rebok, W.G (ed.) Requirements Engineering Body Of Knowledge (REBOK), Version 1.0, Kindaikagakusha (2011). (in Japanese). http://www.re-bok.org/en/

20. Ko, R.K.L.: A computer scientist's introductory guide to business process management (BPM). ACM Crossroads 15(4), 11–18 (2009)

21. van Lamsweerde, A.: Requirements Engineering. Wiley, New York (2009)

22. Lankhorst, M.: Enterprise Architecture at Work. Springer, Heidelberg (2005)

23. Leffingwell, D.: Agile Requirements. Addison-Wesley, Upper Saddle River (2011)

24. Nuseibeh, B., Easterbrook, S.: Requirements Engineering: a roadmap. In: Proceeding of the Conference on The Future of Software Engineering, ICSE 200, pp. 35–46. ACM, May 2000

25. A. Osterwalder and Y. Pigneur, Business Model Generation, Wiley, 2010

26. Paul, D., et al.: Business Analysis, 2nd edn. British Informatics Society, Chippenham (2010)

27. Penzenstadler, B., et al.: The Requirements Engineering Body of Knowledge (REBoK). In: Proceeding of the RE 2013, pp. 377–379. IEEE Computer Society, July 2013

28. Pohl, K.: Requirements Engineering. Springer, Heidelberg (2010)

29. Reynolds, C.: Introduction to Business Architecture. Course Technology (2010)

30. Regev, G., Favre, J., Hayek, E., Wilson, p., Wegmann, A.: Business/IT alignment in practice: lessons learned from a requirements project at P&G. In: Salinesi, C., Pastor, O. (eds.) BUSITAL 2011. LNBIP, vol. 83, pp. 93–101. Springer, Heidelberg (2011)

31. Rosemann, M., vom Brocke, J.: The six core elements of business process management. In: von Brocke, Rosemann, M. (eds.) Handbook on Business Process Management. International Handbooks on Information Systems, vol. 1, pp. 105–122. Springer, Heidelberg (2010)

32. von Rosing, M., et al. (eds.) The Complete Business Process Handbook: Body of Knowledge from Process Modeling to BPM, vol. 1, Morgan Kaufman (2015)

33. Rubens, J.: Business analysis and requirements engineering: the same, only different? Requirements Eng. J. 12(2), 121–123 (2007)

34. Saito, S., Iimura, Y., Aoyama, M.: REO: requirements engineering ontology: spectrum analysis of requirements engineering knowledge and its practical application. In: Proceedings of COMPSAC 2015, pp. 62–70. IEEE Computer Society, July 2015

35. Shull, F., et al.: How perspective-based reading can improve requirements inspections. IEEE Comput. 33(7), 73–79 (2000)

36. Simon, D., Schmidt, C. (eds.): Business Architecture Management: Architecting the Business for Consistency and Alignment. Springer, Switzerland (2015)
37. Ulrich, W., et al.: Business and Dynamic Change: The Arrival of Business Architecture. Future Strategies Inc. (2015)
38. US Office of Management and Budget, Federal Enterprise Architecture Framework, Version 2 (2013). https://www.whitehouse.gov/sites/default/files/omb/assets/egov_docs/fea_v2.pdf
39. Wiegers, K.; Beatty, J.: Software Requirements, 3rd edn. Microsoft Press, New York (2013)
40. Yu, E., et al. (eds.): Social Modeling for Requirements Engineering. MIT Press, Cambridge (2011)

# Quality of Models and Models of Quality

## Preface to the Third Workshop Quality of Models and Models of Quality

Samira Si-Said Cherfi[1], Oscar Pastor[2], and Elena Kornyshova[1]

[1] CEDRIC – Conservatoire National des Arts et Métiers, Paris, France
[2] Universidad Politècnica de Valencia, Valencia, Spain

The third edition of the Quality of Models and Models of Quality workshop aims to continue promoting efforts in the development of methods and frameworks for assessing, managing and maintaining quality of artefacts and deliverable through their conceptual models. Data and information in general need to be of high quality to be valuable. However, this quality, to be ensured, requires reliable IS that can only be designed with a precise ontological commitment. Moreover, in the Internet age, we are witnessing the emergence of a new practices such as collaborative designs, user generated contents, crowdsourcing information systems and other non-traditional methods based Information systems. Consequently, a new challenge facing the researchers as well as practitioners is: "how to ensure the quality of such systems?". We believe that research on quality needs more contributions based on experimentation to provide empirical evidences of successful IS design.

This positions the research on quality at the intersection of a variety of disciplines such as Conceptual Modeling (CM), Software Engineering (SE), Web Semantics, Process Engineering etc. This active research encompasses theoretical aspects including quality frameworks and standards as well as practical/empirical aspects as tools, case studies and empirical research. Quality is also a cross-domain concern involving contribution from academic and practical fields such as universities, medical structures, commercial or governmental organizations.

Our aim within this workshop is to offer an opportunity to cross-fertilization of ideas, research directions and methods by gathering researchers and practitioners from several disciplines and business domains. This should lead to envision new perspectives to the problem of evaluating quality in IS.

The workshop includes a keynote by C. Partridge and S. de Cesare on *Grounding for Ontological Architecture* Quality, three paper presentations and a discussion session.

Out of 9 high quality papers submitted, the workshop international committee se-lected three papers for presentation and publication with an acceptance rate of 33 %. The accepted papers authors come from Belgium, Dominican Republic, Spain and UK.

We would like to thank all authors, presenters and reviewers for their valuable work. We are also grateful to the 2016 ER workshop chairs for giving us the opportunity to organize this workshop.

Samira Si-Said Cherfi    CEDRIC - Conservatoire National des Arts et Métiers, France
Oscar Pastor              Universidad Politècnica de Valencia, Spain
Elena Kornyshova          CEDRIC - Conservatoire National des Arts et Métiers, France

# An Exploratory Analysis on the Comprehension of 3D and 4D Ontology-Driven Conceptual Models

Michaël Verdonck[✉] and Frederik Gailly

Faculty of Economics and Business Administration, Ghent University, Ghent, Belgium
{michael.verdonck, frederik.gailly}@ugent.be

**Abstract.** In this paper, we perform an exploratory analysis to investigate the impact of adopting a 3D and a 4D foundational ontology on the quality of a conceptual model. More specifically, we determine the impact of the metaphysical characteristics of an ontology on the comprehension and understandability of the ontology-driven models by its users. The contributions of this research are: (1) while much effort in ODCM has been devoted into the syntactic and semantic aspects of models for improving their overall quality, this research focuses on the pragmatic aspect of a model; and (2) since little empirical research has yet been performed in this area, we formulated several hypotheses that are derived from the results and observations from our exploratory analysis. These hypotheses can then serve as a testing ground for future empirical research in order to investigate the fundamental differences between 3D and 4D ontology-driven models.

## 1 Introduction

According to Lindland et al. [1], the quality of a model can be defined into three aspects: syntactic quality, semantic quality and pragmatic quality. While *syntactic quality* of a model corresponds to how well the representation equals the language's statements and constructs, the *semantic quality* of a model relates to the validity and completeness of a conceptual model. The last aspect, *pragmatic quality* concerns the comprehension of conceptual models. The better a model is understood, the higher the pragmatic quality of the model, and hence the higher the overall quality of the conceptual model. Since the beginning on the nineties, ontologies have been often applied for improving the quality of conceptual models. Ontologies provide a foundational theory, which articulates and formalizes the conceptual modeling grammars needed to describe the structure and behavior of the modeled domain [2]. In particular, foundational ontologies are frequently applied since they describe general concepts like space, time and matter, and are independent of a particular problem or domain. In this paper we refer to all techniques where ontologies are applied (e.g. evaluation, analysis or theoretical foundation) to improve either the quality of the conceptual modeling process or the quality of the conceptual model, as ontology-driven conceptual modeling (ODCM). Although prior research has focused much on the semantic quality of models, there has been little research examining the pragmatic quality of these models [3, 4].

© Springer International Publishing AG 2016
S. Link and J.C. Trujillo (Eds.): ER 2016 Workshops, LNCS 9975, pp. 163–172, 2016.
DOI: 10.1007/978-3-319-47717-6_14

Since ontological theories form the foundations of ODCM, consequently the metaphysical characteristics of a particular ontology (i.e. its philosophical concepts and structures) influence the conceptualizations that are produced. Moreover, because many different kinds of ontologies exist, their choice should be well motivated. For example, based upon the endurantism-perdurantism paradigm, we can distinguish between 3D and 4D ontologies. *3D ontologies* view individual objects as three-dimensional, having only spatial parts, and wholly exist at each moment of their existence. *4D ontologies* on the contrary, see individual objects as four-dimensional, having spatial and temporal parts, and exist immutably in space-time [5]. The relevance between applying these different paradigms has been demonstrated in several research efforts. For example, in the theoretical research of [6], the 3D object-role modeling (ORM) paradigm was analytically compared to the 4D object paradigm (OP). The conducted comparison reveals that the OP paradigm can provide semantically richer representations of phenomena than the ORM paradigm. Also [7, 8] theoretically examined the way in which a 3D foundational ontology (UFO) and a 4D foundational ontology (BORO) represent temporal changes, concluding that each of the ontologies can lead to different representations and interpretations.

Therefore, in this paper, we intend to investigate the impact of adopting a 3D and 4D ontology on the quality of a conceptualization. More specifically, we regard the pragmatic quality of the model, by determining the influence of the ontology on the comprehension and understandability of the model by its users. Because little empirical research has yet been performed on this topic [3, 4], we intend to conduct an empirical comparison. Further, since it's the goal of this paper to gain more insight on the comprehension of the models generated by these foundational ontologies, and not to test if one is better than the other, we conduct an exploratory analysis. In summary, we can formulate the *research question* of this paper as: which are the differences in comprehension between adopting either a 3D or 4D ontology for the representation of conceptual models?

In Sect. 2, we will explain how the exploratory research will be conducted and which ontologies have been selected for the comparison. Section 3 presents the results of our empirical comparison. Section 4 formulates several hypotheses for further empirical research based upon the outcome and interpretation of the results. Finally, Sect. 5 presents our conclusion.

## 2    Design of Empirical Comparison

Every foundational ontology has their own metaphysical characteristics that define how they describe general concepts such as space, time, matter, object, event, action, etc. [9]. Based upon these characteristics, we can distinguish different kind of foundational ontologies, which represents real world phenomena in their specific way. The main differences between 3D and 4D ontologies depend on how they define spatio-temporal entities, their locations in space-time, and their different modes of persistence. More specifically, these differences can be translated in their ontological interpretation of the following metaphysical characteristics: (1) *The notion of identity and essence defining properties*: defines how the ontology assigns a principle of identity to its entities and how it deals with temporary entities such as roles, states and phases. (2) *The perception and endurance of time*: defines how entities begin and cease to exist over time, and how they perceive events and changes. (3) *The formation of relations*: describes how entities form relationships and how they can become part of each other or be separated from one another. Since we intend to investigate the influence of a 3D and a 4D ontology-driven model on the comprehension by its users, we will develop our empirical comparison on these metaphysical characteristics, highlighting their ontological differences. We will thus compare a specific 3D and a 4D ontology and identify the impact of the differences in their metaphysical characteristics on the interpretation of the ontology-driven models.

The ontologies that will be compared are UFO (Unified Foundational Ontology) [10] and BORO (Business Object Reference Ontology) [11]. While UFO is a 3D ontology, having a focus on endurants, BORO was developed as an ontology of perdurants, i.e. a 4D ontology. They are both foundational ontologies, which are frequently applied in the domain of conceptual modeling. We will not cover all the concepts of both ontologies in this paper. Instead, for a more detailed reading of these ontologies, we refer the reader for UFO to [10, 12] and for BORO to [7, 11].

To perform our comparison, we follow the approaches as defined in [13, 14]. Akin to our purpose, these papers compared the comprehension of different models that were constructed with different techniques. The comprehension of the models was compared through two kinds of questions: comprehension questions (CQ) and problem-solving questions (PQ). While the CQs assess the basic level of understanding, the PQs are more challenging and target a deeper level of understanding. Similarly, we developed three ontology-driven models of both BORO and UFO, where every model emphasizes one of the metaphysical characteristics as described above. Every one of these models has been presented to, and approved by, an expert of the respective ontology. We created two treatments of groups of each six subjects where one group of subjects was given the UFO-driven models while the other group was given the BORO-driven models. All subjects had prior experience and education in the domain of conceptual modeling, and were either completing their Masters or PhD degree at the University of Ghent. None of the subjects had former knowledge of the ontology they had to use.

During the experiment, our subjects were required to first interpret the ontology-driven model, and then answer the CQs and PQs that assessed their level of understanding. To closely follow the comprehension process from our subjects, we examined their progress in the form of a protocol analysis, as performed by [14]. The data obtained from a protocol analysis method reveals the mental processes taking place as individuals work on the interpretation of the models. Subjects are required to verbalize their thought processes and strategies, as well verbalize their answers to the CQs and PQs. In line with other protocol analysis studies [15, 16], the number of subjects was small (12 subjects), as a large volume of data is generated even with this small sample size. The interpretation of the models by the subject is evaluated according to the correctness of the answers. Both the outcome of the protocol analysis and the correctness scores of the subjects' answers are then combined to assess the differences in interpretation between the UFO and BORO models. The comparison of the models was conducted as follows:

1. *Familiarization with the ontology & Interpretation of the models.*

Depending on the treatment, subjects are familiarized with either UFO or BORO. The ontology and its syntax are explained by the aid of a description of the ontology and several modeling examples. For both treatments, we have used the syntax in which they are normally expressed. For UFO we relied on the OntoUML language, a UML profile that reflects the ontological distinctions prescribed by UFO [10], while for BORO we constructed the models in space-time maps as is often employed in the associated BORO literature [11]. Each subject could take as much time as needed to read and understand the description. Overall, there were no issues reported with the misunderstanding of the description of the ontologies or their syntax.

After the subjects were familiarized with the respective ontology, they were given three assignments, each containing a model and a set of CQs and PQs. Each assignment was given without any additional explanation. All models in UFO and BORO were the informational equivalents of each other and represented an identical scenario. The difference between these models originated from the metaphysical characteristics of the respective ontology. Of course it is unattainable to have one scenario deal with solely one metaphysical property. Instead the models and their associated questions were designed so they would focus on a certain characteristic:

- **Assignment 1:** focused on the notion of identity and essence defining properties, where the model represents a scenario where a person 'John' is a customer of a company '4Energy'.
- **Assignment 2:** highlighted the perception and endurance of time. The model represents a scenario where two chemical substances (Zinc and Sulphate) are fused together by an industrial process into a new chemical substance (Zinc Sulphate).
- **Assignment 3:** focused on the formation of relations between entities, where the model represents a scenario of an engine that is first owned by the company '4Energy' but changes ownership after a transaction to the company 'Tesla', where it becomes part of the car 'Model S'.

## 2.  *Comprehension Questions*

After the subjects interpreted the model, they had to answer a set of CQs to assess their interpretation. The CQs serve two purposes: first they aim to evaluate if a subject fully understood what kind of scenario the model was representing. Second, they assessed if the subject could identify every concept in the model to the correct concept of the ontology. A score was given based upon their comprehension and the correct identification of the appropriate constructs of the model to the proper concepts in the ontology. The CQs allowed us to evaluate if subjects not only correctly interpreted the ontology-driven model, but also understood the underlying structure and meaning of the concepts. As an example, the CQs that were asked during the first assignment are the following:

- **CQ1:** Explain the scenario that is being represented by the model;
- **CQ2:** Assign the correct model construct to the concept in [UFO/BORO].

Depending on the structure of the model, all CQs were the same for both the UFO assignments as for the BORO assignments, except for individual differences in the model constructs between BORO and UFO. During the experiment, the time was measured that the subjects needed to complete the CQs. This allowed us to better estimate the difficulty subjects had to complete the questions, and to compare the time difference between the assignments.

### 3. *Problem-solving questions*

After the subjects completed the CQs, they had to answer several PQs. The PQs assess a deeper level of understanding, by letting the subjects make modifications and apply new concepts and relationships to the ontology-driven models. Again, a score was assigned to every answer, depending on the correct modifications in the model. The time each subject needed was measured to estimate the difficulty in completing the PQs, and to compare the time difference between the assignments. During the experiment, all subjects were asked to draw their modifications onto the existing models. This allowed us to better estimate their full understanding of the model and the ontology in answering the PQs. The PQs were identical for both the UFO and BORO assignments. As an example, the PQs for the first assignment were:

- **PQ1**: Consider a competitor of the company 4Energy, named Pearson, which offers electricity utilities to its customers. How would Pearson be represented?
- **PQ2**: If John would end its contract with 4Energy, and start a new contract with Pearson, how would this affect the current model?

### 4. *Post Test Questions*

A post test question was asked at the end of every assignment to assess if the CQs or the PQs were perceived as most difficult. After all three assignments were completed, a final post test question was asked where the subjects had to indicate which assignment was perceived as the most intensive to solve, for either the UFO or BORO-driven models. As such, we could link the difficulty of solving the assignments to the metaphysical characteristics of an ontology and how they are expressed in a model.

## 3   Results

Our results suggest that there are meaningful differences in the comprehension of the ontology-driven models. As a first indicator, we consider the average time needed for all subjects to solve each assignment. The time differences are displayed in Table 1 and are expressed in minutes and seconds. The UFO subjects needed more time to solve the assignments, whereas the third assignment is the exception. When considering their feedback, this is caused by the numerous concepts that exist in UFO and their rather complex hierarchy. Practically every subject reported after reading the description that the ontology was somewhat overwhelming. Several subjects also pointed out that the naming of certain terms in UFO (rigid, sortal etc.) did not have any familiar meaning to the subjects, making it more difficult to remember and apply these concepts. Further, when solving the assignments, we noticed there was often doubt which concepts of a model was associated to which concept in UFO, especially in the beginning of the experiment. On the contrary, since the BORO ontology exists out of only a few concepts, subjects reported the ontology as clear and accessible to comprehend.

**Table 1.** Average time differences between BORO and UFO for solving the assignments (A)

|  | A1 | A2 | A3 |
|---|---|---|---|
| BORO | 09:10 | 14:00 | 15:20 |
| UFO | 15:20 | 17:15 | 12:58 |

Similar observations can be found regarding the CQs of every assignment. In general for both UFO and BORO, most of the subjects had no real difficulties in answering CQ1 and were able to correctly explain what every model was trying to represent. However, when the subjects had to complete CQ2, we noticed explicit differences between both ontologies. In Table 2, we display the average results, on a total of 10, for the identification of the appropriate concepts in CQ2 of every assignment. Subjects scored considerably less in assigning the correct UFO concepts (6.7) compared to assigning the correct BORO concepts (7.7). Especially in the first and second assignments, subjects struggled to find the correct UFO terms. Regarding their feedback, we noticed a great deal of confusion associated with the concepts Role, Kind, SubKind, RoleMixin and Individual. Most of the difficulties can be related to the different kind of identity criteria that UFO dictates, i.e. the principle of application, the principle of identity and the notion of rigidity. Most of the confusion in the second assignment was due to the concepts Relator and Event. Because a Relator can for instance be named as 'Manufacturing', often they were associated as Events, or vice versa, Events that were mistaken as Relators. Several subjects also commented that the structure of the Relator concept, was peculiar, in the sense that the material relationship was deemed unnecessary since the Relator already described what the nature of the relationship between two concepts was. However, when subjects moved to the third assignment, we noticed a growing understanding in the concepts of UFO. Fewer difficulties were reported and we could clearly observe that the subjects became more familiar with these concepts and their meaning.

**Table 2.** Average results (on 10) of CQ2 between BORO and UFO for every assignment (A)

|  | A1 | A2 | A3 | Average Results |
|---|---|---|---|---|
| BORO | 8.1 | 7.3 | 7.7 | 7.7 |
| UFO | 6.5 | 5.5 | 8.0 | 6.7 |

Concerning the CQ2 of BORO, we noticed that most of the faults arose from confusing States with Elements or incorrectly interpreting Temporal and Whole Parts as Elements. We further noticed that subjects slightly experienced more trouble in comprehending the second assignment. Even in the third assignment, there was still often doubt between States and Temporal/Whole part relations, indicating that a full comprehension of these concepts was still lacking. This observation is confirmed when looking at the results and feedback of the PQs.

Table 3 displays the average results, on a total of 10, of the PQs for every assignment of the BORO and UFO-driven models. Contrary to the results of the CQs, subjects scored meaningfully lower on the PQs for the BORO-driven models (6.5) compared to the UFO-driven models (8.2). When completing the PQs related to BORO, again, most of the confusion arose from applying a State or an Element to a new concept. Also modifying the Temporal or Whole part relationships were often perceived as complex. Additionally, the PQs revealed that the subjects experienced difficulty understanding the spatial-temporal extensions of Elements, a specific characterization of 4D ontologies. Our subjects reported it as unnatural that the spatial extension of an element can expand or diminish, with for example the formation or ending of temporal part relationships. Similarly, complications arose when dealing with the time extensions of Elements or States. An often-heard remark was how space can be scaled on an axis in an objective matter.

**Table 3.** Average results (on 10) of PQs between BORO and UFO for every assignment (A)

|        | A1  | A2  | A3  | Average Results |
|--------|-----|-----|-----|-----------------|
| BORO   | 7.9 | 5.4 | 6.2 | 6.5             |
| UFO    | 9.6 | 6.7 | 8.3 | 8.2             |

As for the PQs associated to UFO, it seemed that the difficulties experienced during the CQs, increased the subjects' understanding of the concepts and made them think more thoroughly about the structure of the model. Most of the mistakes that were reported during the PQs could be related to the confusion of identity between Kinds, SubKinds or Roles, and the Relator and Event concepts.

Finally, when considering the post-test questions results, we notice that they are in line with the difficulties experienced in the assignments. Table 4 displays the number of subjects that assigned either the CQs or the PQs as most difficult to complete. We observe that subjects of the BORO group experienced more difficulties with solving the PQs compared with the CQs. Subjects had no real difficulties in relating the concepts in the model to the concepts in BORO. When this knowledge however had to be administered in the PQs, it seems that applying the principles and characteristics of BORO were less straightforward. On the opposite, subjects dealing with UFO struggled more with the CQs and identifying the correct concepts in the model. However, because the subjects had spent considerable time in investigating the model when completing the CQs, the PQs became easier to solve.

**Table 4.** Number of subjects per post-test questions for every assignment (A)

|        | A1 |    | A2 |    | A3 |    |
|--------|----|----|----|----|----|----|
|        | CQ | PQ | CQ | PQ | CQ | PQ |
| BORO   | 2  | 4  | 1  | 5  | 3  | 3  |
| UFO    | 6  | 0  | 3  | 3  | 3  | 3  |

Considering the final post-test question, for the BORO treatment, four of the subjects appointed the third assignment as the most difficult to solve, while two subjects appointed the second assignment as the hardest to complete. As for the UFO subjects, three appointed the first assignment; two subjects indicated the second assignment and one subject appointed the third assignment as most difficult.

## 4   Discussion

The results of our exploratory analysis demonstrate that the conceptualizations that are realized by two different ontologies have a considerable impact on the understanding and comprehension of its users. Our results suggest that depending on the metaphysical characteristics of an ontology, some ontology-driven models are perceived as more easy or difficult to comprehend. Consequently, these metaphysical characteristics determine the quality of the conceptualizations. Since little empirical research has yet been performed in this area, we will formulate several hypotheses that are derived from the results and observations from our exploratory analysis. These hypotheses can then serve as a testing ground for future empirical research in order to investigate the fundamental differences between 3D and 4D ontology-driven models.

**Hypothesis 1:** *The notion of identity and essence defining properties is more difficult to comprehend with 3D ontology-driven models than with 4D ontology-driven models.* As our results indicate, subjects dealing with the 3D ontology-driven models appointed the assignment that focused on identity and essence defining properties as the most difficult to comprehend. This hypothesis is further confirmed when regarding the answers to the post-test questions, where all of our subjects acknowledged that the CQs of the first assignment were the most difficult. Much of the feedback reported that subjects experienced difficulties in distinguishing the many types of identity criteria that are needed to identify the concepts of the ontology-driven models.

**Hypothesis 2:** *The formation of relations between entities is more difficult to comprehend with 4D ontology-driven models than with 3D ontology-driven models.* Our second hypothesis is derived from the observation that most of the subjects of the 4D ontology appointed the third assignment, focusing on the formation of relations between entities, as most difficult. Also, the time needed to solve this assignment was the highest compared to the other assignments. Feedback reported that several concepts were difficult to comprehend and felt unnatural to several of our subjects.

**Hypothesis 3:** *The learning curve in understanding 4D ontology-driven models is higher than for 3D ontology-driven models.* As regards to the comments of our subjects of the 3D ontology, we observe a pattern, where initially the ontology was experienced as complex to understand. However, after the completion of every assignment, subjects reported that they could better comprehend the underlying concepts and structures. For example, the highest score of the CQs is achieved in the last assignment. Further because most of the subjects experienced rather some difficulty in solving the CQs, it made them think more thoroughly about the model. As a consequence, the PQs were easier to complete and achieved higher scores. The opposite tendency was observed for the comprehension of the 4D ontology-driven models. Initially, many subjects reported the ontology as easy to comprehend. When completing the CQs, more doubt could be observed from our subjects. The real difficulties however were experienced during the PQs, where subjects had to append new concepts or modify existing elements. We noticed that a true understanding of the ontology was still lacking. As a result, the subjects scored less on the PQs compared to the CQs. Concerning the post-test questions, the PQs were rated as more difficult to complete. It would thus seem that 3D ontology-driven models are more quickly understood over time in comparison to 4D ontology-driven models.

**Hypothesis 4:**  *There is no clear difference in comprehension between the representation of time in 3D or 4D ontology-driven models.* Contrary to what is sometimes claimed [6, 8], we did not observe any considerable differences in the comprehension of models representing time with a 3D or 4D ontology. Subjects of both the 3D and 4D treatment experienced a similar amount of difficulties with completing the second assignment, which focuses on the metaphysical characteristic of time and change. Both groups received the lowest scores in this assignment, for both the CQs as well as for the PQs. Further, an equal number of subjects from the 3D ontology and the 4D ontology acknowledged the second assignment as the most difficult to complete. We can therefore not deduce from our exploratory study that 4D ontology-driven models are better at representing time scenarios than 3D ontology-driven models.

## 5  Conclusion

This research performed an exploratory analysis on the differences in comprehension and understanding of 3D and 4D ontology-driven models. The results of our exploratory analysis revealed that the conceptualizations that are realized by the 3D or 4D ontology have a considerable impact on the understanding and comprehension of its users. Depending on the metaphysical characteristics of an ontology, some ontology-driven models were perceived as more easy or difficult to comprehend. These results therefore indicate that the metaphysical characteristics of a particular ontology influence the quality of the conceptualizations that are produced. Since little empirical research has yet been performed in this area, we formulated several hypotheses that are derived from the results of our exploratory analysis to serve as a testing ground for future empirical research on this topic.

**Threats to validity.**  Due to the low number of participants participating in the exploratory study validity is threatened, as recognized by the authors. Additionally, more ontologies can be further compared to identify the differences between 3D and 4D ontologies. Therefore, it is the authors' intention to conduct further validation in the form of a full experimental comparison.

**Acknowledgements.**  We would like to express our sincere gratitude to Chris Partridge, of the BORO Solutions Group, and Maria das Graças da Silva Teixeira, of the Ontology and Conceptual Modeling Research Group (NEMO), for their detailed reading and revisions of the respective BORO and UFO ontology-driven models applied in this research.

# References

1. Lindland, O.I., Sindre, G., Solvberg, A.: Understanding quality in conceptual modeling. IEEE Softw. **11**, 42–49 (1994)
2. Wand, Y., Weber, R.: On the ontological expressiveness of information systems analysis and design grammars. Inf. Syst. J. **3**, 217–237 (1993)
3. Moody, D.L.: Theoretical and practical issues in evaluating the quality of conceptual models: current state and future directions. Data Knowl. Eng. **55**, 243–276 (2005)
4. Verdonck, G., de Cesare, F.S., Poels, G.: Ontology-driven conceptual modeling: A systematic literature mapping and review. Appl. Ontol. **10**, 197–227 (2015)
5. Hales, S.D.S., Johnson, T.T.A.: Endurantism, perdurantism and special relativity. Philos. Q. **53**, 524–539 (2003)
6. Al Debei, M.M.: Conceptual modelling and the quality of ontologies: endurantism vs perdurantism. Int. J. Database Manag. Syst. **4**, 1–19 (2012)
7. de Cesare, S., Henderson-Sellers, B., Partridge, C., Lycett, M.: Improving model quality through foundational ontologies: two contrasting approaches to the representation of roles. ER **2015**, 304–314 (2015)
8. Verdonck, M., Gailly, F., Poels, G.: 3D vs. 4D ontologies in enterprise modeling. In: Indulska, M., Purao, S. (eds.) ER Workshops 2014. LNCS, vol. 8823, pp. 13–22. Springer, Heidelberg (2014)
9. Poli, R., Healy, M., Kameas, A.: Theory and applications of ontology: Computer applications. Springer, Heidelberg (2010)
10. Guizzardi, G.: Ontological foundations for structural conceptual models. In: CTIT, Centre for Telematics and Information Technology (2005)
11. Partridge, C.: Business Objects: Re-engineering for Reuse. Butterworth-Heinemann, Oxford (2005)
12. Guizzardi, G., Wagner, G.: Towards ontological foundations for agent modelling concepts using the unified fundational ontology (UFO). Agent-Oriented Inf. Syst. **II**(3508), 110–124 (2005)
13. Gemino, A., Wand, Y.: Complexity and clarity in conceptual modeling: Comparison of mandatory and optional properties. Data Knowl. Eng. **55**, 301–326 (2005)
14. Vessey, I., Conger, S.A.: Requirements specification: learning object, process, and data methodologies. Commun. ACM **37**, 102–113 (1994)
15. Bera, P.: Analyzing the cognitive difficulties for developing and using UML class diagrams for domain understanding. J. Database Manag. **23**, 1–29 (2012)
16. Shanks, G., Tansley, E., Nuredini, J., Tobin, D., Weber, R.: Representing part-whole relations in conceptual modeling: an emperical evaluation. MIS Q. **32**, 553–573 (2008)

# Data Quality Problems When Integrating Genomic Information

Ana León$^{(\boxtimes)}$, José Reyes, Verónica Burriel, and Francisco Valverde

Research Center on Software Production Methods (PROS),
Universitat Politècnica de València, Camino de Vera S/N, 46022 Valencia, Spain
aleon@pros.upv.es

**Abstract.** Due to the complexity of genomic information and the broad amount of data produced every day, the genomic information accessible on the web has become very difficult to integrate, which hinders the research process. Using the knowledge from the Data Quality field and after a specific study of a set of genomic databases we have found problems related to six Data Quality dimensions. The aim of this paper is to highlight the problems that bioinformaticians have to face when they integrate information from different genomic databases. The contribution of this paper is to identify and characterize those problems in order to understand which ones hinder the research process, increasing the time-waste that this task means for researchers.

**Keywords:** Data quality · Data integration · Genomic databases

## 1 Introduction

To gather and integrate data from multiple databases is a problem that has to be faced every day in multiple domains: business, private enterprises, public healthcare, etc. but probably genomic information is much more difficult to handle due to its complexity and heterogeneity. The knowledge is evolving every day and Next Generation Sequencing (NGS) technology allows researchers to sequence DNA and RNA quicker and cheaper than before. All this information is uploaded and spread to online databases in order to be accessible to the research community. A complex part of the research process involves to be able to manage in an unified and holistic way all this complex information. Conceptually speaking, it is essential to gather this wide-spread data under a single information perspective without loosing quality. The lack of standards and strict enough quality controls to submit information to databases drive to an inefficient management of multiple genome databases and a time-consuming for scientists. In this context, the main contribution of this paper is (i) to select a set of data quality dimensions to be used for assessing quality of genome data, and (ii) to apply them to a set of genomic databases to have a perspective of how difficult the integration among them could be.

To achieve these goals the rest of the paper is structured as follows. In Sect. 2 the concept of Data Quality (DQ) is introduced and it is also highlighted its

© Springer International Publishing AG 2016
S. Link and J.C. Trujillo (Eds.): ER 2016 Workshops, LNCS 9975, pp. 173–182, 2016.
DOI: 10.1007/978-3-319-47717-6_15

importance when dealing with genomic information. Next, in Sect. 3 we propose a set of data quality dimensions and how they could be measured, which are interesting in the DQ assessment of genomic databases. In Sect. 4 a set of quality errors found in common genomic databases are shown, classified by dimension and explained with specific examples. Finally, Sect. 5 contains the conclusions and future work.

## 2  Data Quality in Genomics - State of the Art

The great amount of genomic information produced every day requires specific ways of analysing, storing and assuring the quality of data in order to take advantage of the generated knowledge. But what does Data Quality (DQ) mean?

Wang et al. [29] have defined DQ as data that are "fitness for use", i.e. data that are useful for the purpose it was created for. DQ is a multidimensional concept where a data quality dimension is defined as a set of attributes, that can be assessed in order to get a quantitative measure representing the quality of the data that are being managed.

Even though DQ has been studied for decades it has been mainly applied to the business field. DQ in genomics is an emerging field, which is getting very close to the Big Data field. The great amount of data and the diversity of data sources brings abundant data types and complex data structures, which increases the difficulty of data integration. Besides, genomic information is very complex and the current knowledge is changing every day to be adapted to the new discoveries. Some ISO standards have been developed to assess data quality: ISO-8000 is the international standard for Data Quality (under development), ISO-9000 is an standard for quality management systems and ISO-9126-1 has been developed for assessing software product quality. But there is a lack of standards in DQ assessment when using big data and genomic information.

## 3  Materials and Methods

A large list of DQDs proposed to assess DQ can be found in literature. For example, Wang identified four categories containing fifteen DQDs [29]. Because of the characteristics of the genomic domain, not all of them are useful for our purpose. Based on some relevant studies in DQ [1,14,28] a set of DQDs, useful for Data Quality assessment in genomic databases, has been gathered along with their definitions and measures. Once the DQDs have been selected, different types of genomic databases where analysed in order to determine the most common quality errors.

### 3.1  Data Quality Dimensions

There is not consensus in the number, importance and definition of the dimensions needed to assess data quality. But there is a set of common dimensions, proposed by Askham, which can be applied to genomic databases [1]:

- **Accuracy:** Data correspond to real-world values and are correct.
- **Completeness:** The extent to which data is not missing and all necessary values are represented.
- **Consistency:** Data must be consistent between systems and represented in the same format.
- **Uniqueness:** The database won't have redundant data or duplicate records.
- **Currency:** The extent to which data is sufficiently up-to-date for the task at hand.
- **Reliability:** The extent to which data is regarded as true and credible.

There is an important difference between two time-related data quality dimensions - currency and timeliness. As Loshin explains in [10] currency refers to how up-to-date data is, and whether it is correct, despite the possibility of modifications or changes that impact time and date values. Meanwhile, timeliness refers to the time between when data is expected and when it is readily available for use. We have considered that currency dimension fits our purposes better than timeliness dimension.

The dimensions mentioned above are related to each other. For example, consistency errors lead to accuracy and uniqueness problems: if the information are not standardized and does not have rules to store data properly it means that erroneous or duplicated data can be submitted to the database. Besides, if the information is incomplete or obsolete it cannot be considered as reliable. In the same way, if the database is difficult to be maintained there will be more probabilities of having obsolete or erroneous data.

### 3.2   Application to Genomic Databases

In order to gather the most frequent data quality errors affecting to genomic databases, a literature review and specific queries, based on previous studies and personal knowledge, were performed in different databases. Once the errors have been identified, they were classified according to the DQDs previously defined.

The analysed genomic databases belong to different domains:

- **Sequence databases:** RefSeq, Ensembl and GenBank.
- **Protein databases:** BioGrid, UniProt (UniProtKB, UniRef and UniParc).
- **Mutation databases:** HGMD, dbSNP and ClinVar.
- **Other databases:** UCSC, Alzforum Mutation and Niagads.

This heterogeneous set of databases allows us to determine the concrete quality problems which affects to each type.

## 4   Results

In the following subsections we present the most common errors found by dimension, cause and percentage in which the database is currently affected.

## 4.1   Accuracy

Accuracy is a dimension that mainly affects to primary databases. These databases are warehouses where raw genome sequences are submitted by researchers and not reviewed by external experts. This means that they only store data and they can have duplicated information and errors.

**Sequence errors:** Krawetz et al. determined in [9] the Error Rate (ER) of nucleic acid sequence data interpretation by assessing and quantifying the discrepancies reported in the version 55 of GenBank database. His study revealed that the ER was 2.887 errors per 1000 bases. The highest ER was observed in the RNA (structural RNA) with 48.8 errors per 1000 bases. Nowadays, the advances in sequencing procedures and quality checks performed on every sequence submitted to GenBank maintained the error rate <1 in 10,000 bases for the Human Genome Project [2]. Based on the study performed by Krawetz in [9], we have used the suggested keywords to find the well-defined and documented discrepancies (conflict, revision, corrections, differences, error or unsure). In the current version of GenBank database (release 213) only 0.8 % of sequences present documented discrepancies. Attending only to homo sapiens organism, the percentage is 0.5 %. This analysis does not consider entries without a reported discrepancy, correct or incorrect. It means that the percentage of erroneous sequences must be at least 0.8 % but it cannot be established for sure. As Moran highlights in [11], GenBank is full of sequences that are known to be incorrect but the corrections are not always made: "Most of the authors were unwilling to allow changes'cause they weren't aware of the fact that there was a conflict between their sequences and the aligned sequence database. They didn't even know that others had sequenced the same gene and gotten a different sequence.

Attending to protein databases, SwissProt is the reviewed section of the UniProtKB database. Once the sequences are reviewed by experts, any sequence conflict is annotated. Using this knowledge, we have made an analysis of human protein sequences in current release 2016_6. The analysis results indicates that 86.98 % of the reviewed sequences have errors: 54 % of them were sequence conflicts and 23 % were problems in the sequence initiation.

**Taxonomical errors:** Accuracy of taxonomic identifications is crucial because these data serve as basis for large scale analysis of macroecological and biogeographic patterns, and to document environmental changes over time [16]. However, especially for fungi, about 20 % of sequence entries, including approximately 700,000 ITS barcoding sequences, have been estimated to be incorrectly labelled.

**Curation errors:** The information that describes the function of sequences is very important to researchers to do their laboratory investigations and when they are making computational inferences. However, public protein databases have a high-error rate, depending on the method used to annotate the sequences. A study made by Schnoes et al. about the miss-annotation levels for molecular function in four public protein sequence databases [15], reveals that those which use computational prediction for molecular functions have more errors than those which use manual annotations. SwissProt uses manual annotation and the error percentage is almost 0 %, but other databases such as GenBank NR, TrEMBL and KEGG, which use automatic annotations, presents even over 60 % rate of errors. In another study made by Jones in the Gene Ontology database [7], it was estimated that up to 49 % of computationally annotate sequences using sequence similarity methodology ISS are miss-annotated.

We have performed a study of the current state of TrEMBL release 2016_06 (the not reviewed database of UniProtKB). We have chosen a dataset of 134,236 human sequences. The analysis performed have indicated that 35 % of sequences have been marked with a caution annotation, which means that the sequences have been derived and they should be considered as preliminary data. With regard to function, only 9 % of sequences have been annotated but almost 100 % of them have been automatically annotated so, based on Schnoes et al. study in [15] 60 % of these annotations may be erroneous. Corrections to these errors may never occur so new annotations may be based on erroneous miss-annotations, and so on. Such error chains can lead to the progressive increase in annotation error rates.

Even though accuracy errors in primary databases are frequently mentioned in the literature we have found that there is a lack of updated studies about the impact of this kind of errors. The advances in sequencing technologies have increased the number of submitted sequences to databases, making the analysis difficult to perform. But these technologies are supposed to increase quality too. The taxonomic errors (mainly for plants) and functional curation errors (mainly in automatic curation for proteins) stand out among the others, so these are the type of errors that must be taken into account when trying to assess accuracy. However, proper studies about the real impact of sequence errors must be performed because our results show a high percentage of errors in manually reviewed protein sequences. Due to the increase of cross-references among databases errors can be quickly propagated.

## 4.2 Completeness

There are several ways to assess completeness in a genomic database, such as checking for missing values. To assess the percentage of missing values we have looked for human proteins and their function in the SwissProt database 2016_06. From 20,200 entries, only 23,6 % have information about protein function.

UniProtKB also allows users to know how complete the information of an entry is, by consulting a field called "Annotation score". The annotation score provides a heuristic measure of the annotation content of a UniProtKB entry or proteome. It is a number in the range 1 to 5 which help users to get a quick idea of the relative level of annotation of the entries in a search results [22]. Entries which belong to a manually annotated database, like SwissProt, have a higher level of annotations (60 % of entries with annotation score = 5) than those belonging to automatically annotated databases, like TrEMBL (almost 90 % of entries with annotation score = 1). According to the results, SwissProt can be considered much more complete than TrEMBL.

In regard to completeness we have found that a common problem is the one related to missing values. Manually annotated databases are more accurate than automatically curated ones but, because of their cost of maintenance, their number of registers is lower.

## 4.3  Reliability

The reliability of the information stored in a database is very important, particularly when trying to get conclusions from data that are not well supported by published research. For example, genes can be characterized in direct experiments or by transfer of information from the few characterized sequences on the basis of sequence similarity.

UniProtKB provides information about the type of evidence that supports the existence of a protein [27]. A comparison of the distribution of evidence in UniProtKB database have been made. According to the results, 54 % sequences from SwissProt and 93 % sequences from TrEMBL provides experimental evidence. In the same way, 46 % sequences of SwissProt and only 7 % sequences from TrEMBL doesn't have experimental evidence. There is a significant difference in the % of sequences without experimental evidence between SwissProt and TrEMBL. As mentioned before, SwissProt is manually curated and most of the sequences are inherited from TrEMBL. This suggests that maybe most of the sequences annotated as having experimental evidence don't have it really. Regarding to the results, SwissProt can be considered more reliable than TrEMBL.

In databases based on genotype-phenotype relationships like ClinVar, reliability measurement can be done by checking the level of review supporting the assertion of clinical significance, or the type of reports associated to each variation.

Using a dataset for human variations, 94 % of entries do not have assertion criteria to the provided clinical significance. In the same way, the reliability of variations can be measured by checking the type of reports associated to each variation. Using a dataset for Alzheimer's disease, only 4.8 % of sequences are supported for clinical testing reports, 3.2 % are supported for research reports and 92 % are supported by literature only.

Reliability is very important to infer proper conclusions from the information collected, but most of the databases have a lack of experimental evidences. Most of them are derived from other evidences based on similarity sequences.

## 4.4  Consistency

In order to obtain results more biologically meaningful, it is important to incorporate information from different biological repositories into the analysis. If data structures were consistent between systems, the integration from different resources would be easy. But genomic databases are very diverse, making extremely laborious to perform even simple queries across databases. Most of genomic databases provides all their data, or part of them, within text files in different formats, including flat, tabular, XML and RDF formats. Changes in data file structure are frequent and they can produce errors when importing or integrating data. For example, a study made by Soh in pathway databases highlights that the level of consistency for genes in similar pathways across databases ranges from 0 % to 88 % [17]. The corresponding level of consistency for interacting genes pairs is 0 %–61 %.

Following, some specific examples of consistency problems are presented:

- To represent the information related to the type of variation, Ensembl uses the attribute "Class attr id" which references a list of 21 types based on Sequence Ontology, dbSNP uses the attribute "Variation Class" based on 8 types of variations and UCSC uses the attribute "snpType" where only 3 types are referenced. The most common types of variations are Insertion, Deletion and Substitution, but based on the types mentioned above the problem is that each database uses its own term:
  - Ensembl: Insertion, Deletion and Substitution.
  - dbSNP: DIV (Insertion/Deletion Variation) and none for Substitution.
  - UCSC: I (Insertion), D (Deletion) and S (Substitution).
- Sometimes, the problem is the format in which the information is represented. ClinVar represents the chromosome only with the number and Niagads uses the format chr+number (i.e. chr1).

Consistency errors mean that a previous understanding and normalization step is required, which is complicated because of the genomic information complexity. Each database stores information on its own format and without a proper standard, which means that integration becomes a laborious process.

## 4.5 Uniqueness

The number of entries in genomic databases has grown exponentially in the last few years and this increase was accompanied by a high level of redundancy. One of the affected databases was the not reviewed UniProtKB (TrEMBL), specially for bacterial species. In a publication made in their official web page [23] they hinder that it was becoming a noteworthy problem so, since UniProt release 2015 04, a Proteome Redundancy Detector was used in order to discard entries belonging to redundant proteomes of bacterial species in the not reviewed UniProtKB (TrEMBL) set. After applying the method for the first time 46.9 million entries were removed from UniProtKB.

## 4.6 Currency

Currency dimension is related to accuracy and reliability because obsolete data can't be considered as accurate and reliable. It is very common to find cross references among biological databases to complete and improve the information stored. When records are updated, merged or deleted in one database, the reference usually gets obsolete in the others. This situation decreases the data quality of the information. For example, as of September 2016, the integer sequence identifiers known as "GIs" will no longer be included in the GenBank, GenPept, and FASTA formats supported by the NCBI for sequence records [12]. This means that all databases with "GI" references will have to use "accession.version" identifiers instead. If the information stored is not updated, the reference of all affected records will be obsolete.

Another example of currency issues is that proteins may exist in different source databases and in multiple copies in the same database. UniParc [21] avoids such redundancy by storing each unique sequence only once and giving it a unique identifier (UPI). Among the information provided by UniParc it is the UniProtKB references describing each protein. Some of these entries are marked as obsolete which means that they are not active. UniParc version "2016_06" stores 120,721,825 protein sequences with 9,351,506 UniProtKB references and 396,331 of them are marked as obsolete (4.23 %).

To know how old the information are in UniProtKB 2016_06, we performed a search for all active homo sapiens protein sequences. The result was a set of 153,653 entries. Using the fields "Date of creation" and "Date of last sequence modification", several conclusions for the currency were made. The mean age of the sequences are 7 years and 1 % were created 25 years ago at least. We have also found that 2.1 % sequences haven't been modified in the last 20 years and most of sequences have been modified 4–5 years ago.

UniProtKB is an active database, which is updated frequently. The percentage of obsolete and old entries are low so, it can be considered a trustworthy database regarding to currency.

Currency of information is important because of the evolution of knowledge. Even though the number of sequences which are over 25 years old is low, the age of the information should be taken into account too. To measure currency, information about date of sequence creation and modification is needed, but not all databases provide this type of data.

# 5   Conclusions

Biology system databases are becoming quite relevant in finding relationships among the biological information by integrating data from multiple databases. The lack of proper standards for data quality assessment in Big Data and Genomic Data fields, means that each integration system must develop its own quality assessment method. Based on the results of our study, we think that genomic databases should focus in assessing, solving and providing information about (i) taxonomic and functional curation accuracy (ii) completeness, (iii) evidence reliability, (iv) redundancy, (v) data currency and (vi) the use of standards to assure information consistency. This would increase the efficiency of the process, assuring the quality of the information gathered. Besides, it would decrease the time that genomic researchers have to spend, analysing and verifying quality information among crossed databases. This means that they could focus in the core of their research and not in data management.

The refinement of the data quality dimensions proposed, by defining proper attributes and measures adapted to genomic databases, would provide the base to define a framework to assess data quality as a future work.

# References

1. Askham, N., Cook, D., Doyle, M., Fereday, H., Gibson, M., Landbeck, U., Lee, R., Maynard, C., Palmer, G., Schwarzenbach, J.: The six primary dimensions for data quality assessment. Technical report, DAMA UK Working Group (2013)
2. Barker, N., Clevers, H.: Quality control in databanks for molecular biology. BioEssays **22**(11), 1024–1034 (2000)
3. Batini, C., Cappiello, C., Francalanci, C., Maurino, A.: Methodologies for data quality assessment and improvement. ACM Comput. Surv **41**(3), 1–52 (2009)
4. ClinVar. https://www.ncbi.nlm.nih.gov/clinvar/
5. Eckerson W.: Data quality and the bottom line. TDWI Report. The Data Warehouse Institute (2002)
6. Growth of sequence and 3D structure databases. http://www.kanehisa.jp/en/db_growth.html
7. Jones, C., Brown, A., Baumann, U.: Estimating the annotation error rate of curated GO database sequence annotations. BMC Bioinform. **8**(1), 170 (2007)
8. Koh, J., Lee, M., Khan, A., Tan, P., Brusic, V.: Duplicate detection in biological data using association rule mining. In: Proceedings of the Second European Workshop on Data Mining and Text Mining in Bioinformatics (2004)
9. Krawetz, S.: Sequence errors described in GenBank: a means to determine the accuracy of DNA sequence interpretation. Nucleic Acids Res. **17**(10), 3951–3957 (1989)
10. Loshin, D.: The Practitioner's Guide to Data Quality Improvement. A Volume in MK Series on Business Intelligence, pp. 115–128 (2011)
11. Moran, L.: Sandwalk: Errors in Sequence Databases (2008)
12. NCBI is phasing out sequence GIs - use Accession. Version instead! https://www.ncbi.nlm.nih.gov/news/03-02-2016-phase-out-of-GI-numbers/
13. Pastor, O.: Conceptual modeling meets the human genome. In: Li, Q., Spaccapietra, S., Yu, E., Olivé, A. (eds.) ER 2008. LNCS, vol. 5231, pp. 1–11. Springer, Heidelberg (2008). doi:10.1007/978-3-540-87877-3_1
14. Scannapieco, M., Missier, P., Batini, C.: Data quality at aGlance. Datenbank-Spektrum **14**, 6–14 (2005)
15. Schnoes, A., Brown, S., Dodevski, I., Babbitt, P.: Annotation error in public databases: misannotation of molecular function in enzyme superfamilies. PLoS Computational Biology 5(12), e1000605 (2009)
16. Smith, B.E., Johnston, M.K., Lucking, R.: From GenBank to GBIF: phylogeny-based predictive niche modeling tests accuracy of taxonomic identifications in large occurrence data repositories. PLoS ONE 11(3), e0151232 (2016)
17. Soh, D., Dong, D., Guo, Y., Wong, L.: Consistency, comprehensiveness, and compatibility of pathway databases. BMC Bioinform. **11**(1), 449 (2010)
18. The ClinVar record display. https://www.ncbi.nlm.nih.gov/clinvar/docs/details/#review_status
19. The Ensembl project. http://www.ensembl.org/info/about/index.html

20. Triplet, T., Butler, G.: Systems biology warehousing: challenges and strategies toward effective data integration. In: Proceedings of the 3rd International Conference on Advances in Databases, Knowledge and Data Applications, pp. 34–40 (2011)
21. Uniparc. http://www.uniprot.org/help/uniparc
22. Uniprot knowledgebase. http://www.uniprot.org
23. UniProt: reducing proteome redundancy. http://www.uniprot.org/help/proteome_redundancy
24. UniProt: how redundant are the uniprot databases? http://www.uniprot.org/help/redundancy
25. Uniprot key staff. http://www.uniprot.org/help/key_staff
26. UniProt: current release statistics. https://www.ebi.ac.uk/uniprot/TrEMBLstats
27. UniProt: protein existence. http://www.uniprot.org/help/protein_existence
28. Wand, Y., Wang, R.Y.: Anchoring data quality dimensions in ontological foundations. Commun. ACM **39**, 86–95 (1995)
29. Wang, R., Strong, D.: Beyond accuracy: what data quality means to data consumers. J. Manage. Inform. Syst. **12**(4), 5–33 (1996)

# The Design of a Core Value Ontology Using Ontology Patterns

Frederik Gailly[1(✉)], Ben Roelens[1(✉)], and Giancarlo Guizzardi[2]

[1] Department of Business Informatics and Operations Management,
Faculty of Economics and Business Administration,
Ghent University, Ghent, Belgium
{Frederik.Gailly,Ben.Roelens}@UGent.be
[2] Ontology and Conceptual Modeling Research Group (NEMO),
Computer Science Department, Federal University of Espírito Santo,
Vitória, Brazil
gguizzardi@inf.ufes.br

**Abstract.** The creation of value is an important concern in organizations. However, current Enterprise Modeling languages all interpret value differently, which has a negative impact on the semantic quality of the model instantiations. This issue need to be solved to increase the relevance of these instantiations for business stakeholders. Therefore, the goal of this paper is the development of a sound Core Value Ontology. In order to do that, we employ a pattern-based ontology engineering approach, which employs the Unified Foundational Ontology.

**Keywords:** Value · Core ontology · UFO · Ontology patterns

## 1 Introduction

Creating value is an important purpose of the economic activities that are performed by companies to sustain their long-term viability. Therefore, the concept has been studied by a wide range of Enterprise Modeling languages. ArchiMate, which is oriented towards Enterprise Architecture, defines value as *what a party gets by selling or making available some product or service, or it may apply to what a party gets by buying or obtaining access to it* [16]. In the context of Business Model Design, the Value Delivery Modeling Language (VDML) specifies value as *a measurable benefit delivered to a recipient in association with a deliverable* [11]. On an aggregated level, the values that are associated with a deliverable are embodied in a value proposition [11]. A similar idea is adopted in Requirements Engineering by e$^3$-value [4], which uses a value proposition to describe the creation of value in a constellation of multiple actors. This concept is specified as *something that is offered by a party for consideration or acceptance by another party* [4]. These examples show that a general semantic agreement is currently still missing for the Value domain [5], which endangers the semantic quality of resulting model instantiations. Solving this issue is important, as models with a bad semantic quality are not corresponding with the targeted problem domain, which lowers their relevance for business experts [8].

© Springer International Publishing AG 2016
S. Link and J.C. Trujillo (Eds.): ER 2016 Workshops, LNCS 9975, pp. 183–193, 2016.
DOI: 10.1007/978-3-319-47717-6_16

Semantic agreement about the notion of Value can be realized by the development of a core ontology. A core ontology *provides a semantic characterization of the core terms used in a specific field that spans different application domains, with the purpose of minimizing ambiguities and misunderstandings* [10]. In this context, a core ontology should combine the following characteristics: axiomatization and formal precision, modularity, extensibility, reusability, and separation of concerns [15]. These characteristics can be supported by making sure that the developed ontology: (i) is based on a foundational ontology, (ii) follows a pattern-oriented design approach, and (iii) is applicable in arbitrary application domains.

Although a sound core ontology was previously developed in the domain of services [10], it is currently still missing for the Value concept. To this end, the goal of this paper is the development of a Core Value Ontology, which is (i) grounded in the Unified Foundational Ontology (UFO). Furthermore, the development of the ontology will be guided by an engineering approach, which (ii) is explicitly oriented towards supporting reuse by systematically using ontology patterns [13]. Finally, the use of the Core Value Ontology is demonstrated (iii) by applying it on an existing healthcare case.

## 2    Methodology

The Core Value Ontology is developed by following the ontology engineering approach proposed by Ruy et al. [13]. This approach makes use of ontology design patterns, which describe particular recurring modeling problems that arise in specific ontology development contexts and present a well-proven solution for this problem [2]. Specific for the approach of Ruy et al. is that a distinction is made between *foundational ontology patterns (FOPs)* and *domain-related ontology patterns (DROPs)*. A FOP is a fragment of a foundational reference ontology, which spans across many fields and models the very basic and general concepts and relations that make up the world [6]. In contrast, a DROP is a fragment of a core ontology, which captures the core knowledge related to a domain. The ontology engineering process that is followed within this paper also recognizes that DROPs of related core ontologies can be reused while developing a new core ontology. This ontology engineering process consists of three steps, of which the results can be consulted in Sect. 4:

1. First, a set of FOPs are extracted from the UFO foundational ontology. UFO is useful for creating a Core Value Ontology because it comprises a number of notions that fundamentally explain the notion of value including the notions of goals, capabilities, actions, and intentions. As discussed in [13], the FOPs extracted from UFO are considered as the relevant building blocks for the Core Value Ontology and will be either reused during the development of the Core Value Ontology or will be used to analyze existing DROPs of related core ontologies;
2. Second, a set of DROPs is extracted from related core ontologies and existing enterprise modeling languages. For every DROP, it should also be clear how this DROP reuses a FOP that was extracted in the previous step.
3. In the final step, the Core Value Ontology will be constructed by integrating the identified DROPs. This integration is founded on generally accepted domain

knowledge about the Value concept. Moreover, it makes use of the FOPs identified in the previous steps to connect the different DROPs.

## 3  Building the Core Value Ontology

**Foundational Ontology Patterns.** UFO consists of three main modules: UFO-A, UFO-B and UFO-C. UFO-A describes *Endurants* and their ties. In a nutshell, *Endurants* are entities that persist through time, possibly changing qualitatively while maintaining their identity [7]. UFO-B describes *Perdurants* or *Events*. UFO-C uses UFO-A and UFO-B to define a foundational ontology for social entities, which is very relevant for defining enterprise concepts.

Figure 1 depicts the Endurant FOP. These *Endurants* can be divided into *Substantials* and *Moments*. *Substantials* are existentially independent individuals and can be further specialized in *Objects*, *Agents* and *Situations*. *Agents* are substantials that can bear special types of moments, named *Intentional Moments* (see Agent FOP). *Objects* and *Situations* are non-agentive substantial individuals. *Objects* are *Endurants* that are existentially independent (e.g., a Person, a Car, an Organization); *Moments*, in contrast, are individuals that can only exist in other individuals, and are thus existentially dependent on other individuals (e.g., an electric charge in a conductor, John's head-ache). *Moments* can be further specialized in *Relators* and *Intrinsic Moments*. *Intrinsic Moments* are moments that inhere in one single individual. *Relators* are further explained by FOP 2. *Situations* are complex entities that are constituted by possibly many *Endurants* (including other situations). *Situations* are taken here to be synonymous to what is named a *state of affairs* in the literature, i.e., a portion of reality that can be comprehended as a whole. Examples include "John having fever and influenza", "John being in the same location as Paul, while Mary is in the same location as David", and "Mary being married to Paul who works for Ghent University".

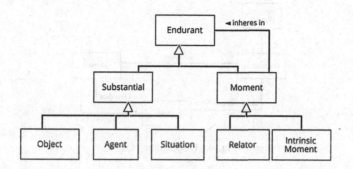

**Fig. 1.** Endurant FOP

In Fig. 2, *Relators* are considered as *Moments* that are existentially dependent on two or more *Endurants*. When mediated by a *Relator*, an *Endurant* plays a role in a certain context.

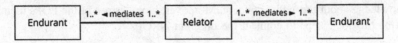

**Fig. 2.** Relator FOP

Figure 3 further specifies the *Agent* concept, which is defined as a specialization of a *Substantial*. As such, an *Agent* represents an entity that is capable of bearing *Intentional Moments*, such as *Beliefs*, *Desires*, and *Intentions*. Every *Intentional Moment* has an associated *Proposition*, which is called the propositional content of the *Moment*. The propositional content of an *Intentional Moment* can be satisfied by *Situations* in reality.

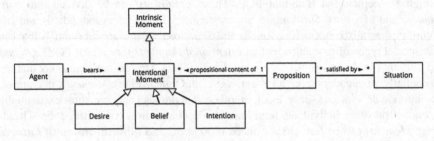

**Fig. 3.** Agent FOP

*Dispositions* are *Intrinsic Moments* that are only manifested in particular *Situations*, but that can also fail to be manifested (see Fig. 4). When manifested, they are manifested through an occurrence of *Events*.

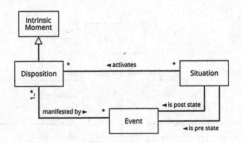

**Fig. 4.** Disposition FOP

In the Intention FOP of Fig. 5, the propositional content of an *Intention* is termed a *Goal*. *Actions* are intentional *Events*, i.e., events with the specific purpose of satisfying (the propositional content of) some *Intention* of an *Agent*.

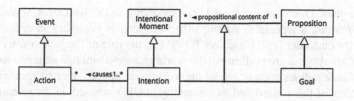

**Fig. 5.** Intention FOP

**Domain-related Ontology Patterns.** Extraction of relevant DROPs for the development of the Core Value Ontology is less straightforward because of the limited availability of related core ontologies (with exception of UFO-S, which is a core ontology for services). In this paper, three relevant DROPs are created by looking at the reference ontologies that were used to develop some well-know enterprise modelling languages (e.g., the Business Model Ontology (BMO) [12], the TOVE ontological framework [4], e3-value [5], the Service Science discipline [9], ArchiMate [1] and ARIS [14]). Some of these sources explicitly define a reference ontology which can be used to extraxt the DROPS's. Others implicitly use a reference ontology to define the concepts of the enterprise modelling language or to analyze the semantics of the modeling language. In the next paragraphs, the DROPs that are extracted from the reference ontologies (see Figs. 6, 7, 8) are described in more detail. Additionally, the UML stereotype mechanism will be used to indicate how these DROPs are related to the previously selected FOPs.

The first DROP focuses on the *Value Proposition* concept. This concept has its origin in the BMO, Service Science, and e3-value. Within the BMO, the concept is defined as *an overall view of a company's bundle of products and services that are of value to the customer* [12]. This view is shared within Service Science who consider the concept as the *potential value that is offered to a customer* [17]. A last important aspect of the *Value Proposition* concept is stressed within e3-value, within which this concept is specified as follows: *something that is offered by a party for consideration or acceptance by another party* [4]. The condition of acceptance is important here as it differentiates the *Value Proposition* from the actual value co-creation between a company and its customers (see DROP 2). In Fig. 6, a *Value Proposition* is identified as an UFO *Relator*, which connects the *Recipient* and *Provider* as two *Agents that are because of their connection with the Value Proposition Relator also Roles.*

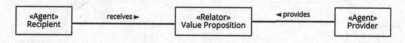

**Fig. 6.** Value proposition DROP

The second DROP is oriented towards value co-creation. The Service Science discipline agrees with the fact that value is always the result of a co-creation between the company (i.e., the *Provider*) and its customers (i.e., the *Recipient*) [17]. Both parties are considered as a dynamic configuration of resources, which apply *Capabilities* during the value co-creation process [17]. According to the BMO, a *Capability* is the ability to execute a repeatable pattern of *Actions* that is necessary in order to create value for the customer [12]. Based on TOVE [3], the role of the *Action* can be further refined. When *Actions* are performed, the world changes from one situation to another. A *Caused state* defines what is true of the world once the activity has been completed. The modeling of this pattern and its grounding in UFO is based on the research in [1], which analyzes *Capabilities* as defined in ArchiMate.

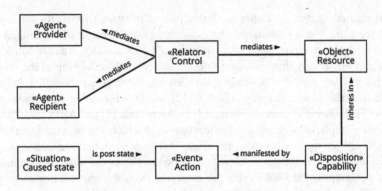

**Fig. 7.** Value co-creation DROP

The third DROP focuses on value measurement. Defining appropriate value measures is important as value is not transferred between a recipient and a provider but is uniquely determined by the customer [17]. In this respect, the measurement is based on their level of satisfaction with a particular value [11]. More specifically, this *Satisfaction Level* is determined by the customer's perception of the solution of a problem in a given situation [3]. The *Satisfaction Level* is a UFO *Belief* that is by means of its *Proposition* connected to the *Goal* of a *Recipient* (i.e., the propositional content of an *Intention*) and a particular *Situation* that is the result of an action.

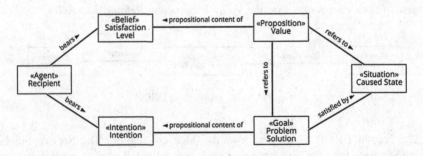

**Fig. 8.** Value measurement DROP

**Core Value Ontology.** The Core Value Ontology that is proposed in this paragraph is the result of an integration of the previously defined FOPs and DROPs (see Fig. 9). Central in the Core Value Ontology is the *Recipient* concept, which is common to the three important value aspects: (i) value proposition (see Fig. 6), (ii) value co-creation (see Fig. 7), and (iii) value measurement (see Fig. 8). While the *Provider* also plays an import role in the offering of the value proposition and in the co-creation of value, this is not the case for the actual value measurement. Furthermore, the *Caused State* (as an instantiation of a UFO *Situation*) appears in both the value co-creation (i.e., DROP 2) and value measurement (i.e., DROP 3) patterns. This can be explained as there is a clear relation between these two aspects. Indeed, the outcome of the *Actions* that are performed during the value co-creation will impact the perceptions of the *Recipient* about the *Problem Solution* and its resulting *Satisfaction Level*.

## 4 Healthcare Use Case Illustration

The healthcare case is a case that studies the value of remote monitoring of high-risk pregnancies, which was originally developed to illustrate the VDML meta-model and notation. In this paper, the description of the case is limited to those concepts that are relevant in the context of the developed ontology[1].

The illustration of the Core Value Ontology by the healthcare use case can be found in Fig. 10. In the context of a high-risk pregnancy, it is not straightforward for a hospital to provide valuable maternity care to a pregnant client. Although the future mother bears the intention to obtain maternity care by having frequent examinations, these trips to the doctor's office pose a possible risk for the unborn child. This problem can have a serious impact on the satisfaction level of the pregnant client with the maternity care service, which is measured by four distinct criteria: (i) the cost of care, (ii) the total duration of the hospitalization, (iii) the risk of death of the mother, and (iv) the risk of death of the child. To better satisfy these conflicting goals, the hospital wants to use new monitoring devices. These devices are lent by the hospital to high-risk pregnant clients as they possess the capability of remote monitoring of the future mother and unborn child by creating and sending automatic health reports. These reports can subsequently be analyzed by the doctor who is responsible for monitoring the high-risk patient. These actions will result in a situation where high-risk patients receive a continuous follow-up by doing limited physical efforts. While the limited physical efforts support the client's goal of minimizing their visits to the doctor's office, the continuous follow-up satisfies the need of having frequent examinations in case of a high-risk pregnancy. This should increase the value of the maternity care that is received by these patients.

---

[1] The interested reader can consult the VDML healthcare use case via: http://files.modelbased.net/vdml/12-11-11.pdf.

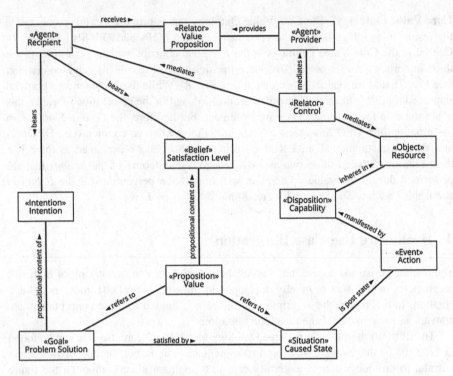

**Fig. 9.** Core Value Ontology

Besides the illustration of the Core Value Ontology, we also want to show how it relates to Enterprise Modeling fragments that are oriented towards the Value concept. Therefore, illustrative fragments can be found for e3-value (see Fig. 11), ArchiMate (see Fig. 12), and VDML values (see Fig. 13). The focus of the e3-value fragment is on the exchange of the maternity care services (i.e., a value object) between the hospital (i.e., an actor) and the high-risk pregnant client (i.e., a market segment). As a compensation for these services, the client will pay money to the hospital. Furthermore, the responsibility of the hospital for executing the activity of monitoring the high-risk patients is also incorporated. This activity is the end of a scenario path, which starts with the need of the future mother to obtain maternity care (see dotted lines).

Within the ArchiMate Business Layer, several constructs comply with the developed Core Value Ontology. Furthermore, the relations between the different concepts can be instantiated as general association relationships. As such, the maternity care services are considered as a business service that is exchanged between the hospital and the high-risk pregnant client (i.e., two actors). Furthermore, the monitoring device can be modeled as a business object that has the function of creating automatic health reports. This business function is manifested by the business event of monitoring the high-risk patient, which results in a situation that determines the maternity care value (i.e., an ArchiMate value). This value refers to two goals of the future mother: (i) have frequent examinations and (ii) minimize visits to doctor's office. These goals are part of

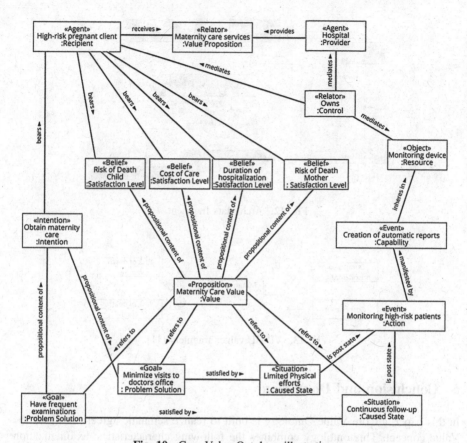

**Fig. 10.** Core Value Ontology illustration

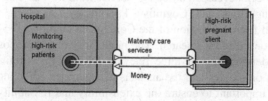

**Fig. 11.** e3-value fragment

the Motivation Extension within ArchiMate. The VDML values fragment focuses on the specific criteria that determine the value of the maternity care service. These criteria are: (i) the duration of hospitalization, (ii) the cost of care, (iii) the risk of death of the mother, and (iv) the risk of death of the child. The negative impact on the resulting value is depicted by the minus sign inside the hexagons.

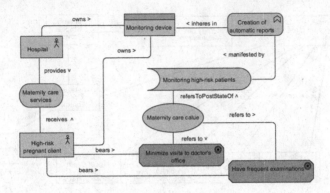

**Fig. 12.** ArchiMate fragment

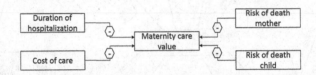

**Fig. 13.** VDML values fragment [11]

## 5  Conclusion and Discussion

In this paper, a Core Value Ontology is built to realize semantic agreement about the Value concept. This ontology combines the following characteristics: axiomatization and formal precision, modularity, extensibility, reusability, and separation of concerns. In this respect, the Core Value Ontology was built on UFO, which is a foundational ontology that has been developed based on theories from Formal Ontology, Philosophy of Language, Linguistics and Cognitive Psychology. As such, we ensured the axiomatization and formal precision of the Core Value Ontology [15], which supports its further validation in future research. The modularity of the proposed ontology was realized by the identification of three relevant DROPs that originate from related enterprise domain ontologies and the analysis of enterprise modeling semantics. This modularization is important to ensure the extensibility and reusability of the proposed ontology [15]. Reusability can be further realized by using the Core Value Ontology to analyze and integrate Enterprise Modeling languages that focus on value. The focus of this analysis is on using the Core Value Ontology to better understand the semantics of these languages with the aim of linking them with related techniques, which focus on business concepts as capabilities, goals, resources, and services. In future research the Core Value Ontology will be formalized in order to improve the formal precision of the proposed ontology.

# References

1. Azevedo, C., Iacob, M., Almeida, J., Van Sinderen, M., Pires, L., Guizzardi, G.: Modeling resources and capabilities in enterprise architecture: a well-founded ontology-based proposal for archimate. Inf. Syst. **54**, 235–262 (2015)
2. Falbo, R., Guizzardi, G., Gangemi, A., Presutti, V.: Ontology patterns: clarifying concepts and terminology. In: Gangemi, A., et al. (ed.) ISWC 2013, vol. 1188, pp. 14–26. CEUR (2013)
3. Fox, M., Barbuceanu, M., Gruninger, M., Lin, J.: An organization ontology for enterprise modelling. In: Prietula, M., et al. (eds.) Computational Model of Institutions and Groups, pp. 131–152. AAAI/MIT Press, Menlo Park (1997)
4. Gordijn, J., Akkermans, H.: Value-based requirements engineering: exploring innovative e-commerce ideas. Requirements Eng. J. **8**(2), 114–134 (2003)
5. Grönroos, C., Voima, P.: Critical service logic: making sense of value creation and co-creation. J. Acad. Mark. Sci. **41**(2), 133–150 (2013)
6. Guarino, N.: Formal ontology and information systems. In: FOIS 1998, pp. 3–15. IOS Press, Trento (1998)
7. Guizzardi, G.: Ontological Foundations for Structural Conceptual Models. UTwente, The Netherlands (2005)
8. Lindland, O., Sindre, G., Sølvberg, A.: Understanding quality in conceptual modeling. IEEE Softw. **11**(2), 42–49 (1994)
9. Maglio, P., Vargo, S., Caswell, N., Spohrer, J.: The service system is the basic abstraction of service science. Inf. Syst. E-Bus. Manage. **7**(4), 395–406 (2009)
10. Nardi, J., Falbo, R., Almeida, J., Guizzardi, G., Pires, L., van Sinderen, M., Guarino, N., Fonseca, C.: A commitment-based reference ontology for services. Inf. Syst. **51**, 263–288 (2015)
11. OMG: Value Delivery Modeling Language (VDML) (dtc/2014-04-05) (2014)
12. Osterwalder, A., Pigneur, Y., Tucci, C.: Business Model Generation: A Handbook for Visionaries, Game Changers, and Challengers. Wiley, Hoboken (2010)
13. Ruy, F.B., Reginato, C.C., Santos, V.A., Falbo, R.A., Guizzardi, G.: Ontology engineering by combining ontology patterns. In: Johannesson, P., Lee, M.L., Liddle, S.W., Opdahl, A.L., López, Ó.P. (eds.) ER 2015. LNCS, vol. 9381, pp. 173–186. Springer, Heidelberg (2015). doi:10.1007/978-3-319-25264-3_13
14. Santos Jr., P., Almeida, J., Guizzardi, G.: An ontology-based analysis and semantics for organizational structure modeling in the ARIS method. Inf. Syst. **38**(5), 690–708 (2013)
15. Scherp, A., Saathoff, C., Franz, T., Staab, S.: Designing core ontologies. Appl. Ontol. **6**(3), 177–221 (2011)
16. The Open Group: ArchiMate® 2.1 Specification (2013)
17. Vargo, S., Lusch, R.: Evolving to a new dominant logic for marketing. J. Mark. **68**(1), 1–17 (2004)

# Conceptual Modelling Education

## Preface to the 4th Symposium on Conceptual Modeling Education (SCME 2016)

The 4th Symposium on Conceptual Modeling Education (SCME 2016) provides a forum for discussing the education and teaching of concepts related to conceptual modeling, methods and tools for developing and communicating conceptual models, techniques for transforming conceptual models into effective implementations, case studies of interesting projects, and pedagogies of modeling education for our next generation.

We received 7 papers in response to the call for papers, each of which went through a thorough review process from a team of 7 reviewers. Three of the submissions were selected for inclusion in the workshop proceedings:

- "YASQLT – Yet Another SQL Tutor: A Tool for Learning by Failing", Ilia Bider and David Rogers
- "Human Factors in the Adoption of Model-driven Engineering: An Educator's Perspective", Jordi Cabot and Dimitris Kolovos
- "Learning Pros and Cons of Model-driven in a Practical Teaching Experience", Oscar Pastor Lopez, Sergio España Cubillo and José Ignacio Panach Navarrete

We would like to thank all of the authors who submitted papers to SCME 2016 for their efforts in promoting education in conceptual modeling. We thank the program committee for their thoughtful and timely reviews of the papers. Finally, we are grateful to the ER General Chairs, Shuichiro Yamamoto and Motoshi Saeki, and to the ER Workshop Chairs, Juan C. Trujillo and Sebastien Link, for their help in organizing the Symposium.

We hope that the interesting contributions of SCME 2016 will contribute to the reader's teaching and practice of conceptual modeling and will foster contributions to future editions of the SCME.

Karen C. Davis
Xavier Franch

# YASQLT – Yet Another SQL Tutor

## A Pragmatic Approach

Ilia Bider[✉] and David Rogers

Department of Computer and Systems Sciences (DSV),
Stockholm University, Stockholm, Sweden
ilia@dsv.su.se, jeffrachov@gmail.com

**Abstract.** The paper describes an ongoing project of creating an automated assessment tool to help novice students learning SQL in a frame of an introductory database course. In difference to other tools of this kind, the project has chosen a pragmatic approach of focusing on catching common semantic errors, leaving syntax control to professional DBMS. Using agile system development, the project successfully completed two iterations, both of which were tested in practice with satisfactory results. The students appreciated the tool and would like to have similar tools for other subjects, including Relational Algebra, and Conceptual Modeling. The latter is planned for implementation in the near future. The tool is considered to be appropriate for Learning by Failure in the situation of large size classes and short courses.

**Keywords:** Database · Technology enhanced learning · SQL · Assessment

## 1 Introduction

Relational databases have a long history starting from the Codd's work in 1970s [1]. Structured Query Language (SQL), which appeared commercially in 1979, remains the mostly widespread language used for defining structure and manipulating data in the databases. Teaching/learning SQL is more or less mandatory for all IT related disciplines, e.g. Computer Science, Software Engineering and Information Systems.

As SQL is an artificial language to be understood by computers, using assistance from the computers in teaching/learning this language seems only natural. Indeed, there is a substantial body of literature devoted to this topic, see, for example, [2–5]. However, when faced with a task of finding appropriate technology for a specific database course, we found no ready-made solution for adoption. Appeal to the AISworld community gave no result. Contacting colleagues who published articles on technology that could be suitable for our course have not been successful, due to the tools they created were not operational (most probably because of their developers where no longer around).

Effectively manage our introductory database course with three rounds a year and large number of students in each round (up to 200) turned out to be difficult without technological support. The main difficulty here was providing timely feedback on students' assignments in general, and assignments on SQL in particular. Having not

© Springer International Publishing AG 2016
S. Link and J.C. Trujillo (Eds.): ER 2016 Workshops, LNCS 9975, pp. 197–206, 2016.
DOI: 10.1007/978-3-319-47717-6_17

found appropriate technology to adopt, we decided to develop our own. The main principle used in the development was pragmatism - create a system that provides the students with timely feedback on common errors without guaranteeing all errors being captured. Another pragmatic principle was to limit the development efforts as much as possible by not trying to repeat functionality that was already present in the existing Database Management Systems (DBMS).

The development of a new assessment tool, dubbed YASQLT (Yet Another SQL Tutor), is being done in an agile manner. We do not use any formalized methodology like Scrum, but directly employ agile principles [6] in interpretation of [7]. As soon as some functionality is ready, the tool is set into operation to be used by the students completing their assignments in the frame of the next round of the course. So far, two iterations have been completed and the results are under evaluation. The quality of submitted assignments has improved, and students appreciate help they get from the new tool. What is more, they would appreciate getting similar tools for other parts of the course, such as Relational Algebra and Conceptual Modeling.

In addition, the students use the tool not only for completing assignments, but also for preparing for exams, and for learning more about SQL in general. Generalizing the results achieved, we call YASQLT a tool for Learning by Failing, and we are planning to extend the experience to other subjects, conceptual modeling in the first place.

The goal of this paper is to report on the progress achieved in the YASQLT project and discuss other areas of Information Systems (IS) education, e.g. conceptual modeling, where the approached used in this project could be of help. The rest of the paper is structured as follows. In Sect. 2, we present the background of the project, giving a short description of the context in which the project has been initiated. In Sect. 3, we described our approach to building YASQLT, while in Sect. 4 we give a short summary of technical architecture of the tool. Section 5 is devoted to results achieved so far, while Sect. 6 summarizes the results and discusses plans for the future.

## 2    Background

### 2.1    The Organization

The project was initiated in the Department of Computer and System Sciences, abbreviated to DSV, at Stockholm University. The department is engaged in research and undergraduate and graduate teaching of about 5400 students simultaneously. It runs bachelor, master, and doctoral programs in the fields of Computer Science and Information Systems. The programs have various orientations, such as Game design, IT in economics, Computer Science, Information Systems (IS). The department belongs to the Faculty of Social Sciences, which is unusual for departments of the DSV type in other universities. Such affiliation brings a social focus to the programs given at the department.

## 2.2   The Course

The course *Introduction to DataBases* (IDB) is given three times a year, once in the autumn and twice in the spring for the first (in spring) and second year undergraduates. There are around 400 students in total attending IDB on the yearly basis. The course length is either 5 weeks, if the students study full time and do not have any other courses in parallel, or 10 weeks, if the students study another course in parallel. The course gives the students 7.5 ECTS points.

The subject of the course is one of the cornerstones in all programs of the department. Most of the graduates will be dealing with databases in their professional life while designing requirements on databases, designing and maintaining databases, programming interface to them, or simply using databases.

Though each course round is directed to a specific DSV program, the students are allowed themselves to choose when they are attending the course, so the classes can be mixed. The size of the classes varies from 50 to 200 students. The level of preparedness also varies in both what is required for students to enroll for a specific program (for example, some programs requires advance mathematics to be enrolled, others do not), and what courses the students have attended before attending IDB. The audience is diverse, and not always academically minded, which makes it impossible to introduce the subject in a theoretical academic manner. Thus, teaching/learning is arranged around project work in groups of (3–6 students) where the students complete a number of assignments.

The course includes conceptual modeling for database design using UML, database design based on the conceptual model, normalization, and query languages. The latter includes SQL and Relational Algebra (RA). The projects the students complete include assignments related to all this issues.

## 2.3   The Project Assignment Related to SQL

The project assignment related to SQL consists of a number of questions in natural language, Swedish in our case, that the students need to convert to SQL. Some of the questions, 5 from 17, they also need to reformulate as RA expressions. The database scheme is predefined and it is the same for all students, see Fig. 1. The questions are related to different themes, like *simple select, join, complex conditions, union, group by*, etc. There are a number of different questions for each theme. These are randomly packed in assignments, so that different groups get different sets of questions.

A typical example of questions is: *Get the national Id, name and city of students who have participated in at least three different courses*. It belongs to the theme *group by*, however, the students can use any other technique to formulate a corresponding SQL, for example, *self-join*.

Currently, we use Microsoft ACESS as a tool for the students to test their SQL translations. The choice is done based on pure administrative reasons - the students can work offline, and then submit the results as an *access* file. To run tests, they get a database filled with data in a way that they almost always get a non-empty result set on any question of their assignments.

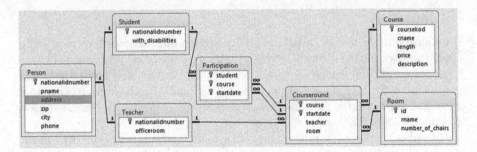

**Fig. 1.** Database schema

## 2.4 Problems with Manual Assessment

As the students test their results in a DBMS, the results they submit are free from syntax errors. However, the assignment they get is quite difficult for them and very few students groups get *pass* on the project assignment without two or three round of corrections based on the teachers' feedback. The feedback consists of the teacher marking questions that were translated incorrectly and giving some advice on how to make corrections. The long cycle of assignment assessment leads to the following (negative) consequences:

1. The assessment becomes a long and tedious process. It is quite boring, as the students make the same kind of errors in each course round.
2. As the calendar time of the course is quite short, the students are not getting the feedback before the exams, thus they cannot use it for the exams preparation.

## 2.5 Project Initiation

A natural way of alleviating the two problems listed in the previous section is through automating the assessment. As database courses in general, and SQL courses in particular, were quite usual (if not mandatory) for IS education, we assumed that we could adopt an automated assessment tool developed by somebody else. Having this in mind, a request was sent to AISWorld mailing list that includes over 1000 academics in IS discipline (the list, besides making announcements, is used for requests and discussions). The posting dated 15th December 2014 is presented below:

*"I wonder whether anybody has a tool in operation for automated assessment of assignments in a database course. In particular, we would be interested to have such a tool for assessing assignments related to SQL, though other tools like converting UML into Relational scheme, or assessing assignments in the area of Relational Algebra would be also good to have. In connection to SQL, assessing assignments connected to learning SELECT has a priority. The tool does not need to make a sophisticated analysis of SQL statements, and it does not need to insure 100 % correctness - it can miss some incorrect statements, but shouldn't mark as incorrect correct statements. The following scheme would do. A database is created in some popular DBMS, like SQLserver, or MySQL, or even Access. A teacher creates a textual question, and a corresponding SQL*

*SELECT. The statement is run and the set of records it gives is saved. The students are not allowed to change the content of the database. When a student creates his/her own SELECT to answer the question, it is run against the same database and the set produced is compared with the one stored when the teacher ran his/her version of SELECT. If the data sets differ, the tool marks the student's SELECT as incorrect. Any help in acquiring such a tool would be much appreciated. As customary, a summary of responses will be reported back to the list."*

The only response received was from a person with a similar problem who asked to share with him any information we would get. As the request was unsuccessful, we searched for and studied the available literature, such as [2–5] (due to the size limitations, we cannot discuss all relevant literature here). Some tools reported in the literature seemed suitable for our needs and we contacted the authors of these papers. Some respondents did not answer, others informed us that their tools where no longer supported. After a couple of unsuccessful tries, we decided to stop the search and develop our own tool. The start of the development was delayed until Autumn 2015 when we got resources to get started. Our department decided to invest in automation of exams, which included assessment of project assignments. We applied with the YASQLT proposal and got resources to start the project.

## 3    Main Ideas Behind YASQLT

The guiding principle of our project is pragmatism. This implies to define what we do not do before deciding on what we do. In particular:

1. YASQLT is not meant as a self-sufficient platform for catching syntax as well as semantics errors, as other tools try to do [2, 5]. The students are supposed to use a standard DBMS to test their SQL queries and get rid of all syntax errors.
2. YASQLT is envisioned to be a tool for introductory courses only. Therefore, no deep semantic analysis of SQL queries and no check of whether the students' queries are optimal or not is done. The main focus is on:
   - checking whether the result of the query is correct and
   - searching for the most common errors made by novices working with the type of assignments that we have. These errors are known to us from our practice, and they are also listed in the literature [8].
3. Only SELECT and CREATE VIEW statements are to be checked.
4. No generic methods for doing semantic analysis of computer languages in general, and SQL in particular, are to be used[1]. Using an SQL parser is considered sufficient to facilitate the development. Catching the common errors is programmed using an ordinary programming language.
5. The tool development is done while following the agile principles [6, 7].

The tool is being built using some assumptions regarding SQL queries to be composed by the students of an introductory course. The main ones are as follows:

---

[1] An example of using general semantic analysis is presented in [3].

- Students are using "classical" SQL without inner joins, though inner joins are not prohibited.
- Tables listed in the FROM clause are to be joined by conditions in the WHERE clause, no Cartesian products are expected.
- Tables are joined based on foreign key - primary key relationships, directly or indirectly (transitively). This means that all possible joins between two tables are known in advance. In addition, self-join can be used based on one or several columns with the same names.

The above assumptions would not hold for assignments in an advanced Database/SQL course, but are not very restrictive as far as an introductory course is concerned.

The first iteration of YASQLT development included only limited functionality:

1. Check whether the result returned by the student's SQL query is correct. This is done based on comparing the result set of rows from running the student's query with the one produced by a reference query composed by a teacher. This is a usual technique used in other tools. However, we use the reference query only to compare the results sets. No comparison between the student's query and the reference query is done (as is the case, for example, in [4, 5]).
2. If the result is not correct, a check for duplicate rows in the result set is done. If duplicates are found a warning about them is issued. Forgetting *DISTINCT* is one of the common errors made by our students.

The next iterations are gradually adding checks for common errors, such as[2]:

1. Disconnected tables, e.g. *SELECT DISTINCT S.nationalidnumber FROM Student AS S, Participation AS P WHERE P.course = 'JAVA2'* – there is no connection between the tables in the *FROM* clause. Note, that unconnected tables or groups of tables do not always produce an erroneous result set; "hanging" tables could be used neither in SELECT, nor in WHERE and thus do not matter.
2. Tables are not connected via *Foreign key – Primary key* relationships (directly or indirectly). More specifically, when a primary key is segmented, our students quite often define a connection between the tables based only on one segment. For example, the following question against the database in Fig. 1: *List national ID numbers of students who have participated in a course in room Jupiter!* is often answered incorrectly as: *SELECT DISTINCT student FROM Participation P, Courseround C, Room R WHERE P.course = C.course AND C.room = R.id AND R.name = 'Jupiter'*. Students are forgetting to connect the tables through *P.start-date = C.startdate*.

---

[2] The full list of errors to be caught by the tool is not presented due to the size limitation.

## 4   Overview of Technical Architecture

YASQLT is being developed as a web-based tool. The students work with it by first choosing a question group (number) and a question inside the group (letter), after which a question in natural language (Swedish in our case) appears, see Fig. 2. After that, the student writes or pastes his/her SQL and presses *Send*. The tool shows whether the result is correct or not and issues warnings, where appropriate. To get warnings, the student needs to check *More detailed analysis*, see Fig. 2. The students are also allowed to create and save views. Some questions require creating views; for others, the students may choose to use or not use views themselves.

Question: `13 ▾`  subtype:
`B ▾`

## Database Model

## Question 13 B

List the national Id, name and location of students who have participated in classes in rum Orion or in room Jupiter (or both)!

Click for larger image

## SQL Query:                                    Created views

```
SELECT DISTINCT P.nationalidnumber, P.name, P.city
FROM Person AS P, Participation AS P, Courseround
AS C, Room AS R
WHERE P.nationalidnumber=D.student AND
(R.name='Orion' OR R.name = 'Jupiter') AND
D.course=C.course  AND C.room=R.id;
```

`Send`   ☑ More detailed analysis (takes longer)

The result is not correct

Warning: The table Participation (P) is not linked to the table Courseround (C) with FK = PK relationship (Note that the keys are composed)

## Your result                          Correct Score

| nationalidnumber | name | city |
|---|---|---|
| 121017-0001 | Bo Dahl | Bromma |
| 121017-0002 | Ann Steel | Kista |
| 121017 0003 | | |

| nationalidnumber | name | city |
|---|---|---|
| 121017-0002 | Ann Steel | Kista |
| 121017-0003 | Ebba Ryd | Bromma |
| 121017 0004 | | |

**Fig. 2.**  User interface of YASQLT

The tool is realized as a server-based application under *Linux* (Debian) and *Tomcat 8* webserver (from Apache) using *Java* as a programming language. A number of Open Source components and libraries are used for facilitating the development, the guiding principle being to use as much of available third party software as possible.

For connection to *Microsoft Access* files the *UCanAcess* library is used (from Marco Amadei), which, in turn, rely on the following components: *Jackcess* (from Health Market Science), *HyperSQL* (from The HSQL Development Group), *Apache Commons Lang* (from Apache) and *Apache Commons Logging* (from Apache). For parsing SQL sentences, the *JSqlPArser* library [9] is used.

For client development, the following languages and tools are used: *HTML*, *CSS*, *Javascript* and *jQuery* (from jQuery Foundation).

The tool is being developed by the authors of this paper, the first authors being a teacher of the database course, and the second author being an MS student having the YASQLT development as part of his MS thesis work.


# 5    Evaluation of Results

So far, YASQLT was used in two course rounds - both in Spring 2016. In the first round, only the initial functionality was implemented (checking whether the result produced by the student's SQL is correct, and checking for duplicates, see Sect. 3). As it was the first release of YASQLT, it had a number of bugs and some performance issues. Therefore, using the tool was not mandatory for the students. Some of them used it intensively; others did not use it at all.

In the second round, the bugs and performance issues were resolved and new functionality was added (check on disconnected tables and join relationships, see Sect. 3). The usage of YASQLT was made mandatory in the second round. The students were requested to include a screen dump from YASQLT when submitting their project work.

As the primary objective of the YASQLT project was to minimize teachers' resources, the focus of evaluation was set on measuring time required for assessing students' submission. Here, we introduced two measurements: (1) percentage of students groups (each consisting of 3–6 students dependent on the size of a class) getting *pass* on the first submission, (2) average time for assessing one assignment (including assessing corrections made by the students in several iterations and registering the results).

As far as the first measure is concerned, the results are presented in Table 1. As far as the second measure is concerned, so far, we have data from one teacher (who is not the author of this paper) that compared the average time for assessing one submission between the Autumn 2015 round (no YASQLT) and the first round of Spring 2016 (first edition of YASQLT). His average time for assessing one submission went down from 46.5 min to 26 min – decrease of 46 %. We do not have full data on the second round of Spring 2016, as the corrections are not fully assessed. However, we can see the improvement indirectly. For example, errors related to segmented keys, which were quite common before, have practically disappeared.

**Table 1.** Numbers of group assignments that passed on the first submission

| Course round | Passed on first submission |
|---|---|
| Spring 2015 – 1st round. No YASQLT | 17 % (5 of 30 groups) |
| Spring 2015 – 2nd round. No YASQLT | 0 % (0 of 21 groups) |
| Autumn 2015. No YASQLT | 0 % (0 of 11 groups) |
| Spring 2016 – 1st round. First edition of YASQLT | 43 % (13 of 30 groups) |
| Spring 2016 – 2nd round. Second edition of YASQLT | 48 % (13 of 27 groups) |

**Table 2.** Students' opinions on Likert scale (based on 30 answers)

| YASQLT | 5 - agree | 4 | 3 | 2 | 1 - disagree |
|---|---|---|---|---|---|
| helped me to prepare for the exams | 20.0 % | 26.7 % | 36.7 % | 0.0 % | 16.7 % |
| helped me to learn SQL | 46.7 % | 26.7 % | 13.3 % | 6.7 % | 6.7 % |
| motivated me to test more SQL | 33.3 % | 26.7 % | 13.3 | 20 % | 6.7 % |

The secondary objective of our project was providing the students with timely feedback, and thus, affecting their learning. To evaluate the results, we use a questionnaire among the students at the end of each round where we investigate: (a) for what purpose they use YASQLT, (b) whether they found it useful, and (c) whether they would like to have similar tools for studying other subjects. In addition, we plan an investigation of whether the introduction of YASQLT have affected the results of the exams by comparing the exam results from the rounds without YASQLT with the ones where YASQLT has been introduced.

Below, we present a summary of answers from the students that used the second edition of YASQLT.

The questions in the questionnaire where of two types: choosing an alternative and assessing a statement on a Likert scale from 1 to 5. From the first type of questions, we can conclude that 60 % (18/30) used YASQLT not only for completing the project, but also for studying for the exams. Besides, 100 % (30/30) would like to have similar tools for other subjects, especially for studying Relational Algebra. The summary of some of the students answers based on Likert scale are presented in Table 2, where 5 means totally agree, and 1 – totally disagree.

In comments, the students asked for more and diverse assignments and for more feedback on what went wrong. From the answers to the questionnaire, we can conclude that for some students, the value of YASQLT goes beyond helping in completing their project assignments.

# 6   Conclusion

The YASQLT project has been started to solve practical problems in a database course with many students and short calendar time. A pragmatic approach is being applied to developing YASQLT, which consists of two principles: (1) aiming at detection of common errors, and (2) agile approach to system development. The first principle clearly differentiates our approach from the works of others.

Two iterations of the development have been completed successfully. The results achieved so far are encouraging, both in terms of diminishing teachers' resources, and providing timely feedback to the students. The students appreciate the tool and would like to have similar tools for other subjects. The usage of the tool is not restricted to completing project assignments; it is also used for learning SQL as such and preparing for the exams. The latter usages might be more important than the official goal of the project - to reduce the assessment time.

An approach that focuses on the common errors adopted for YASQLT development could be helpful in implementing the pedagogical principle of Learning by Failing (LbF) [10]. In LbF, students are encourage to try and learn via own failures, which requires providing timely feedback. In large size classes and short calendar time, this is impossible without employing a tool of YASQLT type. Currently, we are looking to expand our experience to other subjects, conceptual modeling being first in the line. This can be started with capturing errors in multiplicity of associations between UML classes.

**Acknowledgements.** Many thanks to all members of the DSV database teaching team: M. Bergholtz, N. Dimitrakas, J. Snygg, A. Thelemyr and W. Westmoreland for their engagement in the project. The authors are grateful to our prefect U. Fors for allocating resources to the project. We are also thankful to the anonymous reviewers whose comments have helped to improve the text.

# References

1. Codd, E.: A relational model of data for large shared data banks. Commun. ACM **13**(6), 377–387 (1970)
2. Sadiq, S., Orlowska, M., Sadiq, W., Lin, J.: SQLator – an online SQL learning workbench. In: Proceedings of the 9th Annual SIGCSE Conference on Innovation and Technology in Computer Science Education (ITiCSE 2004), pp. 223–227 (2004)
3. Mitrovic, S.: An intelligent SQL tutor on the web. Int. J. Artif. Intell. Educ. **13**, 171–195 (2003)
4. Dollinger, R., Melville, N.A.: Semantic evaluation of SQL queries. In: Proceedings of 2011 IEEE International Conference on Intelligent Computer Communication and Processing (ICCP), pp. 57–64 (2011)
5. Abelló, A., Burgués, X., Casany, M.J., Martín, C., Quer, C., Rodríguez, M.E., Romero, O., Urpí, T.: A software tool for E-assessment of relational database skills. Int. J. Eng. Educ. **32**(3(A)), 1289–1312 (2016)
6. Agile Alliance: Manifesto for Agile Software Development. http://agilemanifesto.org/. Accessed 10 Oct 2013
7. Bider, I.: Analysis of agile software development from the knowledge transformation perspective. In: Johansson, B., Andersson, B., Holmberg, N. (eds.) BIR 2014. LNBIP, vol. 194, pp. 143–157. Springer, Heidelberg (2014)
8. Brass, S., Goldberg, C.: Semantic errors in SQL queries: a quite complete list. In: Proceedings of the Fourth International Conference on Quality Software, QSIC 2004, pp. 250–257 (2004)
9. Manning, R.: JSqlPArser. http://jsqlparser.sourceforge.net/. Accessed June 2016
10. Kebritchi, M., Hirumi, A.: Examining the pedagogical foundations of modern educational computer games. Comput. Educ. **51**(4), 1729–1743 (2008)

# Human Factors in the Adoption
# of Model-Driven Engineering:
# An Educator's Perspective

Jordi Cabot[1,2(✉)] and Dimitrios S. Kolovos[3]

[1] ICREA, Barcelona, Spain
jordi.cabot@icrea.cat
[2] Internet Interdisciplinary Institute, UOC, Castelldefels, Spain
[3] Department of Computer Science, University of York, York, UK
dimitris.kolovos@york.ac.uk

**Abstract.** This paper complements previous empirical studies on teaching Model-driven Engineering (MDE) by reporting on the authors' attempt at introducing MDE to undergrad students. This is important because: (1) today's students are tomorrow's professionals and industrial adoption depends also on the availability of trained professionals and (2) observing problems in the introduction of MDE in the more controlled environment of a classroom setting allows us to identify additional adoption factors, more at the individual level, to be taken into account after in industrial settings. As we report herein, this attempt was largely unsuccessful. We will analyze what went wrong, what we learned from the process and the implications this has for both future endeavors of introducing MDE in both educational and professional environments, particularly regarding human/socio-technical factors to be considered.

**Keywords:** Education · Model-driven engineering · Code-generation · Empirical

## 1 Introduction

Model-driven engineering (MDE) has not been adopted by industry as extensively as many expected. Stephen Mellor (creator of the Executable UML [17] concept) is famously quoted saying that *modeling will be commonplace in three years time* with the only *but* being that he has been giving the same prediction since 1985. Many empirical studies have investigated this phenomenon (see [22] for a recent overview), sometimes even with contradictory results and almost always accompanied with heated discussions e.g. [19]. There is a consensus, though, to point out to organizational and managerial reasons and not only technical concerns as key aspects of this limited adoption, as it has happened before with other technologies [8]. Choosing the wrong project for a first MDE pilot, not having enough internal support, the lack of expertise of the development

© Springer International Publishing AG 2016
S. Link and J.C. Trujillo (Eds.): ER 2016 Workshops, LNCS 9975, pp. 207–217, 2016.
DOI: 10.1007/978-3-319-47717-6_18

team in MDE technologies are often given as examples, based on developers' interviews and surveys.

An initial failure creates a resistance to try again in the future, further hampering the adoption of MDE in industry. To overcome this situation we believe it is important that this first MDE impression is given in a course part of computer science/engineering degrees where the more controlled environment of a classroom setting can be used to isolate students from the contextual problems professionals have to face and maximize the chances to convince students of the potential of MDE and (conceptual) modeling in general. This would also fix the *lack of expertise* adoption challenge mentioned above.

At least, this was the idea. But (on two instances) such an attempt proved largely unsuccessful. The goal of the paper is to describe how an attempt to introduce MDE to undergraduate students by the first author at École des Mines de Nantes failed and what lessons can be learnt from that. As discussed in the sequel, most factors involve regarding the adoption of MDE as a socio-technical problem where human factors/ergonomy aspects of the interaction with the tools play an important role. This study offers a new perspective in this field by complementing other empirical studies more focused on interviewing practitioners. The lessons learned can be useful for any (not necessarily educational) institution or organization that would like to adopt MDE and also for tool vendors to better understand how they can improve their tools.

The rest of the paper is structured as follows. The next section provides a critical review of related studies, Sects. 3 and 4 describe the MDE courses and the feedback students provided on them, Sect. 5 summarizes the lessons learned from the experience, and Sect. 6 concludes the paper and discusses future work.

## 2    Related Work

Many research works have tried to develop insights on how model-driven engineering (and software modeling) is used by practitioners. Some focus on specific languages (mostly on UML [7,11,15,18,19]), specific phases in the development process (like software maintenance [12,13]) or individual (types of) companies or techniques [4,9], while some others aim at getting a more broader picture of why MDE is (not) adopted by looking at a variety of organizations in different domains and categories [14,22,23].

Sometimes these papers show inconsistent results and are often received with heated discussions, as happened with one of the latest works [19]. It is therefore important to continue this line of research by complementing existing empirical studies with new observations, particularly in domains / areas that have not been well-covered so far, as it is the case for this paper.

None of these previous works focuses on an experiment in a classroom setting like the one we report here. Using students as subjects in empirical studies is always controversial but in this context we believe it is valuable to analyze how to improve the first impression of people exposed to MDE for the first time since (1) today's students are tomorrow's professionals and industrial adoption depends also on the availability of trained professionals and (2) observing problems in the introduction of MDE in a more controlled environment allows us to identify additional adoption factors, at an individual level, to be taken into account in industrial settings and that could have been missed when interviewing developers in other studies due to the complex environment (organizational, managerial,...) they work in.

The results we discuss below do not replace previous experiences but complement them, contributing to this global effort in improving (or at least understanding) the role of MDE in general in the software engineering community.

## 3  Introductory MDE Course: Version 1

The first version of the introductory MDE course at École des Mines de Nantes was taught as part of the 2012/13 academic year by the first author and was aimed at providing undergrad students of the engineering degree (CS specialization) with a complete overview of all main MDE aspects using the Eclipse/EMF [21] framework (the standard *de facto* in the community) as base platform to illustrate those concepts with actual MDE tools. The idea was to show students how to build the MDE artifacts (transformations, generation templates and even DSLs) required to integrate MDE in their development process. Using EMF across the course helped save time on the tooling aspects by providing a uniform platform for the whole course. The total number of teaching hours for the course was 45 h (this does not include personal time outside class to work on the personal assignments), given by the first author in combination with external lecturers invited to participate in specific sessions based on their expertise. Students had taken previously an introductory course on UML and design patterns.

The course comprised three sections: MDE Foundations (5 h), MDE Core technologies (30 h), and Methodology and infrastructure (10 h). For each section students were asked to complete a small exercise either individually on in small groups of 2–3 students. These exercises always involved the development of a new MDE artifact (a new model-to-model transformation, a new DSL ...) needed to build a MDE process for the needs of a fictitious company, therefore, students were playing the role of MDE developers during the course. To simplify the assignments, in some cases, skeletons or initial versions of the artifacts to develop were provided alongside the requirements. In a couple of cases, assignments had to be simplified, or even the requirement to build a running product had to be dropped, due to the lack of proper documentation from the tools chosen for the course. No good tooling alternative was available that could be used to replace those problematic tools.

This approach was tried for two consecutive years (2012/13 and 2013/14) until we realized and learned the hard way that you cannot ask people to become MDE developers if they are not first convinced and experienced MDE users (which is what most of them will end up being, if anything). This realization was not linked to poor students' marks. In fact marks were not bad at all but it was because they managed to "fill the gaps" in the individual tasks even when they were not really sure what they were doing (or why they were doing it). By talking to them one could see they had no real understanding or coherent view of MDE as a whole and just went in surviving mode from one tool and assignment to the other until the end of the course. This message was not only our perception as teachers but it was also conveyed by the students themselves to the dean of studies as part of the feedback students are asked to provide about all courses every year.

## 4    Introductory MDE Course: Version 2

After two largely unsuccessful editions of the course we realized that trying to cover all aspects of building MDE artifacts was too much and there was no real practical reason for that since the chances of students working professionally as language designers or similar are rather small. Moreover, they were not convinced about the benefits of MDE in the first place so their motivation was low as well.

Therefore we decided to shift the focus to a more "MDE as users" perspective. The rationale was that this is a more reasonable goal for a first MDE course and one that, if fulfilled, would achieve our goal of increasing the adoption of MDE in software projects. We would like to train students to be at least open to use MDE in their future professional projects, and thus, a course on basic MDE principles from a user perspective seemed more appropriate and a better way to motivate them.

We still wished to cover in the course all the main concepts and components of MDE but now aiming at helping students to understand what each MDE technique was useful for and how they could add it to their arsenal of software tools (even if this could first imply hiring a MDE language designer to adapt the tools to their own specific context before they can start developing software with them). To avoid the *too many too shallow* problem we decided to devote ample time to a couple of case studies, including a large one where students would need to develop a web-based application using MDE techniques (mainly code generation) with the hope this scenario would be a very illustrative and convincing way to demonstrate the advantages MDE could bring to their daily professional practice particularly in terms of productivity and quality gains.

With this new vision, the reshaped course syllabus evolved as follows (in bold the parts that changed from the previous edition, including changes in content and time distribution)

1. MDE Foundations (**4 h**)
2. MDE Core technologies (**8 h**)
3. Methodology and infrastructure (**3 h**)
4. **Case Study 1: Model-driven Reverse Engineering with MoDisco (8 h)**
5. **Case Study 2: Model-driven Software Development with WebRatio (22 h)**

Note the drastic reduction in the core technologies section. Before, the time devoted to this part included the assignments to develop several MDE artifacts. In the revised syllabus students were only provided with an overview of those techniques so they know why/how to use them but not necessarily how to develop them (i.e. they understand the concept of model transformation and know how they could use ATL [16] transformations in their projects and even read them but we don't ask them to write ATL transformations as part of the course).

The first case study was a reverse engineering scenario where students were asked to use MoDisco [6] to reverse-engineer a Java application and write some (OCL) queries at both the Java model and UML model (generated from the Java one also using MoDisco's built-in transformations) level to appreciate the power of reverse engineering as a way to understand complex systems. This scenario was important because this is probably one the most common uses of software modeling in practice and, for instance, in the Nantes region, there are important companies that offer this kind of model-based modernization services.

For the larger case study we chose the development of a CRUD-based web application. That is, given a set of requirements regarding the data that a fictitious company needs to manage, students were asked to create all the forms and reports needed to modify/visualize the data through a web application. This scenario was intended to balance the complexity of modeling a web application compared with the amount of code that could be automatically generated from those models. More specifically, students were expected to specify the data model of the application as a UML class diagram, and its navigation model (showing the web pages of the application, the links between them and the actions/events to execute when following a link) as a standard IFML diagram [5]. Given these two models, the WebRatio tool[1] would automatically generate and deploy a fully-functional web application. WebRatio was not the only tool that could be used on this scenario but was chosen because of its level of maturity and due to strong links with the company and researchers behind the tool which would enable us to ask for help – if at all needed. As studied before [2], tool support seems to correlate with more effective MDE teaching.

And, sadly, we did need their help. The reshaping of the course didn't work as we expected and we even had to invite a WebRatio expert to assist the students with the use of the tool (and to be honest, the feeling is that the same would have happened if we had chosen a different tool). At the end of the course, many students were convinced **not** to use MDE again, which was exactly the opposite effect of what we intended. Thus, we did a postmortem analysis to understand what had gone wrong (again), including a very small (but mandatory) survey for the students to answer. In the following we report on the survey questions and their results.

**Q1 – How would you mark the experience of using the code-generation tool?**

---

[1] http://www.webratio.com/.

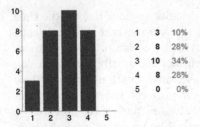

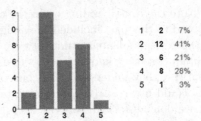

**Fig. 1.** Answers to Q1 from 5 (very satisfactory) to 1 (totally unacceptable). Total number of answers and corresponding percentages shown on the right.

**Fig. 2.** Answers to Q2 from 5 (totally sure) to 1 (no way I'm doing that). Total number of answers and corresponding percentages shown on the right.

Figure 1 summarizes the results. Among the most cited (negative) reasons we had: *lots of installation and configuration problems* (students were eventually allowed to work in pairs to make easier for them to have access to at least one machine were the tool was working smoothly), *lack of optimization of the deployed application* (in terms of the size of the generated files specially due to a default set of generated infrastructure code, quite noticeable for a small application like the one in the course), *sudden crashes and corrupted projects, good for prototyping but unsure if the method scales, lack of documentation* and *difficult to customize the code*. There were also some (but fewer) positive comments like *I think this is the tendency of the future* but we always learn more from criticism.

**Q2 - If you were working in a software company, how likely is it that you would choose to use some kind of code-generation tool in your next web development project ?**

Not very likely according to the results shown in Fig. 2. Here a few students mention that *a MDD tool could be used to generate the back-end part and be a great help for database management or a quick and dirty generation for a prototype but for the front-end part, I think it is a waste of time* particularly because they had the feeling they would need to end up modifying lots of the generated code to polish the result since this kind of tool will never be as configurable (at the model-level) as native HTML/CSS/JS code where one can precisely configure every single graphical aspect of the front-end. A couple of students also mentioned that for the kind of scenario they would find the tool useful (this back-end admin-like generator) most programming frameworks nowadays can already generate a simple scaffolding interface from only a database definition which would be good enough and simpler to use. Clearly, this highlights the need to find a sweet spot between language expressiveness and tool simplicity here. Too complex and developers are concerned that they need to invest too much time learning and modeling. Too simple and they will not perceive the benefits.

**Q3 – In your opinion, what would make MDD tools more useful and attractive to programmers?**

This open question produced good suggestions for some new features for this class of tools, particularly related to having a better and more user-friendly experience with them, like:

1. Being able to build your pages by drag and drop;
2. Ability to change the generated code in a manner that would revert back on the model;
3. Having some common patterns already implemented by default (like login, CRUD tasks, etc.);
4. Easier to build multi-language applications;
5. Requests for non-functional aspects like documentation and better compatibility (result of the problems reported in the first question).

The following comment from one of the students is a good summary of a shared feeling among the cohort: *The concept of generating code seems good in itself. However, I had so many problems with the tool I didn't even think I was saving time.* In the next section we discuss some measures that can be put in place to alleviate this situation and ensure that students do not only think that code generation is a good idea but that they are also convinced that it works in practice. These measures will be directed towards addressing the socio-technical factors that caused this perception.

## 5    Recommendations and Lessons Learned

Based on the previous results, private conversations with colleagues around the world and popular online public discussions[2] we present here a list of lessons learned in the form of recommendations to both MDE instructors (useful for, both, instructors working on companies or in universities and other teaching institutions) and tool vendors to avoid the pitfalls reported earlier.

Recommendations mainly focus on the students perception and experience when interacting with the tools, not on core technical aspects of those tools. For instance, they perceived the tool as generating huge files at the end of the process. This did not really cause any kind of objective efficiency problem when deploying or running the application but they perceived it as a negative value of the tool nonetheless. Therefore, dealing with the reported issues implies considering the

---

[2] It is worth mentioning the discussion in the blog post http://modeling-languages. com/failed-convince-students-benefits-code-generation/ explaining the first author's preliminary observations that ended up with over four thousand visits and thirty comments (from people with different backgrounds like tool vendors: Meta-Case, WebRatio, Softeam, consultants and end-users) and the submission of that same post on reddit https://www.reddit.com/r/programming/comments/2vehhm/ i_failed_to_convince_my_students_about_the/ that brought sixty-five additional comments. Besides these two, additional discussions on these results took place in other forums like a number of LinkedIn groups.

sum of the user and the tool as a sociotechnical system that needs to be improved together. Sometimes, we can improve the tool itself but many other times, we need to change the way (the scenario, the conditions,..) students use the tool to give them a more positive experience.

### Recommendations for instructors

- Start with a very compelling development scenario. Our CRUD exercise was good to generate a full-fledged working application without requiring complex behavioral modeling but it was too small: the investment required to learn the modeling language and corresponding tooling did not pay off during the project. When exposing first-time learners to MDE, they must feel that they save time thanks to MDE from the very beginning. Therefore we would recommend avoiding toy examples and start with a larger one.
- Change the requirements during the development. Beyond making the exercise more realistic, another way to make MDE more compelling would be to change the requirements of the MDE scenario at the last minute. For instance, in the code-generation case study, we could have asked students to adapt the web application to a number of changes (in the names of the attributes, or their types or even associations between classes) two or three days before the due date. It would be very painful for them to implement those changes directly at the code level (looking for all references to the modified classes anywhere in the code) while doing this at the model level and re-generating should be much easier. To make it even more complex, students could be asked to update not their own projects but the project of another student (again, the goal would be to demonstrate that models can be significantly more understandable and maintainable than code)
- Use a repetitive scenario. It is known that MDE pays off in the mid-term due to the initial learning curve [1,10]. Therefore, ideally, students should be asked to complete several similar projects during the course, with the intention of realizing how they their productivity improves at every iteration.
- Compile a set of examples and reference solutions students can refer to and play with. Beyond toy examples, some more complex examples showing that MDE can effectively model and generate non-trivial software should also be provided. In particular, it would be nice to see models simulating popular services like Facebook or Twitter. We believe there should be a community effort to build and share such examples in a public repository. As a side-effect, those same examples could be used as benchmarks to compare the functionality and quality of various MDE tools.
- Keep in mind your target user profile. Introducing MDE to a group of developers in charge of building complex software can be very different than doing so to a group of business users looking for quick – but prototype-level –solutions. WebRatio may work for the former but a solution like Mendix[3] would likely be more appealing to the latter.

---

[3] https://www.mendix.com/.

## Recommendations for tool vendors

- Document, document, document and make sure that documentation is easy to find. The (perceived) lack of proper documentation is what provoked the uprising of students against Acceleo. They did not care whether the tool was the only one properly implementing the OMG standard for model-to-code transformations, they just wanted good documentation to complete the assignment faster.
- Your goal is to hide all underlying technical details. When things go well this is normally the case but, when errors occur in the generation process, tools tend to present users with obscure error messages referencing internal code. This makes finding and correcting the error a daunting task (often involving extensive guesswork as most tools have poor debugging facilities). Even if this happens rarely, when it does, it can cause frustration and disappointment with the tool.
- Offer a well-packaged and standalone installation. For instance, Java-based MDE tools usually ask for the Java environment to use during the installation (even if they have one embedded). This is done to offer more flexibility in the installation process but at the risk of creating unnecessary configuration problems when choosing non-compatible environments. In our case, it turned out that WebRatio was not compatible with the Java version most students had installed as part of another course, so we ended up with over half of the class with an installation of WebRatio they could not use, definitely not a good start.
- Keep up with trends in the software industry. Most software today is an integration of APIs, social components and other kind of services. Students were quickly trying to find components for Google login, Twitter sharing etc. This may not be so relevant for business internal applications but it is for sure something people are now used to find in any web application and will quickly try to replicate when developing their own. Unfortunately, most MDE tools do not offer these features.
- Favor trust in your tool over everything else. Make sure that your tool is reliable and generates optimal code or at least code good enough that users can trust. If the tool crashes regularly, there is no chance users will believe the code that tool generates is good, they will just assume that a bad tool cannot generate good code. It takes only one bad result to lose their trust.

All these recommendations will not fix by themselves one of the major problems when attempting to convince students about the importance of MDE: the lack of job offers stating MDE as a requirement to apply for the position. Compared to any popular programming language/platform, students feel that MDE is unlikely to boost their employability prospects anywhere nearly as much as becoming experts in, e.g. AngularJS would. This is kind of a chicken-egg problem (increasing the adoption of MDE will create more job opportunities for MDE experts and the other way round) but the previous measures should at least help in moving the market in the right direction.

# 6    Conclusions

Teaching MDE, and software modeling in general, is considered positive in itself [18] but there is a lot to be done if we wish that teaching to give students a more complete picture of what MDE can do for them in their future professional life. As reported herein, succeeding in this goal requires a careful preparation of a respective course to ensure students have a positive first experience. We have presented a set of lessons learned, which we believe can help other educators in emphasizing the human factors that come into play when preparing such a course.

As further work we plan to replicate these experiments in other educational institutions. In particular, in the near term, we will focus on the e-learning model of the UOC's (www.uoc.edu) Faculty of Computer Science, in charge of providing online university education in Information and Communication Technologies since 1997 through its fully virtual campus [20]. Additional validation will be done through collaborations with partners from the network of institutions that teach MDE[4]. A more ambitious plan involves following up on some of the (convinced) students to assess whether the experience made any difference in their approach to software development once they started their professional career. On this, the UOC environment can also help since many of the students are already working professionals seeking additional qualifications.

# References

1. Acerbis, R., Bongio, A., Brambilla, M., Tisi, M., Ceri, S., Tosetti, E.: Developing eBusiness solutions with a model driven approach: the case of acer EMEA. In: Baresi, L., Fraternali, P., Houben, G.-J. (eds.) ICWE 2007. LNCS, vol. 4607, pp. 539–544. Springer, Heidelberg (2007). doi:10.1007/978-3-540-73597-7_51
2. Akayama, S., Hisazumi, K., Hiya, S., Fukuda, A.: Using model-driven development tools for object-oriented modeling education. In: Educators' Symposium, 16th International Conference on Model Driven Engineering Languages and Systems (MODELS 2013) (2013)
3. Brambilla, M., Cabot, J., Wimmer, M.: Model-Driven Software Engineering in Practice. Synthesis Lectures on Software Engineering. Morgan & Claypool Publishers, San Rafael (2012)
4. Brambilla, M., Fraternali, P.: Large-scale model-driven engineering of web user interaction: the webml and webratio experience. Sci. Comput. Program. **89**, 71–87 (2014)
5. Brambilla, M., Fraternali, P.: Interaction Flow Modeling Language. The MK/OMG Press, Morgan Kaufmann, Burlington (2015)
6. Brunelière, H., Cabot, J., Dupé, G., Madiot, F.: Modisco: a model driven reverse engineering framework. Inf. Softw. Technol. **56**(8), 1012–1032 (2014)
7. Budgen, D., Burn, A.J., Brereton, O.P., Kitchenham, B.A., Pretorius, R.: Empirical evidence about the uml: a systematic literature review. Softw. Prac. Exp. **41**(4), 363–392 (2011)

---

[4] See an (incomplete) list, taken from the set of instructors that declare to be using [3] in courses, here: https://www.sites.google.com/site/mdsebook/courses.

8. Cataldo, M., Herbsleb, J.D., Carley, K.M.: Socio-technical congruence: a framework for assessing the impact of technical and work dependencies on software development productivity. In: Proceedings of the 2nd International Symposium on Empirical Software Engineering and Measurement, ESEM 2008, pp. 2–11 (2008)

9. Cuadrado, J.S., Izquierdo, J.L.C., Molina, J.G.: Applying model-driven engineering in small software enterprises. Sci. Comput. Program. **89**, 176–198 (2014)

10. Diaz, O., Villoria, F.M.: Generating blogs out of product catalogues: an MDE approach. J. Syst. Softw. **83**(10), 1970–1982 (2010)

11. Dobing, B., Parsons, J.: How UML is used. Commun. ACM **49**(5), 109–113 (2006)

12. Dzidek, W.J., Arisholm, E., Briand, L.C.: A realistic empirical evaluation of the costs and benefits of UML in software maintenance. IEEE Trans. Softw. Eng. **34**(3), 407–432 (2008)

13. Fernández-Sáez, A.M., Caivano, D., Genero, M., Chaudron, M.R.V.: On the use of UML documentation in software maintenance: results from a survey in industry. In: 18th International Conference on Model Driven Engineering Languages and Systems, MoDELS 2015, pp. 292–301 (2015)

14. Hutchinson, J., Whittle, J., Rouncefield, M.: Model-driven engineering practices in industry: social, organizational and managerial factors that lead to success or failure. Sci. Comput. Program. **89**, 144–161 (2014)

15. Iqbal, M.Z., Ali, S., Yue, T., Briand, L.C.: Applying UML/MARTE on industrial projects: challenges, experiences, and guidelines. Softw. Syst. Model. **14**(4), 1367–1385 (2015)

16. Jouault, F., Allilaire, F., Bézivin, J., Kurtev, I.: ATL: a model transformation tool. Sci. Comput. Program. **72**(1–2), 31–39 (2008)

17. Mellor, S.J., Balcer, M.: Executable UML: A Foundation for Model-Driven Architectures. Addison-Wesley Longman Publishing Co., Inc., Boston (2002)

18. Petre, M.: Uml in practice. In: Proceedings of the 2013 International Conference on Software Engineering, ICSE 2013, Piscataway, NJ, USA, pp. 722–731. IEEE Press (2013)

19. Petre, M.: "no shit" or "oh, shit!": responses to observations on the use of UML in professional practice. Softw. Syst. Model. **13**(4), 1225–1235 (2014)

20. Sangra, A.: A new learning model for the information and knowledge society: the case of the universitat oberta de catalunya (uoc), spain. Int. Rev. Res. Open Distrib. Learn. **2**(2) (2002)

21. Steinberg, D., Budinsky, F., Paternostro, M., Merks, E.: EMF: Eclipse Modeling Framework 2.0, 2nd edn. Addison-Wesley Professional, Amsterdam (2009)

22. Vallecillo, A.: On the industrial adoption of model driven engineering. is your company ready for mde? Int. J. Inf. Syst. Softw. Eng. Big Co. **1**(1), 52–68 (2014)

23. Whittle, J., Hutchinson, J., Rouncefield, M.: The state of practice in model-driven engineering. IEEE Softw. **31**(3), 79–85 (2014)

# Learning Pros and Cons of Model-Driven Development in a Practical Teaching Experience

Óscar Pastor[1(✉)], Sergio España[2], and Jose Ignacio Panach[3]

[1] Centro de Investigación en Métodos de Producción de Software - ProS,
Universitat Politècnica de València, Camino de Vera s/n, 46022 Valencia, Spain
opastor@pros.upv.es
[2] Department of Information and Computing Sciences,
Utrecht University, Utrecht, The Netherlands
s.espana@uu.nl
[3] Escola Tècnica Superior d'Enginyeria, Departament d'Informàtica, Universitat de València,
Avenida de la Universidad, s/n, 46100 Burjassot, Valencia, Spain
joigpana@uv.es

**Abstract.** Current teaching guides on Software Engineering degree focus mainly on teaching programming languages from the first courses. Conceptual modeling is a topic that is only taught in last courses, like master courses. At that point, many students do not see the usefulness of conceptual modeling and most of them have difficulty to reach the level of abstraction needed to work with them. In order to make the learning of conceptual modeling more attractive, we have conducted an experience where students compare a traditional development versus a development using conceptual models through a Model-Driven Development (MDD) method. This way, students can check on their own pros and cons of working with MDD in a practical environment. Comparison has been done in terms of Accuracy, Effort, Productivity and Satisfaction. The contribution of this paper is twofold: the description of the teaching methodology used throughout the whole course; and the presentation of results and discussions of the comparison between MDD and a traditional development method. Results show that Accuracy, Effort and Productivity are better for MDD when the problem to solve is not easy. These results are shown to students to promote a discussion in the classroom about the use of MDD. According to this discussion, the most difficult part of using MDD is the learnability and the best part is the automatic code generation.

**Keywords:** Model-Driven · Conceptual modeling · Teaching methodology

## 1 Introduction

We are three teachers of a subject in a master course from Universitat Politècnica de València (Spain) called "Engineering of Information Systems", which deals with the topic of conceptual modelling within a Model-Driven Development (MDD) perspective.

This work was developed with the support of Generalitat Valenciana-funded IDEO project (PROMETEOII/2014/039).

S. Link and J.C. Trujillo (Eds.): ER 2016 Workshops, LNCS 9975, pp. 218–227, 2016.
DOI: 10.1007/978-3-319-47717-6_19

The main goal of the master course is to teach how to abstractly represent system information through conceptual models (CMs) and how this CMs can be used to obtain the final application in a Conceptual-Schema software development context [1]. The subject has been prepared using an MDD tool (INTEGRANOVA [2]). This way, students can focus all their efforts on building conceptual models, relegating the code generation to automatic model to code transformation rules applied by the tool.

During several previous years we have noticed that, in general, the use of conceptual models as a way to represent all system features is new for students. All previous subjects in the software engineering degree were focused on building UML models that only represent data persistence and part of the system behaviour. These UML models guide the manual implementation of the code at best. Most students build UML models at first stages of the software development but once they start to implement the code, these models are forgotten and in most cases, they are not updated with all the characteristics specified within the code. At the end, UML models are a type of heavy-obsolete documentation that nobody (students and teachers) query, focusing on the implementation and the developed system.

Within that context, the topic of conceptual modelling was not motivating for students that are accustomed to focus on writing code and compiling it. In order to motivate the students, we propose teaching conceptual modelling comparing MDD versus a traditional software development method. This should help to wake up a critical spirit in each student, drawing personal conclusions about the pros and cons of conceptual modelling in practice. There are several works that have studied the advantages and difficulties of MDD, such as [3, 4], but we aim to check whether students, which are not familiar with conceptual modelling, perceived the usefulness of MDD. At the end of the course, apart from teaching the students conceptual modelling, we have a set of empirical data that we can use to compare MDD regarding a traditional development. The analysis is based on the study of 4 variables: Accuracy, Effort, Productivity and Satisfaction. The results of analyzing those data statistically are shown to the students as a starting point for a general discussion about the pros and cons of MDD.

We have conducted this teaching experience during two years. The results of the data extracted the first year have been published in [5]. Results showed that MDD obtains better values than a traditional method only when the problem complexity of the system to develop increases. Regarding Effort, Productivity and Satisfaction we did not identify differences. In order to check the idea that the complexity of the problem can affect the results, we increased the complexity of the problems in the second year.

The contribution of this paper is twofold: the description of the teaching methodology used in both years and the summary of results and discussions obtained in the second year. The description of the methodology aims to promote the adoption of future replications in universities different from UPV. The methodology consists in starting with the development of a web application using a traditional method. Next, we have several classes dedicated to learn MDD. Next, students develop another system through MDD. At the end of the course, we compare how much Accuracy, Effort, Productivity and Satisfaction have been experienced by each subject in both treatments, and we conduct a discussion in the classroom. Results of the second year show that when problems to solve are complex, MDD obtains better results not only for Accuracy but also for Effort and Productivity. During the discussion, students claimed that the main cons for using MDD is the high learning curve, while the main pros is the automatic code generation from conceptual models.

The paper is organised as follows. Section 2 discusses related works. Section 3 describes the teaching methodology used during both years. Section 4 shows the results after analyzing data of the second year. Section 5 shows the results of the discussions in the classroom after showing the results to students. Finally, Sect. 6 presents the conclusions.

## 2    Related Works

The topic of techniques to teach conceptual modeling to students has been tackled by several researchers. Muller [6] has elaborated a list of current challenges to teach conceptual modeling. These challenges refer to including conceptual modeling in a multi-disciplinary world to teach that: building systems is an engineering task; customer context and system context is not the same; a system is dynamic; it is important to quantify; systems are not always well-defined; analysts need part of psychology to deal with customers; analysts need a critical attitude. All these challenges show that there is still much work to do in order to better teach conceptual modeling.

Several works explain their experience teaching modeling through Entity-Relationship (ER) schemas, such as Davis [7]. Davis describes that students learn ER models with a combination of individual and team work, including instructor feedback as well as peer interaction. The teacher gives an ER schema and the students must interpret the meaning of constructs used in it; and given a description of requirements, students must design an ER schema. Other similar work has been done by Keberle and Utkin [8], who present a system called "Chen Worlds" to teach ER modeling. The proposal is based on the idea of gaming the environment to accelerate the learning of conceptual models in a course of database information systems. Chen Worlds is a software system for learning, building, visualizing and validating conceptual models in ER notation.

There are other works that have dealt with conceptual models different from ER, such as i*. In this line, Paja et al. [9] have reported their experience teaching i* in a master course. The work concludes that i* analysis allows the students to better understand the activities they perform. This helps to refine models until they are more meaningful and more likely to fulfill their purpose. Other techniques are based on constructivism, such as Zhuoyi et al. [10]. These authors propose a constructive teaching model in a database course where students must learn conceptual modeling under teachers' guidance. Students explore and find knowledge, construct the meaning and learn to cooperate and communicate with others. According to the authors, constructivism arises enthusiasm of the students and improves the ability of solving problems.

Some works have compared two teaching techniques, such as Kung et al. [11] who have compared top-down versus bottom-up approaches to build conceptual models. Results show that with proper experience, students can do it better in a bottom-up design. Sedrakyan et al. [12] define a proposal to build models and generate a prototype of application using those models. The proposal has been compared with other traditional techniques that do not generate prototypes. The results show that the proposal improves the understanding of students.

Some authors teach MDD in their courses, such as Akayama et al. [13], who teach conceptual models through MDD. Akayama compared a development using MDD versus another one without MDD. Results showed the effectiveness of MDD. Our proposal is aligned with this idea, as next sections describe.

## 3  Teaching Methodology

This section describes the teaching methodology that combines MDD with a traditional development (Fig. 1). Sessions took 2 h and there was 1 session per week, with a total of 14 sessions. The course has been designed in such a way that all the students work in pairs for logistic reasons. The three teachers participated at the same time during the course to teach MDD and to report data to analyze the comparison between both methods. Next, we describe each step of the methodology.

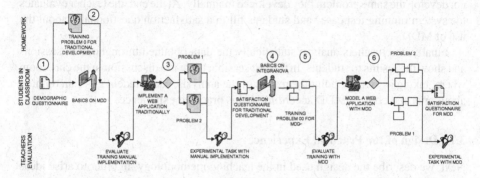

**Fig. 1.** Schema of the teaching methodology

In step 1, students fill in a demographic questionnaire to check the level of experience in a traditional development method and in MDD. The course presupposes that most of the students already know how to develop a system through a traditional method but they know nothing about MDD. We must check this idea with the demographic questionnaire. In step 2, we propose a training problem to develop a web application as homework. This training aims to ensure that students are capable of programming a system from scratch. The time to develop the system is 15 days, students can use the development framework for web applications that they better know and they can draw in a paper any conceptual model that they complementary need. Half of the students drew a UML class diagram and the others used no model. During these two weeks, the teacher teaches the basics of MDD. There is not time inside the classroom to develop the system since we assume that every student has enough knowledge to develop the system on his own. Once the period of the training is over, the teacher evaluates the training through a set of test cases on the system. At this point, we can ensure that all the students have enough knowledge to develop a system with a traditional method.

In step 3, students must develop another web application from scratch in a period of 4 h in the classroom under the teacher supervision. In the same way as in the training, students can choose the programming language and draw in a paper any conceptual model they need. We used two problems to avoid that results were dependent on only one problem. Problems were assigned randomly to pairs such a way they are balanced among groups. At the end of this step, the teacher evaluates the developed problem and students fills in a satisfaction questionnaire about the use of a traditional development method.

Next, in step 4, the teacher explains MDD during 12 h using INTEGRANOVA [2] as tool based on UML models that supports MDD. In step 5, we use a training problem similar to the training problem used in step 2. The students have 15 days to develop the problem as homework using INTEGRANOVA. We use 6 h in the classroom to support this development. At the end of this development, the teacher evaluates the result running test cases. At this point, we can ensure that students have enough knowledge to work with MDD. In step 6, students have to develop a system from scratch using MDD without any help from the teacher. We swap the problems used in step 3 such a way students do not develop the same problem they developed manually. At the end, the teacher evaluates the system running test cases and students fill in a satisfaction questionnaire about the use of MDD.

Finally, the teachers analyze statistically the data obtained throughout all sessions and show the results to students. In the last session, there is a discussion in the classroom where, taking as starting point the results of the analysis, each student gives an opinion about pros and cons of MDD according to this practical experience.

## 3.1 Design of the Practical Experience

Next, we describe the design used in the teaching methodology. In order to arise ideas for and against MDD, we designed a practical experience based on four research questions: (**RQ1**) Is software accuracy affected by MDD?; (**RQ2**) Is developer effort affected by MDD?; (**RQ3**) Is developer productivity affected by MDD?; (**RQ4**) Is developer satisfaction affected by MDD?. All these questions have been extracted from works that claim MDD benefits, such as [14, 15]. The idea is that every student checks all these claims on his own to extract conclusions about the use of MDD. The teacher collects data throughout all the experience to answer the four research questions. At the end of the course, results are shown to discuss in the classroom the pros and cons of MDD.

Research questions are written as null **hypothesis** that the teacher must check statistically: ($H_{01}$) The software accuracy of a system built using MDD is similar to software accuracy using a traditional method; ($H_{02}$) The developer effort to build a system using MDD is similar to effort using a traditional method; ($H_{03}$) The developer productivity using MDD to build a system is similar to productivity using a traditional method; ($H_{04}$) The developer satisfaction using MDD to build a system is similar to satisfaction using a traditional method. We work with the **factor** Method, with two levels: MDD and a traditional method; and 4 **response variables**: Accuracy, Effort, Productivity and Satisfaction. The developed problem is a block variable since we are not interested in studying its effect.

Next, we describe the **metrics** used to check the null hypotheses. We measure Accuracy as the percentage of acceptance test cases that are successfully passed. We used 4 different metrics for Accuracy, from more restrictive to less restrictive:

- All or nothing (AN): we consider that a test case is satisfied only if every item is passed.
- Relaxed all or nothing (RAN): we consider that a test case is satisfied when at least 75 % of items are passed.
- Weighted items (WI): we assign a weight to each test item depending on the complexity of its functionality. When test cases are run, we add the weights of passed items.
- Same weight for all items (SW): we assign the same weight to each item within a test case (independently of complexity) in such a way that the addition of all the weights of the items is 1 per test case. When test cases are run, we add the weights of passed items.

Effort is measured as the time taken by each pair to develop the web applications from scratch. Productivity is measured as the ratio Accuracy/Effort. Finally, satisfaction is measured as the positive attitude towards the use of the development method through a questionnaire based on a Likert scale. Metrics for Satisfaction are based on Moody's proposal: Perceived Usefulness (PU), Perceived Ease of Use (PEOU), and Intention to Use (ITU) [16].

**Problems** used in the experience are a system to manage a company of electrical appliance (Problem 1) and a system to manage a photography agency (Problem 2). Complexity of both problems is similar, Problem 1 has 40 function points and Problem 2 has 35. Complexity of problems used in both training sessions is also similar to complexity of Problems 1 and 2. Since training problems were not analyzed statistically, we do not describe them.

The **design** is a paired design blocked by problems, since we apply both treatments (MDD and a traditional development) to each subject and we are not interested in studying the effect of the problem in the response variables.

We have conducted this experience during two courses. The results of the first course (the baseline experience) was published in [5]. Results of that preliminary study showed that MDD gets better Accuracy the more complex the problem to solve is. We did not identify differences between Effort, Productivity and Satisfaction comparing both methods. In order to study in depth the idea that MDD seems to be more robust to higher complexities, we replicated the experience in a second course with the same procedure, but in this case we used a more complex version of both problems (Problems 1 and 2). Next sections focus on explaining the results obtained after analyzing response variables and the discussion of students in the replication of the second course.

## 4    Results

This section describes the results from the data extracted through the experience. These results were shared with the students to promote the critical thinking regarding MDD.

The teachers have used a Mixed Model [17] to check whether null hypotheses can be rejected or not. In those cases where null hypotheses are rejected, we have calculated the effect size to know the degree of differences between both treatments. The effect size has been calculated through Cohen's Delta [18]. More than 0.8 is a large effect; between 0.79 and 0.5 is a moderate effect; between 0.49 and 0.2 is a small effect.

Table 1 shows the p-values and the effect size of our response variables. **Accuracy** obtains significant results for the four metrics (AN, RAN, WI and SW) since all p-values are less than 0.05. Since effect sizes are around 0.6, we can state that differences between MDD and a traditional method are moderate. So, we can reject $H_{01}$, which means that software accuracy of a system built using MDD is not similar to software accuracy using a traditional method. MDD obtains better averages in Accuracy than a traditional method independently of the used metric.

**Table 1.** p-values and effect sizes.

| | Accuracy | | | | Efficiency | Productivity | | | | Satisfaction | | |
|---|---|---|---|---|---|---|---|---|---|---|---|---|
| | AN | RAN | WI | SW | | AN | RAN | WI | SW | PEOU | PU | ITU |
| p-value | .00 | .01 | .00 | .00 | 0.00 | .00 | .02 | .01 | .01 | .56 | .27 | .85 |
| Effect size | .66 | 0.6 | .62 | .61 | 0.77 | .64 | .58 | .6 | .59 | – | – | – |

**Efficiency** obtains also significant results, since p-value is less than 0.05. Effect size is 0.77, which means that differences between MDD and a traditional method are moderate. So, we can reject $H_{02}$, which means that the developer effort to build a system using MDD is not similar to effort using a traditional method. MDD obtains better averages in Efficiency than a traditional method

**Productivity** obtains significant results considering the four metrics for Accuracy (AN, RAN, WI and SW), since all p-values are less than 0.05. Effect sizes are around 0.6, which means that differences between MDD and a traditional method are moderate. So, we can reject $H_{03}$, which means that the developer productivity using MDD to build a system is not similar to productivity using a traditional method. MDD obtains better averages in Productivity than a traditional method.

**Satisfaction** does not obtain significant results in any of the three metrics (PEOU, PU, and ITU), since p-values are higher than 0.05. So, effect sizes have not been calculated. We cannot reject $H_{04}$, which means that the developer satisfaction using MDD to build a system is similar to satisfaction using a traditional method.

According to these results we can state that the problem complexity affects positively MDD. In the baseline experience, we only got significant results for Accuracy when the problem to solve was complex. In this replication, where problem complexity has been increased regarding the baseline, we obtain better results for MDD in Accuracy, Efficiency and Productivity. This leads to think that the higher complexity we try to solve with MDD, the better results we got. Note that even though problems were implemented significantly better with MDD, students did not feel a better satisfaction. All these results were shown to the student in the classroom for discussion.

## 5   Discussion in the Classroom

The subsequent discussion performed in the classroom arose a set of significant aspects. Figure 2 shows a summary of all the discussed aspects of MDD and the number of students who supported them. The main "pros" are the code generation and the quick software development; while the main "cons" are the difficult deployment and the learnability.

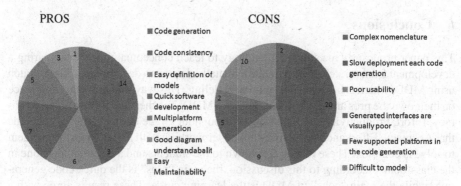

**Fig. 2.**  Pros and Cons of MDD extracted from the discussion session

In the discussion there was a major agreement on a basic fact: the more complex a problem is, the bigger MDD improvements become. Students understood that a "real" conceptual-model compiler can provide a much more efficient and effective software development environment, as capturing the problem complexity in a conceptual (higher-level) model is easier than to do it at a pure (lower-level) programming level. To make true that "the model is the code" instead of "the code is the model", a conceptual programming [19] environment must make possible to specify the full problem complexity in a conceptual model, and this conceptual model must be executable. A main challenge for industrial MDD tools is then to make real this conceptual model compiler goal. The tool used in our experiment –INTEGRANOVA- is a very appropriate example of such a kind of MDD tool.

Another interesting discussion thread was related to know why satisfaction did not improve with MDD. It was again a major agreement in one relevant aspect: using MDD is not at a simple task. It was somewhat assumed that modeling should be easier than programming. The reality was that most of the students had serious problems to switch to a conceptual modeling-based mental strategy to face the problem solution. Conceptual modeling capabilities need to be prepared and to be practiced. While students clearly showed to have a good programming profile, largely practiced during their undergraduate learning experience, their conceptual modeling profile was not at all so good. Current Computer Science degrees mainly focus on programming, not on modeling. Since conceptualizing is an essential task for a software engineer, this lack of conceptual modeling expertise in many curriculas can be seen as a serious handicap to make MDD practices become widely and correctly used.

In any case, a final significant reflection was that after practicing programming for years, practicing MDD only for a few weeks was enough to obtain even better results in 3 of the 4 response variables, while for the fourth one the difference was not significant. A final aspect that we want to explore in future experiments is how personal abilities of the student correlate with the results. We suspect that student that outperform with programing, also do it with modeling. Measuring what precise improvement is achieved in these cases when using MDD will be part of our future analysis.

## 6  Conclusions

This paper proposes a teaching methodology to teach conceptual models comparing a development from scratch using a traditional method versus a development from scratch using MDD, which is based on conceptual modeling. This way, students can experience on their own the pros and cons of working with MDD. Teachers report data about Accuracy, Effort, Productivity and Satisfaction throughout all the classes. Results conclude that Accuracy, Effort and Productivity are better working with MDD when the problem to solve is complex. These results are shown to the students and a discussion is done in the classroom. According to this discussion, the main "pros" is the quick code generation, while the main "cons" of MDD is the learning curve. These results agree with a previous baseline experience we conducted the previous year on the same subject.

Note importantly that there are some characteristics in our proposed teaching method that might affect the results. First, the limitation of 4 h to the development of problems results in a maximum level for Effort. So, we do not know whether differences in time would have been higher without that limitation. Second, we use complex problems to analyze variables, but these problems are still toy problems. Maybe, more differences between MDD and a traditional method might have arisen if we had worked with real complex problems. Third, all the students knew to develop a web application with a traditional method, but the level of knowledge was not the same. Results might have been different if we had worked with professionals.

As future work, we plan to conduct more replications of the same teaching methodology during several years. It would be interesting to get more replications from different universities with other MDD tools.

## References

1. Olivé, À.: Conceptual schema-centric development: a grand challenge for information systems research. In: Pastor, Ó., Falcão e Cunha, J. (eds.) CAiSE 2005. LNCS, vol. 3520, pp. 1–15. Springer, Heidelberg (2005)
2. INTEGRANOVA Technologies. http://www.integranova.com
3. Selic, B.: The pragmatics of model-driven development. IEEE Softw. **20**, 19–25 (2003)
4. Hailpern, B., Tarr, P.: Model-driven development: the good, the bad, and the ugly. IBM Syst. J. **45**, 451–461 (2006)
5. Panach, J.I., España, S., Dieste, Ó., Pastor, Ó., Juristo, N.: In search of evidence for model-driven development claims: An experiment on quality, effort, productivity and satisfaction. Inf. Softw. Technol. **62**, 164–186 (2015)

6. Muller, G.: Challenges in teaching conceptual modeling for systems architecting. In: Jeusfeld, M.A., et al. (eds.) ER 2015 Workshops. LNCS, vol. 9382, pp. 317–326. Springer, Heidelberg (2015). doi:10.1007/978-3-319-25747-1_31

7. Davis, K.C.: Teaching conceptual design capture. In: Parsons, J., Chiu, D. (eds.) ER Workshops 2013. LNCS, vol. 8697, pp. 247–256. Springer, Heidelberg (2014)

8. Keberle, N., Utkin:, I.V.: Teaching conceptual modeling in ER: chen worlds. In: ICTERI, pp. 222–227 (2012)

9. Paja, E., Horkoff, J., Mylopoulos, J.: The importance of teaching systematic analysis for conceptual models: an experience report. In: Jeusfeld, M.A., et al. (eds.) ER 2015 Workshops. LNCS, vol. 9382, pp. 347–357. Springer, Heidelberg (2015). doi:10.1007/978-3-319-25747-1_34

10. Zhuoyi, C., Na, L., Hongjie, Z.: Exploration of teaching model of the database course based on constructivism learning theory. In: 2012 2nd International Conference on Consumer Electronics, Communications and Networks (CECNet), pp. 1808–1811 (2012)

11. Kung, H.-J., Kung, L., Gardiner, A.: Comparing top-down with bottom-up approaches: teaching data modeling. In: Information Systems Educators Conference, Information Systems Educators Conference (2012)

12. Sedrakyan, G., Snoeck, M., Poelmans, S.: Assessing the effectiveness of feedback enabled simulation in teaching conceptual modeling. Comput. Educ. **78**, 367–382 (2014)

13. Akayama, S., Hisazumi, K., Hiya, S., Fukuda, A.: Using Model-Driven Development Tools for Object-Oriented Modeling Education. MODELS (2013)

14. Borland: Keeping your business relevant with model driven architecture (MODEL-DRIVEN ARCHITECTURE) (2004)

15. Singh, Y., Sood, M.: Model driven architecture: a perspective. In: Advance Computing Conference, 2009. IACC 2009. IEEE International, pp. 1644–1652 (2009)

16. Moody, D.L.: The method evaluation model: a theoretical model for validating information systems design methods. In: Ciborra, C.U., Mercurio, R., Marco, M.d., Martinez, M., Carignani, A. (eds.): European Conference on Information Systems (ECIS 03), Naples, Italy, pp. 1327–1336 (2003)

17. West, B.T., Welch, K.B., Galecki, A.T.: Linear mixed models: a practical guide using statistical software. CRC Press (2014)

18. Cohen, L.: Statistical power analysis for the behavioral sciences. Lawrence Earlbaum Associates (1988)

19. Embley, D.W., Liddle, S., Pastor, Ó.: Conceptual-model programming: a manifesto. In: Handbook of Conceptual Modeling, pp. 3–16. Springer (2011)

# Models and Modelling on Security and Privacy

## The 1st International Workshop for Models and Modelling on Security and Privacy (WM2SP-16)

Takao Okubo[1], Atsuo Hazeyama[2], and Eduardo B. Fernandez[3]

[1] Institute of Information Security (IISEC), 2-14-1 Tsuruya-cho, Kanagawa-ku, Yokohama-shi, Kanagawa 221-0835, Japan
okubo@iisec.ac.jp
[2] Department of Information Science, Tokyo Gakugei University, 4-1-1 Nukuikita-machi, Koganei-shi, Tokyo 184-8501, Japan
hazeyama@u-gakugei.ac.jp
[3] Department of Computer Science and Engineering, Florida Atlantic University, 777 Glades Road, Boca Raton, FL 33431, USA
fernande@fau.edu

Concerns regarding secure and/or privacy-aware software development increase. In order to attain such concerns, security and/or privacy have to be addressed in the whole software development life cycle, especially from the early stage of the software development life cycle.

This workshop aims to bring together researchers and practitioners in the areas of modeling for secure and privacy-aware software development to exchange ideas and preliminary results.

This workshop will be organized by paper presentation, tutorial, work-in-progress presentations and in-depth discussions.

# Towards Provable Security of Dynamic Source Routing Protocol and Its Applications

Naoto Yanai[1,2(✉)]

[1] Osaka University, Osaka, Japan
yanai@ist.osaka-u.ac.jp
[2] AIST, Tsukuba, Japan
yanai-naoto@aist.go.jp

**Abstract.** Routing control such as Internet routing is one of the most popular topics that dram many researchers' attention in recent years. However, to the best of our knowledge, there are few works to deal with their provable security, where the security can be mathematically proven under some reasonable assumption. Although the provable security has been discussed in the area of cryptography, we consider that such analysis should also be done to conventional network systems in order to guarantee the security of their specifications. In this work, we aim to construct such a provable framework, and particularly discuss formalization of dynamic source routing (DSR) protocol which is a kernel protocol for sensor networks. Our formalization can be easily extended into secure routing protocols with cryptographic schemes such as digital signatures.

**Keywords:** Routing security · Formal method · Provable security · Dynamic source routing · Ad hoc networks

## 1 Introduction

### 1.1 Backgrounds

Many network services have been developed in recent years, and there are practical applications such as BitCoin or network configurations consisting of directly connected things. Although managing path information via a routing protocol is necessary in such communication, the security of the routing protocol has not been well analyzed from a standpoint of the provable security. In general, the security should be analyzed via mathematically well-defined formalization considering realistic threats and its mathematical proof. Meanwhile, such a proof for a system specification is often difficult in comparison with proofs for the conventional cryptographic schemes. This is because formalizing the system specification is quite complicated. In this work, we challenge formalization of a routing protocol towards their provable security.

Meanwhile, our challenge is mainly for formalizing a system specification of *some* routing protocol. There are several existing works [3,25] ultimately formalizing system specifications towards true generalization. However, each routing protocol in the real world has aimed at each layer, devices and applications,

© Springer International Publishing AG 2016
S. Link and J.C. Trujillo (Eds.): ER 2016 Workshops, LNCS 9975, pp. 231–239, 2016.
DOI: 10.1007/978-3-319-47717-6_20

and their constructions and design principles are drastically different from each other. That is, extremely formalizing these specifications sometimes has a gap from the realistic environments, and the resulting analysis under such formalization may fall into being meaningless even if the security can be proven. We hence consider that forwarding generalization is undesirable, and try to individually formalize each routing protocol.

In particular, we hereafter discuss the *dynamic source routing (DSR)* [16] protocol which is a major routing protocol for wireless sensor networks. When each device sends data in DSR, its neighbor devices behave as routers to relay the received data and forward it. Such a mechanism is known as *multi-hop routing*. The reasons why we focus on DSR are as follows. First, developments of wireless sensor networks including Internet-of-Things (IoT) in recent years are indispensable whereas an adversary can more easily attack the networks rather than the conventional wired networks. For instance, the adversary can intrude in the wireless networks by putting on its own malicious devices. Moreover, because each device in DSR can exchange path information with neighbor devices as a router, the adversary can inject false path information within the networks via the malicious devices. Based on these reasons, we consider that the provable security of DSR is quite important and thus formalize its specification.

## 1.2    Contributions

In this work, we formalize a specification of DSR as a routing protocol on sensor networks. For this purpose, we also formalize a class of ad-hoc networks and a topology-based routing. Our network definition consists of seven components, i.e., nodes, links between nodes, identifiers, relations between identifiers and nodes, destination, and cost evaluation. See Sect. 3 as more details. Based on the network definition, we also define two functions of DSR, *route discovery* and *route maintenance*. These definitions can also be extended into their security extensions with cryptographic schemes. See Sect. 4. We also briefly describe the existing secure routing protocols as instantiations of our definition. We leave as an open problem to prove the security of these protocols.

## 1.3    Paper Organization

In this section, we described the motivation of this work and main contributions. The rest parts of this paper are organized as follows. In the next section, we briefly describe several related works with respect to formal analysis of routing protocols. Next, we define a network configuration of ad-hoc networks in Sect. 3 and DSR in Sect. 4, respectively. In Sect. 5, we show the existing secure routing protocols as further applications of our definition. Finally, we conclude in Sect. 6.

## 2    Related Works

There are two kinds of security analysis of routing protocols in the existing works, i.e., proofs by black-box reduction by human and proofs by formal methods.

In the former approach, Buttyán and Vajda [6] have defined the security model of ad-hoc networks via a simulation-based definition. Their model dealt with each device and a network itself as Turing machines, and an adversary can put only a single malicious node in the network. Their model also assumes that each device communicates with only the network in order to communicate with other devices. In other words, the network behaves as a proxy of any devices. However, we consider that a network should be a simply public channel and hence their model seems to be strange. Although there are several works to discus the security by black-box reduction [1,17,23], all of them have followed the model by Buttyán and Vajda. The strangeness described above, therefore, still exists.

Next, for proofs by formal methods, John and Marshall [15] have analyzed the security of the secure routing protocol (SRP) [21] and Godskesen [9] has analyzed that of the authenticated routing for ad hoc networks (ARAN) [22], respectively. Nanz and Hankin [20] have formalized the network topology and its broadcast communication toward formal analysis. These works do not discuss the black-box reduction which is our main target. Arnaud et al. [2,3] then formalized these protocols as a more generalized form. The most generalization has been done by Zhang et al. [25], and their idea is to define any routing protocol consisting of two entities, an origin and a path. Although these works are elegant, we consider that they are still insufficient because they sometimes have gaps from realistic environments due to too much generalization.

As more results in different layers, Boldyreva and Lychev [4] have proved the security of the border-gateway protocol (BGP) and its security extension. Next, Goldberg et al. [10] have analyzed the security of the next secure (NSEC) in the domain name system security extensions (DNSSEC) to hide dependency relations in domain name system (DNS) during guarantee of that between URL and IP addresses. These works are the closest to our work, and finally we plan to extend our work by following these results.

## 3   Definition of Network Configurations

In this section, we define ad hoc networks and topology-based routing to define DSR later. The following definitions are parts of our contributions.

### 3.1   Definition of Ad Hoc Networks

To formalize DSR, we first define a configuration of networks and a class of a topology-based routing protocol as its idealized class. In particular, we define networks as (**Node, Links, ID, IDforNode, Routeto, Dest, Cost**).

$\mathcal{G}$ = (**Node, Links**) is a finite graph consisting of a set **Node** of nodes and a connected function **Links** : **Node** × **Node** → $\{0, 1\}$. Here, each node $V$ included in **Node** corresponds to a network device, and an existence of an edge between any two nodes $V$ and $V'$, i.e., a connection between $V$ and $V'$, is defined as **Links**$(V, V')$ outputs 1.

**ID** is a set given by $\{0,1\}^*$ and defines a unique identifier for any device.

**IDforNode** is a function represented by **ID** $\rightarrow$ **Node**. Given any identifier $ID \in$ **ID** as input, it returns a device node $V \in$ **Node**.

**Routeto** represents a transitive binary relation between any two routes. In particular, **Routeto**$_V$ for each node $V \in$ **Node** describes relations between routes to an identifier $ID$ corresponding to $V$.

**Cost** is a function defined by **Node** $\times$ **Node** $\rightarrow \mathbb{R}$, and outputs a cost in a real number required for communication between two nodes $(V, V') \in$ **Node** given as input.

In this work, we define a route $R$ as a permutation $(V_n, \cdots, V_1)$ consisting of $n$ nodes for any $n \in \mathbb{N}$ and any node $s(V_1, \cdots, V_n) \in$ **Node**. We call $V_1$ in the permutation $(V_n, \cdots, V_1)$ as a source. Similarly, an index $i \in [1, n]$ for each node means a distance from the source. More precisely, for any $i$, the number of hops for $V_i$ from the source increases in proportion to the value of $i$. We say a node $V$ prefers $R$ rather than $R'$ for any $V \in$ **Node** and two routes $(R, R')$ if $R'$**Routeto**$_V R$. We furthermore say $R = (V_{n-1}, \cdots, V_1)$ for any $ID \in$ **ID** is the $j$-th preferred route to $V_n$ for if there are $j - 1$ routes $R'$s such that $R'$**Routeto**$_{V_n} R$ holds. Similarly, we say that $R$ is the most preferred route for $j = 1$.

## 3.2 Topology-Based Routing Protocol

A topology-based routing protocol is an idealized protocol to deal with multiple routing protocol for sensor networks, and DSR can be discussed in the topology-based routing. As the details described in the next section, we briefly describe capability of the topology-based routing. In this protocol, there are two steps, the route discovery and the route maintenance. The route discovery is utilized to find a route to a destination node when a source node sends data. The availability of the found route can be checked via the route maintenance.

## 3.3 Route Discovery

Route Discovery is a function executed between multiple nodes. Each node $V_i$ is given $(V_i, \mathbf{Neighbors}(V_i), \mathbf{Routeto}_{V_i}, \mathbf{Cost}, \{ID_j\}_{j=1}^{i-1})$ as input, where **Neighbors**$(V_i)$ is a set of nodes which are neighbors of $V_i$ and $\{ID_j\}_{j=1}^{i-1}$ is a set of identities whose nodes appear in a route from a source to $V_i$. $V_i$ then send a route request $(V_i, V_j, R, D, C, W, Aux)$ to all $V_j \in$ **Neighbors**$(V_i)$, where $R$ is a route as described in the previous section, $D$ is a unique identifier of its destination defined in **ID**, $C \in \mathbb{R}$ is a whole cost on $R$, $W \in \{0,1\}$ is a disappearance flag, and $Aux$ is any auxiliary input to hold any additional input. For instance, information about the global positioning system (GPS) for vehicular ad hoc networks can be utilized as $Aux$. For any route request an error $\perp$ only if $V_i$ can discard the request. We say $V_i$ accepts a route request if $V_i$ does not discard the request.

## 3.4   Route Maintenance

Route maintenance is a function executed between multiple nodes. Each node $V_i$ is given $(V_i, \textbf{Neighbors}(V_i), \textbf{Routeto}_{V_i}, \textbf{Cost}, \{ID_j\}_{j=1}^{i-1}, N, s)$ as input, where $N$ is an expire date defined in an integer set $\mathbb{N}$, $s$ is state information defined in $\mathbb{N}$. $V_i$ sends a route information $(V_i, V_j, R, D, C, W, Aux)$ on a route $R$ to all $V_j \in \textbf{Neighbors}(V_i)$, and then checks if $V_j$ accepts the request. If so, $V_i$ keeps the route and resets $s$. Otherwise, $V_i$ increments $s$ as $s = s + 1$ and sends the route information again until $s \leq N$. For $s > N$, $V_i$ discards the route information and returns $W = 1$ to its source node as disappearance of the route.

# 4   Dynamic Source Routing Protocol

The dynamic source routing (DSR) protocol is a routing protocol on ad-hoc networks. It does not require network infrastructures but is able to autonomously configure wireless networks. Algorithms of DSR are defined in the protocol described in the previous section in general. In this section, we define a routing table of DSR below and then describe functions extended from the definitions in the previous section.

## 4.1   Routing Table

Each device node $V$ owns a routing table $T_V$ to store route information. This $T_V$ is defined as an bidimensional array $T_V[i][j]$ for any integers $i, j \in \mathbb{N}$, where each column $i$ contains an identifier $ID \in \textbf{ID}$ and each row $j$ contains the $j$-th preferred route to $V$.

## 4.2   Route Discovery

When any node $V$ with an identifier $ID$ starts with the route discovery, $V$ sends a route request $(V, V', R = (ID), D, 0, 0, Aux)$ to $V_j \in \textbf{Neighbors}(V)$. Given the request $(V, V', R, D, 0, C, Aux)$ by $V$, $V_j \in \textbf{Neighbors}(V)$ checks if $R$ includes its own identifier $ID_j$. If so, $V_j$ discards the request and returns nothing. Otherwise, $V_j$ executes the following processes:

1. For $D = ID'$, return a route reply $(R, W = 0, Aux)$ to a source.
2. For $D \neq ID'$, set $R = R \cup \{ID'\}$ and $C = C + \textbf{Cost}(V)$. Then, for any $i$, retrieve a cost $C_i$ on the $i$-th preferred route to $D$ from the routing table $T_{V'}[D][i]$ and then compare it with $C$. If some $i$ such that $C > C_i$, then store the route request $(V, V', R, D, 0, C, Aux)$ in $T_{V'}[D][i + 1]$ as the $(i + 1)$-th preferred route. If there is a route in $T_{V'}[D][i + 1]$ already, then previously set $T_{V'}[D][j + 1] = T_{V'}[D][j]$ for any $j \geq i + 1$.

### 4.3   Route Maintenance

Each node $V$ retrieves route information $(V, V_j, R, D, C, 0, Aux)$ from a routing table $T_V[D][i]$ for any destination $D \in$ **Node** and any $i \in \mathbb{N}$. Then, set state information $s = 0$ and the route information to $V_j \in$ **Neighbors**$(V)$ as a request. If $V_j$ accepts the request, then $V$ resets $s$ and keeps $T_V[D][i]$. Otherwise, $V$ sets $s = s + 1$ and sends the request again until $s \leq N$. For $s > N$, $V$ sends $W = 1$ as disappearance of the route to a source node, and then sets $T_V[D][i] = T_V[D][i + 1]$ for all $i$.

## 5   Application to Secure Routing Protocols

In this section, we briefly describe intuition that our formalization includes secure routing protocols where the validity of routing information can be guaranteed by cryptographic schemes [12,24]. We also describe several secure routing protocols as instantiations.

### 5.1   Overview of Secure Routing Protocols

The overhead due to the use of cryptographic schemes is sometimes large, but their guarantee of the security is quite useful. These cryptographic schemes are able to provide the provable security under both reasonable assumptions and their reduction proofs. In general, a secret key to generate message authentication codes (MAC) or digital signatures is unknown information except for a node which generates route information. Hence, the validity of the route information can be guaranteed by verification of these schemes.

Our formalization described in the previous section contains such secure routing protocols. In particular, each intermediate node $v$ generates MAC or digital signatures on $(R, D, C)$ included in route information and then can append it as a part of $Aux$. For the use of MAC, since a forwarding node shares a key for MAC with its received node, the received node can verify the validity of the information from the neighbor. For the use of digital signatures, a received node can verify digital signatures whereby each intermediate node appends not only their signatures but also public key identifiers in $Aux$. These constructions are applicable to both the route discovery and the route maintenance although we omit the detail due to the page limitation.

### 5.2   Instantiations of Secure Routing Protocols

Secure routing protocols are roughly classified into two constructions, MAC-based construction and digital-signature-based construction. In the both constructions, the validity of routing information can be guaranteed because their authenticators are generated. Since MAC are quite faster and need lower memories than digital signatures, the conventional secure routing protocols in wireless sensor networks have adopted MAC [3,12,13,21,25]. In spite of this fact, many secure routing protocols with digital signatures have been proposed [7,8,17,22] in more recent years. Indeed, European Telecommunications Standards Institute (ETSI) has suggested the use of digital signatures for IoT services in order to provide publicly verifiability [11].

We hereinafter describe several major protocols. Papadimitratos and Haas [21] proposed the secure routing protocol (SRP). Next, Hu et al. [12,14] have proposed Ariadne with both MAC and digital signatures. While SRP deals with authentication for only a source and a destination, Ariadne enables intermediate nodes to authenticate route information in order to prevent threats by malicious intermediate nodes. As more recent results, Gosh and Datta [8] have proposed the secure dynamic routing protocol (SDRP) via short signatures by Boneh et al. [5]. These are mainly for DSR and thus become strict applications of our definition. In particular, MAC and digital signatures for each protocol are sequentially attended in a part of packets. They can be then embedded into $Aux$ of our definition as described above in a manner of $Aux = Aux \bigcup \{(R_i, D, C, x)\}$, where $(R_i, D, C)$ are parts of route information such that $R_i = (V_i, \cdots, V_1)$ for any $i$ and $x$ represents a set of MAC and/or digital signatures.

Meanwhile, as a furthermore application, our definition is extendibles to the ad hoc on-demand distance vector (AODV), which utilizes sequence numbers to strengthen the availability. In particular, the sequent numbers are utilized to represent a unique identifier for each entry in a routing table, and then can be embedded into $Aux$ as a part of route information in a manner of $Aux = Aux \bigcup \{(R_i, D, C, S_i)\}$, where $S_i$ is a sequence number related to $R_i$. There are several secure routing protocols for AODV. For instance, Zapata and Asokan proposed the secure ad hoc on-demand distance vector (SAODV) protocol with both MAC and digital signatures. Next, Sangiri et al. [22] pointed out the vulnerability of SAODV and then proposed the authenticated routing for ad hoc networks (ARAN) by utilizing public key cryptography. Gosh and Datta [7] have proposed the identity-based secure ad hoc on-demand distance vector (IDSAODV) from sequential aggregate signatures [18] to combine individual signatures into a single signature. The most recent result is secure routing protocols by Muranaka et al. [19], which is closed to IDSAODV but is almost generic. MAC and digital signatures in these schemes can be also embedded in a similar manner of the secure protocols for DSR, i.e., $Aux = Aux \bigcup \{(R_i, D, C, S_i, x)\}$.

We leave as a future work to prove the security of these protocols.

## 6    Conclusion

In this work, we formalized a specification of DSR, which is a routing protocol on sensor networks, towards the provable security. Although we focused on DSR, our definition can be extended into a class of topology-based routing protocols and ad-hoc networks. Meanwhile, our definition is far from routing protocols in other network layers. This is consistent with our motivation, i.e., formalization of specifications of existing protocols. Our future work is to prove the security of the existing secure routing protocols.

**Acknowledgement.** The author is supported by JSPS KAKENHI Grant Number 16K16065. We would like to appreciate their supports.

# References

1. Ács, G.: Secure routing in multi-hop wireless networks, Ph.D. thesis. Budapest University of Technology and Economics (2009)
2. Arnaud, M., Cortier, V., Delaune, S.: Modeling and verifying ad hoc routing protocols. In: Proceedings of CSF 2010, pp. 59–74. IEEE (2010)
3. Arnaud, M., Cortier, V., Delaune, S.: Modeling and verifying ad hoc routing protocols. Inf. Comput. **238**, 30–67 (2014)
4. Boldyreva, A., Lychev, R.: Provable security of S-BGP, other path vector protocols: model, analysis and extensions. In: Proceedings of ACM CCS 2012, pp. 541–552. ACM (2012)
5. Boneh, D., Lynn, B., Shacham, H.: Short signatures from the weil pairing. In: Boyd, C. (ed.) ASIACRYPT 2001. LNCS, vol. 2248, pp. 514–532. Springer, Heidelberg (2001). doi:10.1007/3-540-45682-1_30
6. Buttyán, L., Vajda, I.: Towards provable security for ad hoc routing protocols. In: Proceedings of SASN, pp. 94–105. ACM Press (2004)
7. Ghosh, U., Datta, R.: Identity based secure AODV and tcp for mobile ad hoc networks. In: Proceedings of ACWR 2011, pp. 339–346. ACM (2011)
8. Ghosh, U., Datta, R.: SDRP: Secure and dynamic routing protocol for mobile ad-hoc networks. IET Netw. **3**(3), 235–243 (2013)
9. Godskesen, J.C.: Formal verification of the ARAN protocol using the applied Pi-calculus. In: Proceeings of IFIP ITS, pp. 99–113 (2015)
10. Goldberg, S., Naor, M., Papadopoulos, D., Reyzin, L., Vasant, S., Ziv, A.: Nsec5: provably preventing DNSSEC zone enumeration. In: Proceedings of NDSS 2015. Internet Society (2015)
11. Guillemin, P.: ICTSB - RFID networks internet of things. In: ETSI 2007 (2007). http://docbox.etsi.org/Partners/ICTSB_Open/RFID/ICTSB_RFID_seminar_2007-10-24/P.Guillemin_ICTSB%20on%20RFID_Oct.07.pdf
12. Hu, Y.-C., Perrig, A., Johnson, D.: Ariadne: a secure on demand routing protocol for ad hoc network. In: Proceedings of MobiCom 2002. ACM (2002)
13. Hu, Y.-C., Perrig, A., Johnson, D.: SEAD: secure efficient distance vector routing for mobile wireless ad hoc networks. In: Proceedings of WMCSA 2002, pp. 3–13. ACM (2002)
14. Hu, Y.-C., Perrig, A., Johnson, D.: Ariadne: a secure on demand routing protocol for ad hoc network. Wirel. Netw. **11**, 21–38 (2005)
15. John, I., Marshall, D.: An analysis of the secure routing protocol for mobile ad hoc network route discovery: using intuitive reasoning and formal verification to identity flaws (2003)
16. Jonhson, D., Maltz, D.: Dynamic source routing in ad hoc wireless networks. Mobile Comput. **353**, 153–181 (1996)
17. Kim, J., Tsudik, G.: SRDP: secure route discovery for dynamic source routing in manets. Ad Hoc Netw. **7**(6), 1097–1109 (2009)
18. Lysyanskaya, A., Micali, S., Reyzin, L., Shacham, H.: Sequential aggregate signatures from trapdoor permutations. In: Cachin, C., Camenisch, J.L. (eds.) EUROCRYPT 2004. LNCS, vol. 3027, pp. 74–90. Springer, Heidelberg (2004). doi:10.1007/978-3-540-24676-3_5

19. Muranaka, K., Yanai, N., Okamura, S., Fujiwara, T.: Secure routing protocols for sensor networks: construction with signature schemes for multiple signers. In: Proceedings of Trustcom 2015, pp. 1329–1336. IEEE (2015)
20. Nanz, S., Hankin, C.: A framework for security analysis of mobile wireless networks. Theor. Comput. Sci. **367**, 203–227 (2006)
21. Papadimitratos, P., Haas, Z.J.: Secure routing for mobile ad hoc networks. In: Proceedings of CNDS, pp. 27–31 (2002)
22. Sanzgiri, K., LaFlamme, D., Dahill, B., Levine, B.N., Shields, C., Belding-Royer, E.M.: Authenticated routing for ad hoc networks. IEEE J. Sel. Areas Commun. **23**(3), 598–610 (2005)
23. Vajda, I.: A proof technique for security assessment of on-demand ad hoc routing protocol. Int. J. Secur. Netw. **9**(1), 12–19 (2014)
24. Zapata, M., Asokan, N.: Securing ad hoc routing protocols. In: Proceedings of WISE, pp. 1–10. ACM Press (2002)
25. Zhang, F., Jia, L., Basescu, C., Kim, T., Hu, Y., Perrig, A.: Mechanized network origin and path authenticity proofs. In: Proceedings of ACM CCS 2014, pp. 346–357. ACM (2014)

# Tool Demonstrations

## Demo Papers of the 2016 ER Workshops

Aditya Ghose[1] and Takashi Kobayashi[2]

[1] Decision Systems Lab, School of Computing and Information Technology,
University of Wollongong, Wollongong, NSW 2522, Australia
aditya@uow.edu.au
[2] Department of Computer Science, Tokyo Institute of Technology, 2-12-1
Ookayama, Meguro-Ku, Tokyo 152-8552, Japan
tkobaya@cs.titech.ac.jp

Progress in conceptual modelling is necessarily underpinned by model-ling and model management tools. A session that affords the opportunity for researchers and practitioners to demonstrate the latest in tool developments has been a long-standing feature of the ER conference series.

All of the submissions to this session bear testimony to the vibrant and effective community building tools in this space.

Of the 4 tools to be demonstrated at the ER-2016 Conference Tool Demonstration session, one submission was selected for publication as a tool description paper.

# A Tool for Analyzing Variability Based on Functional Requirements and Testing Artifacts

Michal Steinberger[1], Iris Reinhartz-Berger[1(✉)], and Amir Tomer[2]

[1] Department of Information Systems, University of Haifa, Haifa, Israel
mnachm04@campus.haifa.ac.il, iris@is.haifa.ac.il
[2] Kinneret Academic College, Jordan Valley, Israel
tomera@kinneret.ac.il

**Abstract.** Analyzing differences among software artifacts is beneficial in a variety of scenarios, such as feasibility study, configuration management, and software product line engineering. Currently variability analysis is mainly done based on artifacts developed in a certain development phase (most notably, requirements engineering). We will demonstrate a tool that utilizes both functional requirements and test cases in order to analyze variability more comprehensively. The tool implements the ideas of SOVA R-TC method.

**Keywords:** Variability analysis · Feature diagrams · Natural language processing · Ontology · Software product line engineering

## 1 Introduction: Research Background and Application Context

*Variability analysis* aims at determining the degree of similarity of different software artifacts belonging to the same development phase (e.g., requirement documents) [9]. Such an activity is important in a variety of scenarios, including feasibility study, configuration management, and software product line engineering. The outcomes of variability analysis are commonly represented in some visual way, most notably in feature diagrams [6]. Those are trees or graphs whose nodes are features – user or developer visible characteristics – and their edges are relations or dependencies among features (e.g., mandatory and optional sub-features, alternatives, and OR-related features). The inputs of variability analysis approaches are quite diverse: they can be requirements, design artifacts, or even the code itself.

Due to the complexity and diversity of software, manually conducting variability analysis is time consuming and error prone. Therefore, approaches have been suggested to automate or semi-automate variability analysis (e.g., see [2] for a recent systematic review of requirements-based variability analysis). These approaches concentrate on single development phases and commonly use one source of inputs (e.g., requirements in the studies reviewed in [2]).

© Springer International Publishing AG 2016
S. Link and J.C. Trujillo (Eds.): ER 2016 Workshops, LNCS 9975, pp. 243–250, 2016.
DOI: 10.1007/978-3-319-47717-6_21

As artifacts of particular development phases may be incomplete or focus on a certain view, our underlying hypothesis is that using artifacts from different, but related, development phases may improve variability analysis and make it more comprehensive. Particularly, concentrating on the two sides of the development process – requirements engineering and testing, we developed a tool that automates variability analysis based on functional requirements and their associated test cases. The tool implements the ideas of SOVA R-TC method [11], which promotes comparing behaviors based on ontological and semantical considerations.

## 2  Key Technologies and Technical Challenges

SOVA R-TC extends SOVA [5], which analyzes and presents variability based on textual requirements only, and considers in addition test cases associated to the input requirements. The four-phase process of SOVA R-TC is depicted in Fig. 1, while screenshots from the supporting tool are provided in the appendix. The inputs of the process are requirements and test cases (see examples in the appendix, Fig. 4). In the first phase the (functional) requirements and test cases are parsed using a general purpose ontology – of Bunge [3] – and NLP techniques (particularly a Sematic Role Labeling (SRL) technique [4]). Based on Bunge's ontological model, a behavior is composed of three components: the initial state of the system before the behavior occurs (s1), the sequence of external events triggering the behavior (E), and the final state of the system after the behavior occurs (s*). The different components are extracted after annotating the text of requirements and test cases with meaningful semantic labels (such as actors, actions, objects, instruments, and adverbial and temporal modifiers). The outcomes of the first stage are demonstrated in Figs. 5 and 6 in the appendix.

The second phase integrates the representation which was extracted separately from the requirements and test cases. As latter explained, this is done by identifying state variables for the requirements and the test cases and integrating them (see Fig. 7 in the

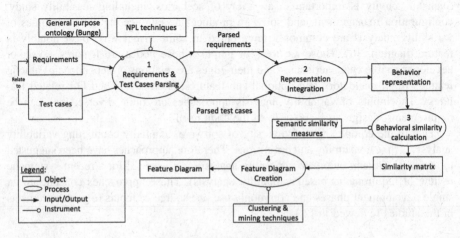

**Fig. 1.** SOVA R-TC process

appendix for an example of the outcome of this stage). In the third phase, the integrated behavior representations are compared utilizing semantic similarity measures. The results of this stage is a matrix showing for each pair of requirements their similarity value – a number between 0 and 1, where 1 denotes very similar or even identical behaviors. As can be seen in Fig. 8 in the appendix, the similarity is separately calculated for the initial state, external event, and final state of the behavior, as well as overall. Finally, the similarity results are used for clustering requirements, identifying features and their dependencies (in the form of optional vs. mandatory features, XOR- and OR-related features) and organizing the features into feature diagrams. The feature diagrams are created in FeatureIDE format [7] enabling their convenient visualization in a common feature modeling tool. An example of a feature diagram created by the tool is depicted in Fig. 9 in the appendix.

SOVA R-TC tool faces two main challenges: (1) How to store and manage the information required to conduct variability analysis? (2) How can artifacts from different development phases (requirements and test cases in our case) be compared and integrated?

The first challenge is addressed utilizing an Application Lifecycle Management (ALM) environment. ALM environments [8] aim at planning, governing, and coordinating the software lifecycle tasks. Particularly, they store and manage requirements, test cases, and the relations among them. Utilizing existing ALM environments further makes our approach usable and accessible, as it does not require the developers to work in new, dedicated development environments. The inputs to our approach, as demonstrated in Fig. 4 in the appendix, can be directly exported from existing ALM tools.

The second challenge of information integration is addressed by identifying state variables and corresponding values for the initial and final states of the underlying behaviors. These are directly obtained from the *(action, object)* pairs of the parsed requirements and test cases. An example of this extraction process is depicted in Fig. 2. The integration is done by mapping similar state variables and unifying their values (separately extracted from the requirements and test cases).

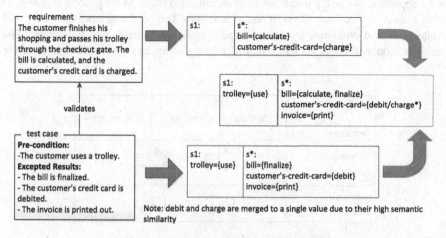

**Fig. 2.** Integrating the extracted information

## 3 Novelty and Relations to Pre-existing Work

Currently, variability analysis is conducted on artifacts developed in a single development phase, most notably requirements engineering [2]. Requirements variability analysis is commonly conducted on Software Requirements Specifications (SRS), but product descriptions, brochures, and user comments are also used due to practical reasons. The outputs of the suggested methods are commonly feature diagrams, clustered requirements, keywords or direct objects. The phases utilized in those approaches can be divided into: (1) requirements assessment, (2) terms extraction (using different techniques, such as algebraic models, similarity metrics, and natural language processing tools), (3) features identification, and (4) feature diagram (or variability model) formation.

Other development artifacts, e.g., design artifacts [1] and code [12], have also been analyzed to find differences between software products. In contrast, testing artifacts seem to attract less attention in variability analysis. This may be due to less agreement on the way testing artifacts need to look like and their reliance on other development artifacts (most notably, requirements). Only a few approaches propose utilizing several distinct sources of information for analyzing variability. However, these sources commonly belong to the same lifecycle phase (e.g., requirements engineering phase [10]) or used to verify correctness of the inputs [9].

Based on the reviewed work, the main novelty of SOVA R-TC is its support for analyzing the variability of artifacts from different lifecycle phases, particularly, requirements engineering and testing, making the outcomes more comprehensive.

## 4 Demonstration

The demonstration, which is targeted to both researchers and practitioners, will present each intermediate outcome, as well as the final output of the approach – feature diagrams representing the variability extracted from the requirements alone and from the requirements and their related test cases. The main screenshots of SOVA R-TC tool are provided in the appendix. We will particularly demonstrate each phase in the process (see Fig. 1) using e-shop applications, physical and virtual ones. During the demonstration we will explain how the outcomes are created, and discuss the benefits and limitations. The demonstration will focus on cases in which introducing test cases information to the

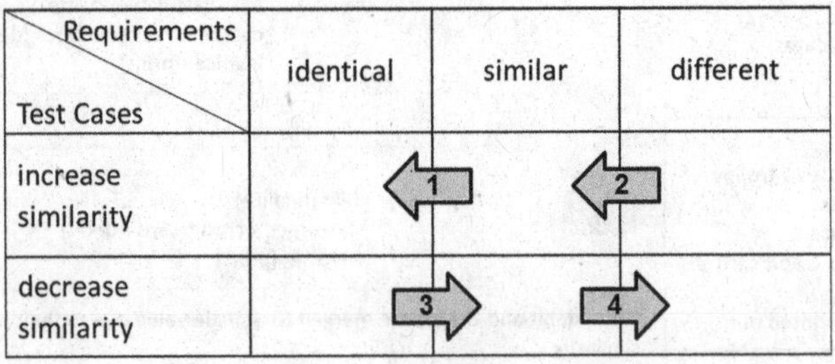

| Requirements / Test Cases | identical | similar | different |
|---|---|---|---|
| increase similarity | ⬅1 | ⬅2 | |
| decrease similarity | 3➡ | 4➡ | |

**Fig. 3.** Main cases for demonstration

variability analysis process results in remarkable differences. Those cases are summarized in Fig. 3. For example, the second case (#2) refers to a situation in which different requirements become similar due to high similarity of their corresponding test cases.

## 5 Conclusions

SOVA R-TC is a powerful tool which supports variability analysis based on functional requirements and test cases. The inputs arrive from ALM environments, parsed and integrated to represent behaviors (and particularly the transitions from the initial states of the analyzed systems to their final states). The behaviors are then compared utilizing semantic measures and clustered to create feature diagrams. The resultant feature diagrams present a more comprehensive view of variability that considers related test cases information and not just the requirements which might be partial and incomplete.

## Appendix: Screenshots from the Supporting Tool

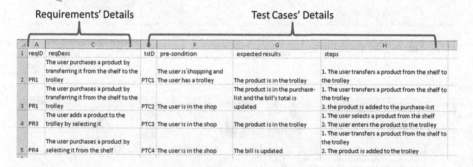

**Fig. 4.** An example of an input file

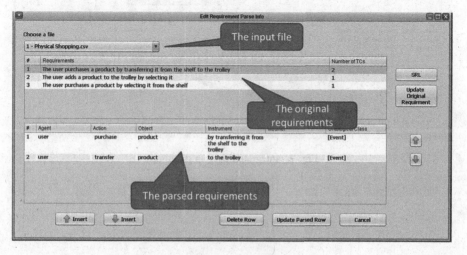

**Fig. 5.** The parsed requirements

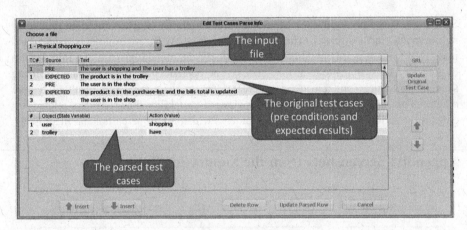

**Fig. 6.** The parsed test cases (pre = precondition, expected = expected results)

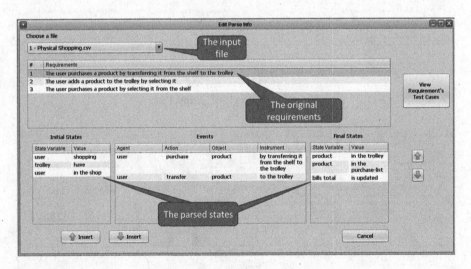

**Fig. 7.** Integrated parsing outcomes

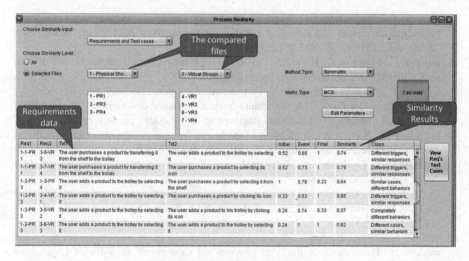

**Fig. 8.** Similarity calculation results

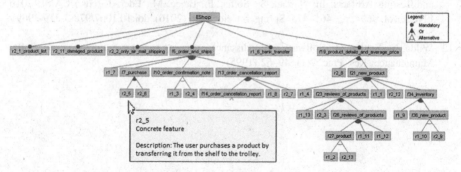

**Fig. 9.** An example of a created feature diagram (The requirements' codes are in the form of rX_Y, where X is the number of product and Y is the number of the requirement in that product. Going over a leaf with the mouse will present the text of the requirement.)

# References

1. Acher, M., Cleve, A., Collet, P., Merle, P., Duchien, L., Lahire, P.: Reverse engineering architectural feature models. In: Crnkovic, I., Gruhn, V., Book, M. (eds.) ECSA 2011. LNCS, vol. 6903, pp. 220–235. Springer, Heidelberg (2011)
2. Bakar, N.H., Kasirun, Z.M., Salleh, N.: Feature extraction approaches from natural language requirements for reuse in software product lines: a systematic literature review. J. Syst. Softw. **106**, 132–149 (2015)
3. Bunge, M.: Treatise on Basic Philosophy, vol. 3, Ontology I: The Furniture of the World. Reidel, Boston (1977)
4. Gildea, D., Jurafsky, D.: Automatic labeling of semantic roles. Comput. Linguist. **28**(3), 245–288 (2002)

5. Itzik, N., Reinhartz-Berger, I., Wand, Y.: Variability analysis of requirements: considering behavioral differences and reflecting stakeholders perspectives. IEEE Trans. Softw. Eng. (2016). doi:10.1109/TSE.2015.2512599

6. Kang, K.C., Cohen, S.G., Hess, J.A., Novak, W.E., Peterson, A.S.: Feature-oriented domain analysis (FODA) feasibility study. Technical report (1990)

7. Kastner, C., Thum, T., Saake, G., Feigenspan, J., Leich, T., Wielgorz, F., Apel, S.: FeatureIDE: a tool framework for feature-oriented software development. In: 31st IEEE International Conference on Software Engineering (ICSE 2009), pp. 611–614 (2009)

8. Lacheiner, H., Ramler, R.: Application lifecycle management as infra-structure for software process improvement and evolution: experience and in-sights from industry. In: 37th EUROMICRO Conference on Software Engineering and Advanced Applications (SEAA 2011), pp. 286–293 (2011)

9. Li, Y., Rubin, J., Chechik, M.: Semantic slicing of software version histories. In: 2015 30th IEEE/ACM International Conference on Automated Software Engineering (ASE), pp. 686–696. IEEE (2015)

10. She, S., Lotufo, R., Berger, T., Wasowski, A., Czarnecki, K.: Reverse engineering feature models. In: Proceedings of the 33rd International Conference on Software Engineering (ICSE 2011), pp. 461–470 (2011)

11. Steinberger, M., Reinhartz-Berger, I.: Comprehensive Variability Analysis of Requirements and Testing Artifacts. In: Nurcan, S., Soffer, P., Bajec, M., Eder, J. (eds.) CAiSE 2016. LNCS, vol. 9694, pp. 461–475. Springer, Heidelberg (2016). doi:10.1007/978-3-319-39696-5_28

12. Wilde, N., Scully, M.: Software reconnaissance: mapping program features to code. Softw. Maintenance: Res. Prac. 7(1), 49–62 (1995)

# Author Index

Printed in the United States
By Bookmasters